# THE GWR EXPOSED

## SWINDON IN THE DAYS OF COLLETT AND HAWKSWORTH

# THE GWR EXPOSED

## SWINDON IN THE DAYS OF COLLETT AND HAWKSWORTH

*Jeremy Clements*

An imprint of Ian Allan Publishing

First published 2015

ISBN 978 0 86093 666 4

Published by Oxford Publishing Company,
an imprint of Ian Allan Publishing Ltd, Hersham, Surrey, KT12 4RG

Printed in Malta

Visit the Ian Allan Publishing website at
www.ianallanpublishing.com

**Picture Credits**
Every effort has been made to identify and correctly attribute photographic credits. Should any error have occurred this is entirely unintentional. All uncredited pictures are from the author's collection.

**FRONT COVER TOP** The most revolutionary proposal to emerge in the High Acceleration Project of 1932 was a 4-cylinder 4-6-2T that would have combined a 'Star'-type chassis with mixed traffic-sized driving wheels and a modified Standard No 1 boiler. *National Railway Museum*

**FRONT COVER BOTTOM** An abortive attempt at modern styling was the treatment meted out to No 5005 *Manorbier Castle* (and also to 'King' No 6014). The result had little merit, except in helping to discourage further initiatives into 'streamlining'. *Stephenson Locomotive Society*

**BACK COVER** The clean lines (on the left hand side at least) of No 1000 *County of Middlesex* were complemented by the large, but ineffective, double chimney. Later, the whole class received squatter double chimneys that helped improve performance.

**PAGE ONE** No 6873 *Caradoc Grange* is on a down freight at Laira Junction on 30 August 1961. *R. C. Riley*

**PAGE TWO** Following transfer of the Lickey route to Western Region control, some of Class '94xxs' were drafted in to replace ex-LMS 3F 0-6-0Ts on banking duties. Here No 8400 breasts the summit and heads for Blackwell station with a fast freight in August 1963. From the angle it is impossible to determine whether the engine is acting as pilot, or is the train engine. *S. Grounds*

# CONTENTS

# INTRODUCTION

Much of the Great Western story is familiar territory that has been covered many times, but there remain inconsistencies whose causes still await a rational explanation. Two events serve as examples of adventurous developments that were totally out of character with the company's conservative management at both Paddington and Swindon.

The first was the appearance of pioneering diesel-mechanical Railcar No 1, a culmination of investigative work that had anticipated more grandiose diesel-electric train formations as early as 1926. The initial stages of this fascinating exercise seem to have been promulgated by Felix Pole, but its continuation, albeit on a more modest scale after his departure, seemed paradoxical. The conclusion would appear to be that others were determined not to let the initiative founder on the rocks of Collett's antipathy towards new ideas, outside influences, and collaboration with commercial manufacturers.

The second was the decision to develop new motive power that harnessed cutting-edge technology derived from the aircraft sector. The sequence of events that led to the placement of orders for two machines shows that Board and management were prepared to move fast. The technology was revolutionary enough in the aeronautical world, and it was quite extraordinary that traditionally restrained senior GWR officers should have enthusiastically accepted the implicit risks.

This dichotomy in mechanical engineering policy was technically motivated rather than commercially inspired. Indeed, at Swindon there appeared to be virtually no appreciation about what was happening to the business at large, and how urgent was the need to instigate far-reaching changes. Issues such as the placement of locomotive valve gear inside or outside, or to what degree should steam be superheated, were trivia compared with the waste that was endemic in new capital investment, and in the manner that routine mechanical engineering affairs were managed.

Statistical ratio comparison may not be an exciting subject, but it is vital to the assessment of how an enterprise is performing within the market at large, and in measuring its efficiency against similar businesses. Analysis of conditions in the inter-war years shows that the railway companies were barely holding their own volume-wise in an expanding transport market, i.e. their market share was diminishing. Comparisons between the 'Big Four' reveal that the GWR's response to this alarming trend was the least impressive. Had not international events taken centre stage, by the end of 1939 Collett and his team should have been facing some very uncomfortable questions.

A further manifestation of the perennial road v rail debate, the causes of changing social patterns and transport economics were subsidiary to the reality that passengers and freight shippers had formed their own judgements and were voting with their feet. In 1938 the 'Big Four' responded with the abortive 'Square Deal' campaign that sought a 'level playing field' from which to compete with road freight transport. Ironically, the GWR had already effectively capitulated by expanding its own road motor fleet, and by reorganising to maximise the opportunities offered by inter-modal distribution networks.

By deduction rather than specific identification, it seems probable that Hawksworth was engaged in the evaluation of alternative traction from around the time of Stanier's departure to the LMS, as well as in the few fresh initiatives in steam power that were essayed in the 1930s. This contention is supported by his seeing the two railcar pairs, Nos 35 to 38, through to completion in the midst of the war, when there were plenty of sound reasons not to complete this project. Combined with his clearly documented participation in the gas turbine exercise, it seems certain that he was an enthusiastic supporter of new technology. Nevertheless, it is apparent that once he gained the necessary authority, he was keen to reinvigorate the steam construction programme with pragmatism and economy.

In some respects there were parallels with the career of William Dean, the pre-eminent member of that select group of six that held command at Swindon. Both were conscious of the need for reform and both saw implementation of their ideas delayed by factors beyond their control. Dean faced the complexities of managing a dual gauge system, while instigating courageous and essential experimentation in face of Daniel Gooch's financial stringencies. Hawksworth restored objectivity to steam locomotive planning and construction while sponsoring new methods against the background of demand and supply crises emanating from the need to keep a railway running under extreme war conditions.

Hawksworth showed a refreshing clarity of purpose that was a welcome contrast to some practices of preceding years. The 1938/39 building programmes had displayed muddled thinking, and the 'Manors', unquestionably the worst of all the two-cylinder 4-6-0s, were a lamentable epitaph to the format pioneered with No 98 in 1903. Even so, these issues were minor compared with the broader problems he confronted. Acceptance of outside influences to help cope with prevailing demands was first apparent in the well-received 'Modified Halls'. Equally, when the 'Counties' failed fully to sustain this progress, reversion to more of the earlier type showed realism and common sense. His enterprising approach was also evident in the novel exploration of gas turbine-electric traction. The visit to Switzerland with Sir James Milne in 1946 was timely in pursuit of this and other new technologies – an initiative that G. J. Churchward, an arch-opponent of parochialism, would have applauded.

On the negative side, Hawksworth remained as unaware of the financial implications of Swindon's inefficiencies as had his predecessor. Despite his welcome changes in design and engineering practice, there was little sign that he appreciated the broader issues of unit optimisation or efficient fleet management. This contention is supported by simple statistics drawn from before, during and after his tenure. The steam fleet totalled 3,688 as at 31 December 1940, peaked at 3,889 in 1944, and stood at 3,127 as late as 1958, despite service reductions, route closures, dieselisation and continuing encroachment by the road lobby. In seeking a cause of British Railways Western Region's operating losses, look no further.

For all his technical and academic talents, Hawksworth's suitability for the role of Chief Mechanical Engineer was unusually contained by the pattern of his earlier career. A lifetime's working association with a single corporation in the same locality, without the interruption of military service, was rare by 20th-century standards. With an extended focus on the disciplines of the drawing office, this experience was so confining as to classify him a specialist, a serious disability for someone destined to become a chief executive.

Equally, advancement to Swindon's highest office that had been facilitated by the premature passing of three more senior colleagues did not augur well. These tragedies were blows for the company at large, but the first two were also unfortunate in denying opportunities for broader experience that would have been invaluable later. The conditions of the 1940s would have daunted a more widely based chief executive, but it is to his considerable credit that Frederick Hawksworth did not flinch from the obligations that circumstance thrust upon him.

Having coped with the stresses of war, the interlude of hope and enthusiasm was brief. Nineteenth-century profligacy had yielded a railway network of duplicated routes, extravagant structures, and financially underperforming assets that exemplified the futility of excessive capital investment without sustaining cash flow. The earlier trading histories of the 'Big Four' had been unimpressive, and now they faced the added challenge of reconstruction. The railway companies had been lucky to retain independent ownership in 1923, with the GWR doubly fortunate in retaining its core structure. The circumstances of the 1940s allowed no alternative to public ownership. None of this made the passing of the Great Western any less unpalatable and, more than most, Frederick Hawksworth would have been conscious of what was being lost.

It is a chastening thought that while the preservation movement keeps its spirit alive, the GWR ceased to exist as a legal entity two-thirds of a century ago. A work of this nature inevitably necessitates reference to the standard sources, but while many of the facts have appeared previously, an attempt has been made to interpret them from a different angle in the hope that the 'why?' of key events might be better understood. Those who insist on rose-tinted spectacles may doubtless consider elements of what follows as revisionist or even polemical. The author makes no apology for his stance. The GWR was a large and complex organisation, and it would be unrealistic to pretend that it was perfect. Some aspects were in desperate need of improvement over several years, and it is a moot point how long, but for the war, the company could have survived in the absence of such measures being implemented.

Many different sources were drawn upon in this project, but beyond general acknowledgement of their contribution some deserve specific mention. The grey monochrome years of austerity sit on the distant horizons of the author's memory, so the publication *Next Station* was invaluable in helping illustrate the vicissitudes of that period. Peter Lugg and Amyas Crump offered wise counsel that was of considerable help, and they must not be held to account for errors and omissions, for these are solely the fault of the undersigned.

The public availability of so many important Swindon locomotive records through 'Search Engine' at the National Railway Museum was of enormous help, and the courtesy and assistance of the NRM staff is gratefully acknowledged.

Particular thanks are due to Kevin Robertson for generously providing drawings and statistical data from his own sources that either have not previously been published, or at least have erstwhile received little attention. The undersigned is solely responsible for the comments and conclusions based on this material.

Finally, the publisher's uncanny ability adroitly to tickle the ego at times of flagging enthusiasm and incipient despair must not go unrecognised. Prospective authors be warned.

*Jeremy Clements*
County Meath
Ireland
May 2014

# CHAPTER 1
# ONE MAN'S DOMAIN

The decision taken by Messrs Brunel and Gooch in 1841 to establish an engineering works near the ancient, small country town of Swindon was heavily influenced by its suitability as a point at which to change engines on London-Bristol services. Convenience was enhanced by the prospect of it becoming the junction with the planned Great Western Union Railway, by which trains would reach Gloucester. Further, at a time when heavy loads could only be conveniently moved by water, the remoteness of the sea was offset by the existence of the North Wilts Canal, then little more than 20 years old, which linked nearby with the Wilts & Berks Canal and which was eventually straddled by the Works site. This canal system provided short-term benefit for evacuation of stone from Box Hill, used in the construction of the facility and its attendant settlement.

Against these advantages, there were drawbacks associated with the location. The 1851 census recorded that only 254,000 people resided in Wiltshire (which remains a relatively under-populated county to this day), and they were from an essentially agricultural background. Able manufacturing labour thus had to be imported, and housed in one of the earliest purpose-designed company towns. This successful social experiment added considerably to the

costs borne by the fledgling company – but then Brunel, for all his genius, was not noted for sound financial husbandry.

In a demographic sense, immigration brought considerable benefits. The company's growth attracted skilled workers with the motivation to break the mould of their lives, uproot themselves from familiar surroundings, and take a risk. Early validation of Swindon's fledgling role as a centre of excellence concerned the treatment of the company's first 19 steam locomotives. Supplied by five contractors to Brunel's specifications, which seemed to owe much to prevailing paddle steamer technology, these unsuccessful engines were a financial and mechanical headache at an awkward time. Originally serviced in the London area, it was at Swindon that the expense was mitigated by rebuilding and by recycling of component parts that yielded some machines with quite respectable working lives.

As creator of the new town and as the major employer in the area, the company was intertwined with the local population and economy, as emphasised by the vertically integrated nature of the company's manufacturing and repair activities. Unlike 21st-century railway systems, which rely upon outsourced services from independent contractors, the GWR (and other major railway companies) produced virtually all manufactured components and equipment in-house. Works expansion under Joseph Armstrong consummated the objective of manufacturing self-sufficiency, as demonstrated by the 'Beyer' 0-6-0s of 1866, which were the last locomotives supplied by contractors until the 1920s.

Despite consolidation and expansion of the Works under Gooch and Joseph Armstrong, the suitability of Swindon's location was reviewed together with other pressing matters, following elimination of the Broad Gauge. There was a proposal that locomotive engineering be transferred to Wolverhampton in an expansion of the Stafford Road complex. Closer proximity to sources of raw materials (particularly coal, iron and steel) and plentiful skilled labour in the Birmingham area were powerful incentives. The existing infrastructural investment at Swindon would have been retained for carriage and wagon work, it being judged that removal of these activities offered fewer savings opportunities.[1]

The Wolverhampton proposal failed not for any inherent disadvantage in the concept but because there was insufficient land available at Stafford Road. The idea was not unprecedented, as establishment of new facilities in greenfield locations took place elsewhere, as with the London & South Western at Eastleigh (carriage and wagons in 1891, locomotives in 1910) and with the Lancashire & Yorkshire at Horwich (1884). Significantly, in both those examples the chosen locations were close to existing engineering communities.

The need to import manpower to Swindon is demonstrated in microcosm by the origins of the company's Locomotive Superintendents. Gooch and Joseph Armstrong were from the North East, Dean was a Londoner, Churchward a Devonian, and Collett came from Worcestershire. F. W. Hawksworth was the sole Swindonian in this sextet, living his entire life in the town. He was also by family background the most 'Great Western'. His grandfather had been a shed foreman in the Shrewsbury district. As owner of a steam launch on the River Severn and a builder of model locomotives, it was from him that the young Hawksworth learned the basics of steam design and construction. Hawksworth's father was a draughtsman at Swindon, and it was under his tutelage that his son first acquired draughting experience.

The wide range of skills needed in the Works meant that, on leaving school, the key question for every young male Swindonian was whether he would 'go inside'. For those who already had a relative employed by the company, it was customary for the recruit to take up the same skills or disciplines. The apprentice system was the training mechanism for young recruits, reflecting prevailing

social standards. Sons of the well-to-do, or of parents with influence, became premium apprentices upon payment of a prescribed sum to the Locomotive Superintendent, who then assumed direct responsibility for their training. In modern terms, this privileged group were on the 'fast-track' to career advancement, but despite the elitist connotation it was not exclusive. Hawksworth, whose background was more modest, joined the company as an ordinary engineering apprentice.

A by-product of Swindon's geographic isolation and its developing self-sufficiency in manpower was the export of trained and talented personnel to other railways. Individuals such as Robinson, Holden, Pearson and Lucy went on to important positions with other companies, while transfers to Swindon from other organisations were rare. A striking feature of the management succession was the harmony with which leadership passed across the generations, as proven by the few cases where significant disagreement did arise. One instance was the appointment of William Dean in 1877 and the reaction of George Armstrong, who, as Northern Division Locomotive Superintendent, objected to reporting to a younger boss who had been his erstwhile subordinate. There would have been plenty of instances of minor

dissent as is inevitable in any large organisation, but the George Armstrong/Dean stand-off was notable as being one of the few that warranted particular notice. Management stability and the smooth pattern of succession thus avoided disruption, as typified by Deeley's departure from Derby, F. G. Smith and the 'River' Class affair on the Highland Railway, and the unseemly treatment meted out to Hughes on the LMS.

## Reorganisation

Notwithstanding constancy in governance, the senior management structure was in dire need of overhaul by the Grouping. Sir Daniel Gooch had run the company as executive chairman, from which had evolved an structure whereby the Chief Mechanical Engineer, the Chief Civil Engineer, the Chief Accountant, the Company Secretary, and the company's Solicitor all reported direct to independent committees of directors. This was less of a problem with the administrative functions in accounting, secretarial and legal matters, but the independence accorded the two engineers was unacceptable in a modern corporation. With direct command of the principal areas of capital expenditure, they could circumvent the General Manager at will. It has since been established that both accrued their own departmental reserve funds, thereby allowing deployment of tranches of the company's financial assets without administrative oversight.

Felix Pole, very likely the first senior manager with a modern, commercially orientated mind-set, recognised the dangers. With the blessing of the Chairman, Viscount Churchill, he introduced a new structure whereby all departments reported direct to him. From Pole's appointment in 1921, the General Manager could at last be effective in the role of chief executive officer without being outmanoeuvred through duality in reporting lines. A more logical organisation resulted that was better structured to cope with the Grouping, thereby avoiding mayhem that could have seriously threatened the enlarged company.

Unsurprisingly, Pole's changes were inimical to conservative elements and he has since been criticised in the context of failing to 'take his people with him'. Capable chief executive officers know that such sentiments are naïve where rapidly changing environmental circumstances threaten the status quo. The CEO is obliged to look beyond the immediate and to anticipate future problems, and Pole's astute foresight brought about vital changes at a crucial time. In an administrative sense, his was the greatest contribution to the company's fortunes since Sir Daniel Gooch's success in staving off bankruptcy in the 1860s. Regrettably, the Pole style was too progressive for some and he left to become executive chairman of AEI Ltd in 1929. It is testimony to his competence that he filled that role until 1945, retiring at the age of 68, by which time he was completely blind. (His allegiance to the Old Company apparently never wavered, as in the early 1950s he remarked that one of the few benefits of his condition was that he would never see a blue 'King'.)

Considering later developments, it is clear that Pole's departure and its timing was a disaster for the company. Trading conditions had been difficult in the 1920s, but the Great Depression brought a new raft of challenges, as reflected in the adverse business trends analysed below. By 1938 the way in which the Chief Mechanical Engineer and his department were mismanaging a major element of the company's capital expenditure budget was increasingly obvious. Pole, with his innate business acumen, would have recognised the warning signs and would have enacted corrective action much earlier.

The high priest of the conservative fraternity had been G. J. Churchward, to whom the Pole changes were anathema. This aspect, coupled with his distaste for impending revisions in the way labour relations were to be handled, induced him to retire three months early. Little has been recorded of the gyrations during this tumultuous period, but it can be deduced that Churchward saw the reorganisation as a personal slight. He had regarded himself as the company's most important executive officer, and thus interpreted the new order as tantamount to constructive and unwarranted demotion. It is unlikely, therefore, that he was overly cooperative in discussions about his succession, for which there were three possible candidates. F. G. Wright (aged 60 years) had joined the company as an apprentice in 1876, became Chief Draughtsman in 1892, Assistant Works Manager in 1896, Works Manager in 1901, and finally Chief Assistant to the CME in 1903. The other two contenders were C. B. Collett (50 years) – Deputy CME since 1919 – and W. A. Stanier (45 years) – Works Manager since 1920.

Wright apparently had strong expectations but his age counted against him, and he retired in August 1921. Apparently on grounds of seniority (by age and appointment), Collett was appointed to the surprise of some observers. Whether Churchward participated in the selection process is unknown, but subsequent history confirmed Stanier as the better man in combining engineering competence, willingness to innovate, diplomatic leadership, qualities, and social skills. As a sound judge of character, Churchward must have acknowledged Stanier's superior qualities, if only to himself. However, relative seniority was an important criterion by the standards of the time, and difficulties following Dean's preferment over George Armstrong might have stayed fresh in the memory.

In any event, once matters had settled down the *Great Western Railway Magazine* published a pictorial organogram in 1922 setting out the company's senior management structure, which left little doubt about reporting responsibilities and relative seniorities.

(The explosive nature of G. J. Churchward's language could be well imagined, had there been any public implication in his day that he was junior in the pecking order to the Chief Goods Manager, despite that post being responsible for the company's primary revenue source!)

The CME's responsibilities covered the locomotive, carriage and wagon shops at Swindon, the divisional running and repair operations, and all outdoor machinery and docks equipment. The Grouping multiplied their scale, with motive power fleet numbers growing by

The Chairman, Deputy Chairman, & Chief Officers of the Great Western Railway Company.

Supplement to GREAT WESTERN RAILWAY MAGAZINE. JANUARY 1922.

Officers of the Great Western Railway Chief Mechanical Engineers' Department

Supplement to GREAT WESTERN RAILWAY MAGAZINE. JANUARY 1923.

some 25% between 1921 and 1923. Many of the new arrivals were non-standard and of diverse age and quality, while enlargement of the rolling stock fleet added yet more variety. Also, the South Wales companies were effectively integrated transport organisations focussed on the export of coal and other minerals with extensive docks facilities, operational responsibility for which passed into the CME's hands. An extra burden came through the increase in route mileage, as Swindon also manufactured equipment for the Civil Engineer.

With this expansion, the CME had charge of more personnel than did any of his peers within the 'Big Four'. He was now directly subordinate to the General Manager and it is hard to see how the pre-Grouping independent fiefdom could have remained tenable. However, there seems to have been no consideration whether so much in the hands of one man was in the best collegiate interest. Size, geographic diversity, and technical complexity combined to create an unwieldy organisation that would have tested an individual with more management and leadership skills than either Collett or his successor could muster. The company was to pay a heavy price in consequence.

**ABOVE LEFT** The senior officers of the Great Western Railway, following the reorganisation initiated by Felix Pole concurrent with the Grouping. *GWR Magazine*

**ABOVE RIGHT** The senior officers of the Chief Mechanical Engineer's Department following the appointment of C. B. Collett. It is notable that Hawksworth at that point was too junior for inclusion. His rapid advancement followed the premature death of G. H. Burrows, Chief Draughtsman, then that of his assistant, O. E. F. Deverell (who was also insufficiently senior to appear). *GWR Magazine*

Although the CME was responsible for running as well as the workshops, it was traditional to appoint an officer with a predominantly works background – Churchward, Collett, Wright and Stanier all fitted this mould. Senior management thus behaved with a works engineering mentality, which risked operations being treated as a secondary consideration. There was thus a strong case for appointment of an independent Running Superintendent with seniority matching that of the CME, as was adopted by the LMS.

Such an arrangement has been questioned in light of the Anderson-Fowler stand-off on the LMS in the 1920s. However, ingredients *inter alia* in that fractious relationship were Anderson's growing frustration with lack of adequate motive power and Fowler's amiable ineffectiveness. In contrast, Stanier, on joining the LMS, established a working rapport with Anderson based on mutual respect, despite holding some differing technical views. The saga underlined the attraction of splitting accountability, even though this arrangement might periodically suffer through individuals' shortcomings.

Although theoretically demoted through the reorganisation, practically speaking Collett suffered minimal diminution in real authority by virtue of the two general managers for whom he worked. Felix Pole saw motive power as a promotional weapon and ensured maximum publicity for the achievements of *Pendennis Castle* in the 1925 Exchanges (to the annoyance of the LNER), and for the 'Kings' in their early days. His successor, James Milne, was of more restrained temperament, but was empathetic through his Swindon training as a locomotive engineer. These natural allies helped Collett to protect his realm, as did also the company's internal accounting methods.

The Works used a costing system based on a simple formula that embraced direct labour and material expense plus a fixed margin for central overheads. However suspect might have been the information generated by this primitive methodology, it was better than nothing and importantly was accepted by the Civil Engineer as a reasonable charging basis for manufacturing done on his behalf. More significantly still, it was superior to Paddington's standards for the company at large.

The Chief Accountant argued that the business was too complex for application of management accounting systems and that imposition of the requisite disciplines would be expensive, rendering no appreciable net benefit. Thus recourse to historic figures comprising the annual accounts was considered the only feasible means of monitoring the company-wide financial condition. The outcome was that, regardless of the accuracy of the CME's departmental accounting information, it was better than anything available to the General Manager. The CME thus had an informational advantage in refutation of any challenge about how he ran his affairs.

## The Collett style

Understanding something of the way in which Collett worked is crucial to forming judgements about Hawksworth, who so long stood in his shadow. Collett was a competent engineer whose skills had been honed in a hard school. He joined the GWR from Maudslay, Sons & Field Ltd of London (marine engineers) in 1893 at the age

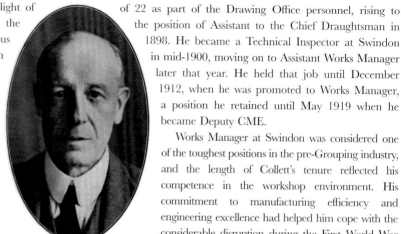

C. B. Collett at retirement in mid-July 1941. *GWR Magazine*

of 22 as part of the Drawing Office personnel, rising to the position of Assistant to the Chief Draughtsman in 1898. He became a Technical Inspector at Swindon in mid-1900, moving on to Assistant Works Manager later that year. He held that job until December 1912, when he was promoted to Works Manager, a position he retained until May 1919 when he became Deputy CME.

Works Manager at Swindon was considered one of the toughest positions in the pre-Grouping industry, and the length of Collett's tenure reflected his competence in the workshop environment. His commitment to manufacturing efficiency and engineering excellence had helped him cope with the considerable disruption during the First World War that had stemmed from governmental manufacturing orders. He therefore spoke with authority when objecting to proposals that the Works should assume a similar role in the later conflict.

The tradition whereby the CME should have a predominantly Works background had been less of a disadvantage for Dean and Churchward, as both had experience of smaller organisations with less of a divide between the technician and he who operated the technician's products. Dean had successfully held three important management appointments concurrently at the more compact Wolverhampton Works, while Churchward had started in the intimate environment of the South Devon Railway's works at Newton Abbot. As the company matured into a more structured organisation in the last quarter of the 19th century, Dean and Churchward by their earlier experiences retained understanding of operational issues at grass roots level. Collett, by contrast, was at a disadvantage in being responsible for a geographically large and varied constituency beyond Swindon Works of which he had virtually no practical experience, and only limited comprehension.

The narrowness of Collett's career background is well illustrated through comparison with that of the popular and competent Richard Maunsell, his senior by three years and his opposite number on the Southern Railway. Maunsell had commenced at the age of 17 as a pupil to H. A. Ivatt on the Great Southern & Western Railway while concurrently reading for an MA (in pursuit of a possible law career) at Trinity University, Dublin. In 1891 he moved to the Lancashire & Yorkshire Railway under an arrangement between Ivatt and Aspinall to exchange promising young men. He became Locomotive Foreman in charge of three Blackpool sheds at the age of 21, and two years later became Assistant Divisional Locomotive Superintendent with the East India Railway. Rising quickly to become District Locomotive Superintendent at Asansol near Calcutta, he returned to the Great Southern & Western in 1896, becoming Assistant Locomotive Engineer and Works Manager at Inchicore. He succeeded Coey as Locomotive Superintendent in 1912, and in 1914 made his final move by taking charge of the SECR Works at Ashford.

RIGHT Two views of the Great Western Railway Chief Mechanical Engineer's Drawing Office at Swindon, taken in 1931. The office was shaped like a letter 'L', and two negatives have been used to render both sides of the office in one picture. The left-hand office was the General Drawing Office, where all the design work was undertaken for machinery and plant throughout the GWR system that was under the responsibility of the CME. The right-hand office was the Locomotive and Carriage & Wagon design office. This was where all the famous GWR locomotives were designed, and is where Hawksworth carried out his calculations and made his drawings for the GWR 'Pacific' locomotive *The Great Bear*.

This breadth of experience contrasted with Collett's time confined to the workshops and drawing office. Without minimising the demanding nature of those roles, Collett would have been helped by a spell away from Swindon as he climbed the ladder. For example, two years as a Divisional Locomotive Superintendent would have taught him a lot about life on the other side of the moon.

Quite unlike Churchward's robust, open-handed leadership, Collett's unappealing style was that of a wily political animal. He was also masterful in deftly manipulating situations to his own advantage, especially in fending off unwelcome suggestions from directors. He was known in such cases to make haste slowly, allowing a proposal to fester without taking firm action until the sponsor lost interest. With more formalised demands, he was well-equipped to cope with penetrating enquiries by virtue of his department's accounting processes.

There was also a ruthless side to his character, as highlighted by an incident at the launch of the 0-6-2T '56xx' class in 1924. Managers and works employees gathered to watch No 5600's first steaming, during which the unlucky engine moved a few yards before coming to an ignominious halt through failure of a valve gear component. The cause was a design oversight that was soon rectified, but not before revised drawings with falsified dates had been prepared and every witness warned that any subsequent reference to the matter would result in instant dismissal. This embargo had effect, as it was years before the matter became

common knowledge. Collett was innately conservative and the embarrassment probably induced even greater reluctance to innovate. The class was the only design that could be uniquely attributed to him and even then it followed a well-trodden path laid down by the Welsh companies. All his other creations were variations on the Churchward theme.

Collett had a devious side that helped him get his own way, apart from his delaying tactics concerning instructions from above. There is a suspicion that he intentionally designed for failure with certain projects, as exemplified by rotary cam valves and streamlining. Another concerned the rumour that he stubbornly refused to acknowledge the advantages of roller bearings. To prove his point, he apparently had two coaches prepared, one with and one without roller bearings. By way of a comparative test, each was uncoupled and given a shove. To the surprise of many, the standard bearing vehicle moved faster and further – but only because Collett had allegedly arranged for the roller-bearing equipped vehicle to be 'fixed' by deliberate assembly as a tight fit.

## The succession issue

Collett's deft hand was also at work in self-preservation, as evident in his attitude towards his immediate subordinates. William A. Stanier had been effectively his No 2 since February 1924, holding the title of 'Principal Assistant to the CME' (note that Collett had been Deputy CME under Churchward). In this role, Stanier willingly

LEFT The Swindon Drawing Office had its own cricket and football teams. This view, dated about 1906, is of the cricket team. F.W. Hawksworth is third from the right in the back row. His brother, who is sixth from the left in the same row, later left railway service and became the Rev J. Hawksworth, Vicar of St Philip's Church, Stratton, Swindon.

undertook most of the social and civic obligations that since Joseph Armstrong's time had traditionally been the lot of the Locomotive Superintendent/CME. Reporting on Stanier's departure for the LMS, the *Great Western Railway Magazine* noted in January 1932 his wide community interests and his active role in many of the company's social organisations. He was involved in the Medical Fund Society, Mechanics' Institution, GWR Athletic Association, Swindon Branch of the Social and Educational Union (as President), and Swindon Works Sick Fund Society (as a Trustee). Outside the company milieu, he had a prominent role with the YMCA, was a Governor of Toc H, a Borough Magistrate, a Governor of Swindon College, and a patron of sports in all its branches, particularly athletics.

John Auld.
*GWR Magazine*

Collett shunned such commitments and, beyond some involvement in the GWR Musical Society in the 1920s, confined himself to a quiet home life. On becoming CME he continued to live modestly, while Churchward stayed on in the grandeur of Newburn House. His wife Ethelwyn was the focus of his existence outside work, and his world fell apart with her death following a short illness in March 1923 at the age of 47. An already deeply private man, he withdrew even more into himself following this tragedy. His work was an essential psychological prop as he had no evident outside interests beyond a fascination with medical matters and an obsession with re-establishing contact with Ethelwyn through the medium of the paranormal.

Following Stanier's departure, Collett ensured that John Auld was appointed in replacement. Auld was an unusual character within the Swindon establishment, regarded initially as even more of a foreigner than his Scottish origin might imply. His career had started in 1887 as an apprentice with the Glasgow & South Western Railway before moving to the Great North of Scotland, then the London Tilbury & Southend. He left the latter prior to the Midland Railway takeover, returning to the G&SWR as Locomotive Superintendent at Glasgow, before becoming CME of the Barry Railway in 1910. In the management realignments of the immediate post-Grouping period, he was appointed Mechanical Engineer, Barry Docks, in June 1922, then Docks Assistant to the CME in August. In February 1924 he became Docks & Personal Assistant to the CME.

Auld's advancement was convenient for Collett. Apart from operating experience that complemented Collett's minimal exposure in that field, Auld was also knowledgeable in management of the inherited harbour empire. Further, his affable manner helped him to blend into the Swindon scene and to assume roles similar to those that Stanier had filled. He was keenly interested in bodies devoted to the benefit of railway employees and at different times was president of the Medical Fund Society, the Mechanics' Institute, the Engineering Society, and the Athletic Association.

There was another facet that was to Collett's personal advantage. Auld was slightly the senior by a matter of months and therefore presented no competitive threat. From about 1936 onwards, it has been alleged that Collett's afflictions of loneliness and recurrent depression grew more acute, significantly eroding his working competence. Auld's role thus developed into rather more than that of senior assistant as he 'carried' his boss through until 1941. By then aged 70 years, Auld was doggedly and quite reasonably set upon retirement, which left Collett exposed and lacking the support necessary to maintain the pretence of continuing ability.

Succession had been a sensitive matter from the early 1930s. After Stanier's departure, the matter was raised indirectly in a chance conversation at Paddington between Collett, Sir James Milne and Viscount Churchill, Chairman of the Board. The latter remarked that, as he expected Collett to go 'the full course', there would have been no chance of Stanier becoming CME. As Stanier was five years younger with an expectation of normal retirement at 65, Collett manipulatively chose to infer that the chairman expected him to remain until at least the age of 70. Subsequently, if the matter of departure came up, he would cite the chairman's remark as being a formal request for him to stay on until then.

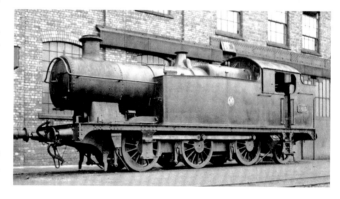

**ABOVE** Hard upon the heels of the new 'Castles', Collett introduced the 0-6-2T '56xx' Class specifically for use in South Wales. Rationalisation of the Welsh motive power fleets was a major priority in the mid-1920s, and the appearance of No 5600 heralded a wheel arrangement previously unprecedented in Swindon design history but very familiar in the Welsh valleys. This was the only class solely attributable to Collett, as all others introduced during his tenure were variations on themes initiated by Churchward. The spectacular failure of the prototype at its first steaming would have reinforced Collett's innate caution and reluctance to risk too much innovation ever again. No 6615 was built in December 1927, and has since acquired the distinctive 'shirt button' totem. *Stephenson Locomotive Society*

Stanier had been gone for more than a year when in 1933 there were two significant events. On the positive side, the first diesel railcar appeared, but the cause of Swindon steam suffered a setback through a tragedy. G. J. Churchward, still in residence at Newburn House, was struck and killed by a train on 19 December. His passing, widely mourned throughout the industry, led to a change of which the 'Old Man' would definitely not have approved.

Churchward had been a leading participant in the Association of Railway Locomotive Engineers, a body formed during the First World War to initiate designs suitable for use nationwide, should nationalisation proceed in the 1920s. Although that objective soon fell by the wayside, ARLE continued as a useful forum for the exchange of ideas among the industry's senior mechanical engineers. Despite having been re-elected as President in 1932, Collett withdrew from any further involvement in ARLE soon after Churchward's death.

From this it may be concluded that Collett had never been keen on sharing knowledge with his opposite numbers, and that he had only participated at his predecessor's behest. Once free to exercise his own will, his withdrawal marked the commencement of Swindon's self-imposed isolation from the industry's mainstream. It can only be speculated how matters might have differed had there remained a free exchange of views in the open-handed Churchward manner. The GWR's motive power policy might have been more progressive. The other companies might have gained useful knowledge derived from the diesel railcar programme. Collett's assistants might have been better informed and thus better equipped to take over the reins when he did eventually relinquish control.

Much has been written of Swindon's technical stagnation in steam design during the 1930s, but with little analysis of the attendant senior management dynamics. On return visits to Swindon, Stanier tried to appraise Collett of perceived shortcomings in GWR practice, but these views, based on hard empirical evidence garnered with the LMS, were abruptly rejected. However, circumstances suggest that Stanier's message was spread more widely within the GWR camp. As will be considered later, he worked with Hawksworth on a significant project (crushed by Collett) as early as 1926, and it seems likely that the pair collaborated on other novel ideas before, and perhaps after, the move to the LMS. Further, Stanier was James Milne's brother-in-law (they had both married daughters of Levi Morse, a native of Highworth, Swindon). It seems entirely possible that this trio discreetly shared reservations about motive power practice.

Usually adherence to low degree superheat serves as the metaphor for the stagnation period, but the issues were much broader and more deep-seated. With Collett's recurrent depression,

Frederick Hawksworth on his appointment as Chief Mechanical Engineer, 7 July 1941. *GWR Magazine*

declining physical condition and growing dependence upon John Auld, Milne and others should have recognised the implications for a large industrial combine led by an ailing chief executive in his mid-60s, helped by a deputy of the same age. There must have been thoughts about Collett's enforced departure when another unfortunate event had a serious impact on manpower planning. R. A. G. Hannington had been Works Manager since 1922, and in the traditional path of career advancement was regarded as Collett's natural successor. He was slightly older than Hawksworth and had much wider practical experience. These expectations were dashed by Hannington's accidental death at the age of 54 in June 1937; a biographical note appears as Appendix B.

Thus were exposed the risks of an inflexible promotional policy. Collett was no longer capable of properly fulfilling his role yet there was no obvious replacement candidate. Hannington's death helped ensure Collett's retention of office when other factors favoured his replacement. This situation meant that a considerable debt was owed to Auld for staying in post, and it is remarkable that his vital role in the Swindon story has been so little recognised.

## The last of the sextet

A group photograph of the seven most senior managers at Swindon dated 1938 clearly defines their respective rankings. Collett sits front and centre with Auld on his right and Hawksworth on his left. Thus the hierarchical tradition ensured that Hawksworth could anticipate the future course of his career, subject only to the CME's departure date. If Collett's earlier career experience had been narrow, Hawksworth's history was positively cloistered:

| | |
|---|---|
| 10 February 1884 | Born in Swindon |
| August 1898 | Joined GWR as apprentice in Locomotive Department |
| Circa 1903 | Period in Swindon Testing House |
| February 1905 | Draughtsman |
| August 1919 | Assistant to Chief Draughtsman |
| July 1923 | Assistant Chief Draughtsman |
| April 1925 | Chief Draughtsman |
| 1 January 1933 | Assistant to CME |
| 7 July 1941 | Chief Mechanical Engineer |
| 31 December 1949 | Retired |
| 13 July 1976 | Died in Swindon |

The key stage in Hawksworth's advancement occurred between 1919 and 1925. His appointment as Assistant to the Chief Draughtsman plucked him from the ranks, but in the normal course it would have been some years before he could expect further promotion. However, G. H. Burrows, who had become Personal Assistant to the CME and Chief Draughtsman in August 1922, passed away 11 months later at the age of 53. O. E. F. Deverell, previously Assistant Chief Draughtsman, took over, but he in turn died aged 50 in April 1925. These losses led to Hawksworth's elevation to senior management in less than six years. It is not known if he had tried earlier to broaden his experience, but these moves effectively denied him any such opportunity.

He held the post of Chief Draughtsman for almost eight years, a period that saw the introduction of the 'Kings' and the new generation of pannier tanks, together with the commencement of the production-series 'Halls'. The next important management realignment followed Stanier's departure, when he became Assistant to the CME, while Auld became the Principal Assistant. At that stage further promotion prospects would have seemed minimal in the face of Collett's determination to stay in office.

The situation that so unexpectedly came about in the summer of 1937 was a reminder of the opportunity lost in failing to back Stanier in 1921. K. J. Cook, who had been Assistant Works Manager since 1923, acceded to the late Hannington's position in August 1937. With Collett close to the end of his career, Cook would have been a better candidate to succeed him through being more in touch with the manufacturing and operational realities. It could be argued that yet again the precedence of seniority resulted in preferment of the second-best option.

While the implications of Swindon's period of stagnation may not have then been fully appreciated, wartime conditions swiftly revealed the urgent need for change. Early in the conflict there was debate between government authorities and Collett on how the company's considerable manufacturing capacity could be harnessed to help with the war effort. The authorities sought wholesale redeployment into munitions production, while Collett resisted on the grounds that the national interest was better served by giving priority to maintenance of a competent motive power and rolling stock fleet. He had been long accustomed to behaving autocratically, and to his views not being questioned. Although later proven to be essentially correct, he handled this debate with little diplomatic aplomb, leading to official questions over his possible pacifist tendencies. This situation, combined with his advancing years and Auld's retirement intentions, enforced his withdrawal from the scene at the age of 70 years, just as he had always intended.

Assessment of Frederick Hawksworth as CME should take account of the breadth and complexity of the responsibilities he assumed and his determination, despite his background, to confront numerous unprecedented challenges during a time of unprecedented national crisis. A less obvious but more longstanding challenge lay in the need to rationalise construction policy to arrest the wastages of the late Collett era. In those trying circumstances, John Auld's varied practical experience would have been invaluable. Thus were the crisis conditions surrounding Hawksworth's appointment exacerbated.

About a month after the new CME took over, F. C. Hall slipped into the shoes previously occupied by Auld. A close contemporary of Hawksworth, his career had taken a different course:

| | |
|---|---|
| July 1900 | Joined GWR as apprentice in Locomotive Department |
| February 1908 | Drawing Office |
| June 1919 | Assistant Divisional Superintendent, Old Oak Common |
| 1922 | Divisional Superintendent, Neath |
| August 1924 | Assistant to Locomotive Running Superintendent & Outdoor Assistant to CME |
| October 1929 | Divisional Locomotive Superintendent, Bristol |
| September 1931 | Locomotive Running Superintendent & Outdoor Assistant to CME |
| August 1941 | Principal Assistant to CME |

His practical experience was a valuable counterbalance to Hawksworth's specialised, 'ivory tower' background. If his boss appeared aloof and remote, Hall in contrast was popular with the common touch. This was demonstrated once with regard to his namesake tribe of 4-6-0s. Those in charge of finding new names were running out of options – in GWR territory at least – and the Drawing Office was asked to make suggestions. The response was less than helpful, including a proposal to use the name 'Fred Hall'.

Pressures from outside sources in the war years were immense. Hawksworth's burden was relieved by the appointment of two more Assistants – R. W. Woolacott in July 1941 and A. W. J. Dymond in July 1945. The latter had joined the Taff Vale company in 1918 as a pupil and, with extensive service at divisional level in South Wales, he was particularly useful at a time of escalating difficulties with coal supplies. Nonetheless, Swindon for the management team and for the rank and file remained the CME's fiefdom, in which his word was law. Establishing how Hawksworth exercised command has proven difficult, as there is little contemporary written record.

Among the next generation of Swindon management, there seems to have been little recalled of a positive nature in the form of stories and gossip, suggesting that Hawksworth had a bland personality with a scholarly disposition. The latter characteristic is deduced from his activities outside the company. A source who had worked in the Drawing Office in 1958/59 said that there appeared to have been little respect for his practical engineering abilities among those who had worked for him. With minimal lasting or favourable impressions left on the corporate memory, some commentators have recorded somewhat negative opinions. One view expressed was that 'Hawksworth was a jumped-up draughtsman'. This assessment might have been rather cruel but, considering his career path, there was perhaps a grain of truth in it.

**ABOVE** The Great Western legacy of Frederick Hawksworth: 'County' Class No 1016 *County of Hants* on the 'Cambrian Coast Express' in BR days. The date is pre-March 1957 as this locomotive was one of the first to be fitted with the standard double chimney in that month. The livery was the generally unpopular BR 'mixed traffic' lined black that was reminiscent of that carried by London & North Western locomotives. The train, apart from the older catering vehicle, appears to be made up entirely of the handsome and comfortable Hawksworth passenger coaches. Difficulties in obtaining materials meant that only about 25% of the planned production run was actually completed before construction ceased in favour of what later became known as the BR Mark 1 stock, which was considered to be inferior. *Ian Allan Library*

Certainly Frederick Hawksworth was technically talented, with an academic bent. As an apprentice he had won the Gooch Prize for machine drawing and the GWR Chairman's prize for the best aggregate results at the Swindon Technical Institute. Later, at the Royal College of Science, he gained first class honours in machine design. He acknowledged how much he had been helped by his studies by later giving back to the education system. For several years he taught various engineering subjects at the Swindon Technical Institute and was also organiser of the machine drawing and design classes. He participated in an advisory committee appointed by the board of that institute and also served for three years as Chairman of the Swindon Junior Engineering Society. He was also a member of the Swindon Education Committee, one of the Wiltshire County Council representatives on the Higher Education Committee, and a member of several committees of the City and Guilds of London Institute. He also served as a council member of the Institution of Mechanical Engineers.

Beyond these technical commitments, he resumed the tradition that Collett had ignored by participating in social affairs. He was President of the Social and Educational Union, and a lifelong member of the choir at St Mark's. He was tall and muscular, which helped him become an accomplished rugby player in his younger years. Later he became a Justice of the Peace, and from 1951 until 1959 he was Chairman of Swindon Borough Magistrates. His services to the community were recognised by his appointment as a Freeman of the Borough in 1960.

Collett had chosen to command from his office, passing instructions down through his immediate subordinates. Hawksworth also adopted an autocratic style, which was hardly surprising since this had been typical of his role model for 20 years. He apparently had little time for ideas and proposals that he did not 'own', or that did not conform with his own views. With respect to proposals initiated without his approval in areas where he might hold counter views, he did not hesitate to exercise his authority.

Hawksworth held untrammelled power so far as his subordinates were concerned, in the fashion that stretched back to the days of Gooch. While the CME's power base had a long history, its demise as an independent command actually preceded Hawksworth's appointment and can be measured precisely – 3 September 1939. With the formation on the outbreak of war of the Railway Executive Committee, acting as agent of the Minister of Transport, the management teams of the 'Big Four' found themselves answerable to a new body that initially comprised Sir James Milne, Sir Ralph Wedgwood, C. H. Newton, Frank Pick, E. J. Missenden and Sir William Wood.

This change left the CME subject to direction by faceless authorities who dictated much of the Works' non-railway productive effort, who drained the enterprise of experienced labour, who exerted increasing demands upon locomotives and rolling stock, and who withheld at crucial points the raw materials for maintenance and improvement of the assets needed to get the job done. Never again would Swindon be one man's domain.

# CHAPTER 2
# THE PRICE OF STAGNATION

Hawksworth took over as CME in 1941, the year generally regarded as the nadir of the Second World War. Although conditions were to improve, from then until his retirement two years after nationalisation the working environment was less benign than it had been the 1930s. Many of the problems that beset Hawksworth during his tenure stemmed from outside influences over which he had little or no control, but less recognised were internal issues embedded in the manner by which Swindon's affairs had been managed prior to his appointment.

Since the Grouping, the peacetime economic environment could be divided into three distinct phases. Appendix A briefly summarises the background conditions and provides a fuller digest of the inter-company comparative data referred to below. However, the dominant issues for the GWR in the three phases were:

**1923-1930:** rationalisation, refurbishment, modernisation of assets acquired at the Grouping
**1931-1933:** containment of activity enforced by the adverse conditions of the Depression years
**1934-1939:** gradual resumption of momentum in the face of acute road transport competition

**ABOVE** Showing them how. The display of a GWR 'Castle' alongside an LNER Class 'A1' Gresley 4-6-2 at the 1924 Empire Exhibition at Wembley led to exchange trials between the two types in April 1925. The GWR was represented on the LNER by No 4079 *Pendennis Castle*, which worked expresses between King's Cross and Leeds. The 'Castle' was a visibly smaller engine, encouraging some cynics to doubt its ability to lift a 475-ton train up the difficult climb out of King's Cross. In fact, the 'Castle' consistently passed Finsbury Park station in less time than the best recorded by a 'Pacific'. More importantly, using unfamiliar Yorkshire coal the 'Castle' outperformed the LNER engine in fuel consumption. On the GWR, where both used Welsh coal, the home engine outshone the visitor by an even greater margin, although it was largely overlooked that the LNER engine performed impressively over the challenging Paddington-Plymouth road.

This was an important event in the history of 20th-century steam from which the LNER drew more profit in the long term. Gresley took note of the results and modified his 'Pacifics' – most importantly with regard to valve design. Collett interpreted the contest as affirmation of the superiority of Churchward's principles, and as a premise for maintaining the status quo. The trials very likely marked the commencement of Swindon's stagnation period in steam development. *Ian Allan Library*

ABOVE At the Grouping the Great Western had a fine locomotive fleet bequeathed by Churchward, which eased Collett's burden in sorting out the diverse fleets acquired from the absorbed companies. At the pinnacle stood the 'Star' Class, of which No 4013 *Knight of St Patrick* was a member, seen here at Old Oak Common on 24 May 1913. The programme of post-construction improvements – superheating and top feed – was implemented with larger locomotives as efficiently as the new fleet had been introduced. No 4013 has received these improvements. *Lens of Sutton*

ABOVE At the other end of the motive power spectrum, no new 0-6-0 tank classes were introduced during Churchward's tenure, but the versatile small pannier '2021' Class continued under construction until 1905. No 2088 was one of the later survivors, staying in service until 1955. *B. V. Franey*

The conditions of the Depression years were extraordinary, but the slower pace of recovery by the railways in the succeeding period did not bode well. Assessment of the social causes lies outside the scope of this work, but it was unavoidable that the changing transport market would exert increasing influence on the manner in which railways invested and then extracted maximum return on the funds so deployed.

Collett and his team, with their 'works focus' secure within the stability of Swindon's traditions, lived in a paradigm where running issues were a secondary consideration to manufacturing quality. This mental isolation helped keep them remote from the effects of an increasingly hostile environment upon the company as a whole. For Swindon it was largely a matter of business as usual although, as the 1930s progressed, the principle of asset replacement by renewal on a like-for-like basis partially metamorphosed into new construction labelled as rebuilding. Unfortunately any resultant savings, perceived or real, were camouflaged by fleet management practices that were later proved inferior to those of the other companies.

Retention of inside valve motion, adherence to low degree superheating, and the yielding of the 'blue ribbon' for power and speed to the LMS and LNER often serve as metaphors for the stagnation that took hold at Swindon in the late 1930s. However, these factors had little relevance to the reality of running an efficient fleet. Having to burrow between the frames to service valve motion was unpleasant but, from a hard-nosed management perspective, of little consequence in an era of cheap, plentiful labour. Superheating was beneficial, but the number of locomotives

ABOVE Churchward's modern 4-4-0 for secondary express work was the 4-4-0 'County' Class. These engines were potent performers for their size, but suffered from poor riding qualities. Also, it was never entirely clear what was the purpose of the original 30, especially with ample numbers of larger-wheeled outside-framed 4-4-0s in service. In 1911-12 ten more were built with curved drop ends. No 3828 *County of Hereford* was one of this series, the purpose for which was even more obscure than those introduced 1904-06. *Ian Allan Library*

that could fully exploit the advantages in everyday service was comparatively few. High-speed stunts with a small group of pampered 'Pacifics' captured the headlines, and imparted an illusion of modernity that was at odds with the everyday reality.

For the GWR, the causes of decline in the inter-war years were multi-faceted and Collett must bear much of the blame, although not exclusively. The process of enlargement brought a host of additional responsibilities and it is easy with the benefit of 20/20

**ABOVE LEFT** Just as the intended purpose of the final ten 4-4-0 'Counties' was unclear, so was that of 'County Tanks' Nos 2241-50 built in 1912. By then the 'Large Prairies' were becoming available in significant numbers and were definitely better suited to heavy suburban work. Again, the curved drop end styling was applied, making for a handsome engine as apparent with No 2242 seen here at Swindon on 10 September 1933. The lives of the 4-4-2Ts, like the 'County' 4-4-0s, were quite short, and this engine was the penultimate example to remain in ordinary service, being withdrawn in September 1935. *A. C. Roberts*

**BELOW LEFT** Sometimes confused with the 'County Tanks' but actually a quite different design was the beautifully proportioned, one-off 4-4-2T No 4600 built in 1913. The excellent 2-6-2T Class '45xx' had by then established itself as a versatile and speedy performer on those services for which this engine might have been planned, and it only survived until 1925. *F. Moore's Railway Photographs*

was in the final stages of withdrawal. The disparate contingent from the economically insignificant Midland & South Western Junction Railway also received disproportionate rebuilding attention despite limited life expectancy.

On a broader front, new standard boilers were designed for absorbed engines deemed suitable for retention – the No 9 was used with Barry and Cambrian engines, and the No 11 for those from the Cardiff, Midland & South Western Junction and Taff Vale (most Rhymney rebuilds received Standard No 10 boilers). There were cases where new boilers were not fitted to entire classes, resulting in uncharacteristic visual variations. Adherence to tradition meant that the new boilers were tapered, and it is doubtful whether the extra construction cost was justified by these engines' typical duties. Other cases saw attempts to improve doubtful performers by fitting taper boilers while leaving features undisturbed that were the real cause of shortcomings.

The most extreme example of waste concerned the ex-Barry Railway 0-6-4T Class 'L' locomotives built in 1914. These ten engines were handsome, powerful and much liked by crews, although the bogie suffered from an unexplained proneness to derail on uneven track. Four were selected for rebuilding with Standard No 4 superheated boilers in 1923, presumably to provide for spares of the original type. The class was stored during the 1926 General Strike, then withdrawn in September/October of that year. Collett claimed to learn only after they had been broken up that these competent engines had been but 12 years old with low mileages.

This was a modern design in quite a different category from some obscure types that had been acquired. Further, the early selection of four for 'Great Westernisation' showed that their potential had already been recognised. Strangest of all, they had been designed by John Auld who, at the time of their scrapping, was one of Collett's assistants. The implication was that oversight of the expanded fleet was inadequate, that management

hindsight to be critical. Nonetheless, from 1923 onwards it is apparent that his tenure was marked by inadequate appreciation of strategic planning, and by adherence to Churchward principles that sometimes rendered at best only marginal economic gains. Early evidence of these shortcomings emerged in addressing the unprecedented challenge of assimilating the large, diverse fleet acquired at the Grouping.

In general, inclusion of the Welsh companies was sensitively conducted. Several of their officers went on to senior appointments with the GWR, while local preferences were recognised in the '56xx' Class, whose 0-6-2T wheel arrangement was new to Swindon but familiar in the Valleys. Recognition came also in a tangential but gracious manner with the new 'Castle' Class. These engines were destined for services to the West Country yet the first six were named after Welsh establishments. Caerphilly was the home of the Rhymney Railway works, an organisation well respected by the GWR (and also the home area of Collett's wife's family).

These gestures aside, wasteful errors suggested that certain standards were lacking in the absorption process. Early on, three Cambrian 0-6-0s that were significantly younger than their similar Dean Goods counterparts were condemned on superficial grounds, suggesting unrealistic expectations of the average condition of the new acquisitions. In contrast, undue attention by way of modernisation was accorded to some undeserving cases, such as the rebuilding of an ex-Taff Vale 0-6-0 Class 'L/M' when the type

**ABOVE LEFT** The Grouping presented unprecedented organisational challenges in rationalising the diverse locomotive fleet that had been acquired, and there were some early mistakes. Three members of the Cambrian Railways 'Large Belpaire Goods' were summarily scrapped at Swindon in 1922 on grounds of condition, despite being only 19 years old. No 892 (ex-Cambrian No 93) was luckier, staying in service until 1953 on its home turf. *Historical Model Railway Society*

**ABOVE RIGHT** Ex-Rhymney Railway 0-6-2T Class 'A' No 117, as BR No 73, is seen at Swindon in August 1952 following withdrawal the previous month, in company with the rather sorry-looking 'Saint' No 2954 *Tockenham Court*. This Rhymney engine is in more or less original condition with only a minor degree of 'Great Westernisation'.

**RIGHT** Ex-Rhymney Railway 0-6-2T Class 'AP' No 37 is seen as BR No 80 following withdrawal in February 1954. This engine received more extensive treatment than did No 73, being fitted with a Standard No 10 boiler in September 1928. As a result, it looks similar to the GWR Class '56xx'.

information systems were poor, and that, with the Auld factor, the left hand had no idea what the other was up to.

By the 1930s there was little to suggest that overall management direction had improved. Difficult economic conditions were reflected in contraction of new construction from 223 locomotives in 1930 to around a third of that total in 1932. A bellwether was the Class '42xx', whose principal *raison d'être* was South Wales coal traffic. Nos 5275-94 (a slightly modernised version) were constructed in 1930 but, apart from trial trips, never worked as 2-8-0Ts. They went straight into store before later conversion to 2-8-2Ts. Plans for another 20 were cancelled altogether.

Creation of the 2-8-2T Class '72xx' presaged a programme under which 'new' locomotives were introduced through rebuilding of older types, or by adaptation of components. This process was distinct from genuine new classes that were sensible reincarnations of 19th-century designs (e.g. 0-4-2T Classes '48xx'/'58xx'). (See Table 1 overleaf).

The motivation for these programmes appears to have been to combine modernisation with economy. More than 200 engines were involved, but there is evidence that even wider application was considered. By the late 1930s there was a need for more eight-coupled freight engines for roles that could not be adequately met by the 2-8-2T type. Alternatives included fitting a Standard No 1 boiler to Class '42xx' chassis, recycled as a 2-8-0, and to ROD Class '30xx'.

Apart from minor items such as outside steam pipes and cabs, the only major design improvement in this programme concerned the improved steam passages with the 'Granges', i.e. it was essentially a case of more of the same. Nevertheless, Collett's approach introduced some curiosities. The Locomotive Scheme of 1901 envisaged four standard driving wheel diameters (4ft 1½in, 4ft 7½in, 5ft 8in and 6ft 8½in), but effectively only three, as the smallest had limited application. In contrast, Collett injected variety: 5ft 3in (new Class '31xx'), 5ft 6in (Class '81xx'), 6ft 0in ('Hall') and 6ft 6in ('King'). The 18-spoke wheel for the new Class '31xx' was connected with the significant High Acceleration Project, which is considered

| TABLE 1 | | | | |
|---|---|---|---|---|
| **Original class** | **Original Nos** | **Built** | **New class** | **Conversion/rebuild year** |
| '42xx' | 5275-5294 | 1930 | '72xx' | 1934 |
| '42xx' | 5255-5274 | 1925-26 | '72xx' | 1935-36 |
| '42xx' | Various '42xx' series | 1912-16 | '72xx' | 1937-39 |
| '2021' | 2062 | 1930 | '54xx' | 1930 |
| 'Bulldog'/'Duke' | Various | 1895-1906 | '32xx' | 1936-39 |
| 'Star' | 4063-4072 | 1922-23 | 'Castle' | 1937-40 |
| '43xx' | '43xx'/'53xx' series | 1911 | 'Grange' | 1936-39 |
| '43xx' | '43xx'/'53xx' series | 1911 | 'Manor' | 1938/39 |
| '3150' | Various | 1907 | '3100' (new) | 1938/39 |
| '5100' | Various | 1903-06 | '81xx' | 1938/39 |

later. Nevertheless, it looked curious beside the Dean-era 5ft 2in-diameter 16-spoke wheel used for Classes '2251', '54xx' and '48xx', as obviously not even the tyre was interchangeable.

Another questionable practice that dated from Churchward's time was the concurrent construction of similarly sized but structurally different classes for ostensibly the same sort of work. This was particularly apparent with the 'Granges' and later 'Halls', but reached its most extreme in 1938/39. In those two years, through new build and rebuild processes, 33 'Large Prairies' entered service to handle similar duties with three different driving wheel diameters and two different boiler sizes.

The introduction of No 5087 *Tintern Abbey* into service in November 1940 saw closure of these rebuilding exercises, and a significant change in new build policy. Although Hawksworth was challenged by shortages of capital and materials, he undertook no rebuilding of earlier locomotives during his extensive construction programme. From this it might be concluded that he had disagreed with his predecessor's policy and that the financial advantages of rebuilding had been overstated. Collett's obsession with accounting minutiae had deflected attention from changing traffic demands, as was proven in 1938 by the exposure of unsettling trends in the management of the locomotive and rolling stock fleets.

Efficient fleet management was hampered by systemic failure that penetrated the CME's department from depot level upwards. It was standard practice to record mileages for locomotives on secondary duties (e.g. branch, shunting, pilot work, etc) on the formula of notional miles per hour in steam; in one authenticated case, a locomotive was habitually recorded as covering 25 miles in a day when the reality was fewer than 2. The risk of error was less with engines working clearly defined, longer-distance duties, but for the bulk of the fleet the capacity for distortion of key records was profound. The resultant overstatement of mileages led to more frequent usage-based maintenance schedules than physical condition actually justified. It also helped create an illusion of engineering quality where dismantling revealed little component wear as the machine had actually done less work than officially recorded.

The organisational structure of the CME's department meant that the financial performances of the workshop and running activities were blended together. Splitting these responsibilities in 1922 would have provided transparency concerning how and where money was being spent or wasted. In the absence of such an organisational realignment, at least a spell away from Swindon would have opened Collett's eyes to the uncomfortable reality that the system for which he became responsible relied on figures fabricated at depot level and thus unreliable as an aid to accurate management of capital assets.

The factor most immune to change in any corporate reorganisation is 'culture', which at Swindon was orientated around manufacturing engineering. This was accentuated by the background of the CME, which made him ill-equipped to cope with pressures exerted on the company by external forces. Awareness of such impact would have come from factors that dictated the use of locomotives and rolling stock, as encapsulated in responsibilities for running that, within the Swindon management philosophy, played second fiddle.

Nevertheless, drawing upon information sources quoted extensively below, base data suggests that the average GWR locomotive continued to perform impressively, measured in coal consumption (lbs per engine mile):

| | 1930 | 1937 |
|---|---|---|
| **GWR** | 44.93 | 44.03 |
| **LMS** | 56.73 | 56.34 |
| **LNER** | 56.51 | 56.49 |
| **SR** | 43.37 | 43.50 |

Obviously, many factors were influential, and predominantly the GWR's greater use of higher calorific Welsh fuel bestowed a considerable advantage. In this respect, there was no sign that stagnation had any impact on individual unit efficiency. (The Southern performed better, but that company's differing structure and profile made it less useful as a basis for objective comparison.)

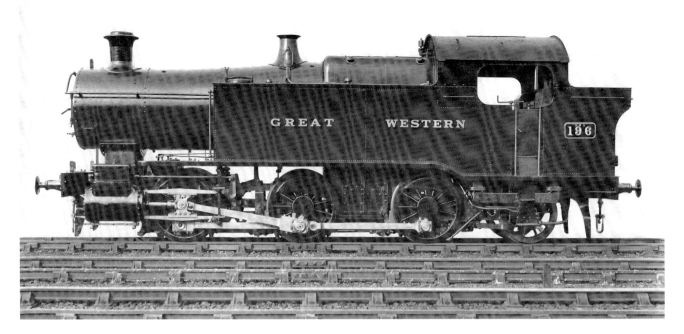

It was in fleet usage that the GWR was below par. Following the post-Grouping need for rationalisation, adverse economic conditions of the 1930s called for a radical reduction in the numbers of underperforming assets. It was soon evident that poor trading conditions would be more than a short-term aberration stemming from the Depression, as rail usage was waning in real terms, and as a proportion of the total transport market. It followed that contraction in fleet numbers was essential, and in terms of percentage reduction between 1930 and 1937 inter-company comparisons are revealing:

|  | No of steam locomotives | No of carriages |
|---|---|---|
| **GWR** | -2.3 | -5.2 |
| **LMS** | -16.6 | -21.3 |
| **LNER** | -7.4 | -11.9 |
| **SR** | -2.1 | -4.1 |

A vital element of transport activity (be it an airline or a tramp steamer operator) is the degree to which income is extracted from expensive capital assets. In the inter-war period, efficiency in keeping mobile assets fully engaged in productive work was as critically important as it is in the 21st century.

## Market background

The rationalisation programmes of the 1920s had been helped by a decade of relative prosperity, other than during the General Strike year of 1926. Despite the sense of enterprise and optimism, broader economic indicators were a source of concern. With the GWR, aggregate receipts (freight and passenger traffic) in 1923 were £32.7 million, but had shrunk to £29.6 million by 1930. This contraction was partly due to deflation (an alien concept for later generations accustomed to inflation as a constant, unpalatable fact of life), but even on the most favourable assessment the company was only holding a static position volume-wise within an expanding market.

Between 1923 and 1930 nationwide growth in numbers of road vehicles was substantial: motorcycles were up 68%; passenger-

**ABOVE** Another case of poor decision-making leading to waste occurred with the 0-6-2T Barry Class 'K', a type that had been built in 1899 by Cooke Loco & Machine Company, New Jersey. This was an unusual blend of American and British design practice with a typically Barry Railway-style rear-end superstructure. However, they had bar frames and a characteristic American front end – outside cylinders and a balanced slide valve actuated by long valve spindles and rocking shafts. The combination of short valve lap at seven-eights of an inch and long valve travel at 5½ inches made late cut-offs and heavy fuel consumption inevitable. Some modifications were made by the Barry company, but the poor front-end design was never properly addressed, and they remained generally unsatisfactory. In 1923 Nos 194 and 196 (Barry Nos 118 and 120 respectively) were sent to Swindon, where they were fitted with Standard No 3 boilers. All five of the class had received new or reconditioned boilers between 1909 and 1919. The need for new standard boilers was unclear when poor performance stemmed from the inadequate front end, which was left untouched. During GWR days they were confined to banking, short trip and pilot duties; No 196 survived until 1932, while the others disappeared between 1927 and 1930. *Official GWR photograph*

carrying vehicles (cars, coaches, buses) were up 130%; and freight vehicles up 91%. With fixed freight rates, railway income levels moved in closer correlation to tonnages shipped, but the changing profile of passenger traffic was ominous. There was diminution in journey numbers (the 1930 total was 12% less than 1923) but, more insidiously, the value of individual ticket sales was reducing. Industry-wide, 56% of passenger revenue was through tickets sold at full tariff in 1923, whereas by 1930 this had shrunk to less than 12%. Thus passengers with the resources and discretion to choose were finding it preferable to travel by road.

The years 1931-33 were severe for the transport market generally. The road vehicle population remained virtually static (2.28 million in 1930 and 2.24 million in 1933), but there was an important change in its composition, with an increase of 130,000

in passenger-carrying vehicles, mainly at the expense of motorcycle numbers. During the same period the railways suffered a 7% fall in passenger journeys (revenue 13% down) and a 17% fall in freight volumes (revenue 19% down), showing that road transport was less vulnerable to adverse economic conditions.

From 1934 onwards, steady economic recovery was apparent in the changing composition of the road population that reflected users' growing affluence. Comparisons of 1933 against 1937 showed that motorcycles were down 13%, passenger vehicles up 46%, and freight vehicles up 24%. Over the same period the railway industry's fortunes also improved (passenger receipts up 15% and freight receipts up 17%). While recovery was welcome, it was clear that road transport was more responsive to growth opportunities.

## Financial decline

Comparison of the aggregate trading results in 1923 and 1937 for the 'Big Four' are shown in Table 2.

The railways were at a disadvantage through inflexible statutory controls that regulated freight rates and obliged them, as common carriers, to handle all cargoes that could be accommodated within the loading gauge. A new licensing regime for road hauliers had been introduced in 1933, but these operators had discretion to negotiate rates as they saw fit, and could thus competitively quote against the railways' fixed, published rates. Ironically, the GWR also recognised the economic advantages conferred on road hauliers by investing heavily in motor transport. The motor lorry fleet grew from 392 in 1923 to 2,324 in 1937, enabling rationalisation in the handling of smaller loads. Goods were transported by rail to and from a reduced number of depots, then distributed or collected by road.

The fleet of directly owned motor omnibuses, which had peaked at 108 vehicles in 1929, was completely eliminated by 1932. They had been replaced by controlling or significant shareholdings in

**ABOVE** Hawksworth became Assistant Chief Draughtsman in July 1923 and Chief Draughtsman less than two years later, in the midst of addressing repairs arrears and determining priorities with the absorbed locomotive fleet. In this hectic period it was understandable that mistakes could be made, but the case of the 10-strong ex-Barry Railway 0-6-4T Class 'L' was distinctly strange. They were handsome, powerful, much liked by crews, and very effective on heavy coal trains; their only shortcoming was a propensity to derail when moving forward at slow speeds over points in docks and colliery areas. Four were among the first absorbed engines to be rebuilt at Swindon when they were fitted with superheated Standard No 4 boilers, as shown with class prototype No 1347 (ex-Barry No 139). The entire class was stored during the General Strike of 1926 and only a couple worked thereafter. In September/October of that year they were withdrawn and scrapped.

Collett claimed later that he had not known at the time that these engines had been built as recently as 1914, otherwise withdrawal would not have been authorised. There is something disingenuous in this as the class had been identified early on as meriting Swindon's attention for rebuilding, so they were hardly an obscure type. Even odder, they had been designed by J. M. Auld who, by 1926, was an Assistant to the CME and who would surely have been aware of the situation facing 'his' engines. If Collett was truly unaware, then the case should have raised uncomfortable questions about the manner of his management, and the adequacy of internal communications, reporting and information systems.

seven major omnibus operators based in GWR territory, which yielded in 1939 an average investment return of just under 10% p.a.

While these road transport activities contributed welcome revenue, the malaise afflicting rail freight operations continued, and in 1938 the 'Big Four' mounted the 'Square Deal' campaign that sought charging flexibility commensurate with that enjoyed by road hauliers. Attempts to increase sales revenues by price or

| TABLE 2 | | | | |
|---|---|---|---|---|
| | 1923 (£ millions) | 1923 (% of total) | 1937 (£ millions) | 1937 (% of total) |
| **Receipts** | | | | |
| - Passengers | 68.9 | 35.2 | 56.7 | 34.0 |
| - Parcels | 17.4 | 8.9 | 16.3 | 9.8 |
| - Merchandise | 51.2 | 26.2 | 41.7 | 25.0 |
| - Minerals | 15.3 | 7.8 | 14.6 | 8.8 |
| - Coal | 38.9 | 19.9 | 34.4 | 20.6 |
| - Other | 3.9 | 2.0 | 2.9 | 1.7 |
| **Total revenue** | **195.6** | **100** | **166.6** | **100** |
| | | | | |
| **Expenses** | | | | |
| - Way & works | 23.5 | 15.0 | 19.7 | 14.9 |
| - Rolling stock | 27.6 | 17.6 | 23.3 | 17.6 |
| - Locomotives | 38.3 | 24.4 | 33.1 | 25.0 |
| - Traffic | 52.1 | 33.2 | 45.3 | 34.3 |
| - other | 15.4 | 9.8 | 10.8 | 8.2 |
| **Total expenses** | **156.9** | **100.0** | **132.2** | **100** |
| **Net trading income** | **38.7** | | **34.4** | |

| TABLE 3 | | | | | | | | | |
|---|---|---|---|---|---|---|---|---|---|
| | Total locomotive fleet size | | | Total under or awaiting repair | | | Under repair as % share of total fleet | | |
| | 1923 | 1937 | % reduction 1923-37 | 1923 | 1937 | % reduction 1923-37 | 1923 | 1937 | % reduction 1923-37 |
| **GWR** | 3,944 | 3,632 | 7.9 | 774 | 344 | 55.6 | 19.6 | 9.5 | 51.5 |
| **LMS** | 10,289 | 7,657 | 25.6 | 1,958 | 362 | 81.5 | 19 | 4.7 | 75.3 |
| **LNER** | 7,388 | 6,576 | 11 | 896 | 337 | 62.4 | 12.1 | 5.1 | 57.9 |
| **SR** | 2,258 | 1,814 | 19.7 | 266 | 156 | 41.4 | 11.8 | 8.6 | 27.1 |

volume as a means of corporate salvation often fail through the costly interval before any net improvement is realised. 'Square Deal' (which achieved nothing before being dropped on the outbreak of war) was a gamble that political hurdles and the objections of vested interests could be quickly overcome while making assumptions about continuing customer loyalty.

In the operating expenses of the 'Big Four', the constituent parts as portions of the whole remained basically constant between 1923 and 1937. It followed that with virtually no upward flexibility in revenue levels at the operators' discretion, the only means of improving profitability was in containment of expenditure. Theoretical options included savage contraction in employee numbers, deferral of expenditure on infrastructure (effectively only in the short term), or reduction of mobile operating assets. The last course was the most readily implemented, and the 'Big Four' had been active in this regard since 1923. This meant modernisation, reduction in unit numbers, increase in load capacities, and improved

utilisation. In crude terms, success demanded improvement of efficiency at a faster pace than that of revenue decline.

With the GWR, activities that were the direct responsibility of the Chief Mechanical Engineer accounted for approximately 42% of expenses. Collett delighted in arcane calculations to determine how best to account for individual tasks, e.g. whether a locomotive project should be designated a rebuild or a new build, and how this should be best recorded in the books. Such financial gymnastics might have been intellectually stimulating for individual cases, but this was the tactician rather than the strategist at work. Micro-management risked ignoring the broader picture, and here the evidence suggests chronic failure to appreciate the implications.

Collett's achievements on a factory-wide scale were unimpressive, as reflected in a statistical survey prepared by the Railway Research Service (an independent body), which compared the businesses of the 'Big Four' in the years 1923 and 1929 to 1937. These figures consistently revealed the GWR as the poorest performer. Details of the results as they affected the locomotive, carriage and wagon fleets appear in Appendix A, but the key conclusions (shown in Table 3) should have deeply alarmed Board and senior management.

Allowing that the Southern was a different case, here was evidence that the LNER, let alone the LMS, was consistently outperforming Swindon in fleet optimisation and availability. A particularly damning statistic is the percentage of locomotives under or awaiting repair in 1937 (9.5% for the GWR, 4.7% for the LMS). In absolute terms, had the GWR been able to match the performance of the LMS an immediate reduction of approximately 200 in the locomotive fleet total would have been possible.

Regarding carriage fleets, all companies made advances through replacement of 19th Century 4-wheel, 6-wheel and bogie coaches, and by adoption of modern construction methods. However, Table 4 reveals that the GWR made poor progress in reducing total numbers and thus in improving the utilisation factor but at least managed to out-perform the LNER in some respects. The efforts of the LMS were markedly superior across-the-board.

The trends in the wagon fleet (as reflected in Table 5) were perhaps the most depressing in this dismal suite. The company generated substantially more gross income from freight than from passengers, yet had manifestly failed to match the other companies in fleet rationalisation and utilisation. Just as significantly the others, led by the LMS, had made considerable improvements in the carrying capacity of individual vehicles. There is a perception that the GWR pressed hard for shippers to contract for larger individual wagonloads, as exemplified by the Pole 20-ton coal wagon, but under the common carrier regime of standard freight rates the other companies were generating superior profits through lower capital and current expenses with every train they ran.

## Summary

The Great Western's business was large and complex, and there were more reasons for encroaching financial difficulties than inept strategic management of mechanical engineering. In 1926 Pole had instigated a review of branch-line services that sought to correlate direct income with operating expenses, with the intent of pruning those that that were losing money. This initiative failed, evidently encountering resistance from vested interests at divisional level that did not wish to see erosion of individual empires. This initiative, which pre-dated Beeching by 37 years, stands testimony to his foresight. He recognised that the company's outmoded structure needed fundamental revision to cope with growing economic adversity and basic changes to the nature of the market. It can only be speculated what he thought about the company's dividend policy following his departure.

Despite the vicissitudes of the early 1930s, the ordinary stock dividend was held at 3% from 1931 (down from 5.5% in 1930), despite the fact that trading was not supporting such generosity to shareholders. The dividend was evidently a source of pride – not the most prudent basis for a key financial policy – and was maintained by drawing more than £4 million from revenue reserves between 1930 and 1935. If the directors were impervious to the financial impact, then equally they would not have appreciated the longer-term consequences of running a network with declining traffic volumes served by under-utilised locomotive and rolling stock fleets.

Reduction of the dividend to ½% for 1938 showed some recognition of market reality, but this was stimulated more in reinforcement of the 'Square Deal' campaign's message. There is no evidence that the Railway Research Service's findings had any

| TABLE 4 | | | | | | | | |
|---|---|---|---|---|---|---|---|---|
| | Total carriage fleet size | | | Yielding total seat numbers (000s) | | | Average seats per carriage | | |
| | 1923 | 1937 | % reduction 1923-37 | 1923 | 1937 | % change 1923-37 | 1923 | 1937 | % increase 1923-37 |
| GWR | 6,768 | 6,248 | 7.7 | 350 | 362 | 3.4 | 52 | 58 | 12.0 |
| LMS | 19,663 | 17,409 | 11.5 | 1,018 | 1,057 | 3.8 | 52 | 61 | 17.3 |
| LNER | 14,314 | 12,430 | 13.2 | 721 | 681 | -5.5 | 50 | 55 | 8.8 |
| SR | 7,469 | 6,682 | 10.5 | 401 | 404 | 0.7 | 54 | 60 | 12.6 |

| TABLE 5 | | | | | | |
|---|---|---|---|---|---|---|
| | Total wagon fleet size (000s) | | | Average capacity per wagon (tons) | | |
| | 1923 | 1937 | % reduction 1923-37 | 1923 | 1937 | % increase 1923-37 |
| GWR | 83.9 | 81.4 | 3.0 | 10.44 | 11.34 | 8.8 |
| LMS | 297.2 | 276.3 | 7.0 | 9.82 | 11.65 | 18.6 |
| LNER | 277.2 | 249.2 | 10.1 | 11.23 | 12.60 | 12.2 |
| SR | 34.7 | 33.0 | 4.9 | 9.97 | 11.22 | 12.5 |

ABOVE 'Manor' 4-6-0 No 7811 *Dunley Manor* heads a quite lengthy passenger train. Collett seems to have been reluctant to place his creations under scrutiny on the Swindon Testing Plant, despite spending a considerable sum on having the facility upgraded. Otherwise he might have become aware just how poor was the steam-raising capacity of this final development of the classic Churchward two-cylinder 4-6-0. Undoubtedly the least satisfactory of the modern 4-6-0 fleet, these engines were made into good performers after being shown up by BR Class 4 4-6-0s some 14 years after their introduction in 1938. *Ian Allan Library*

LEFT The Midland & South Western Junction Railway contributed 29 locomotives in seven different wheel arrangements at the Grouping. Twenty-two were rebuilt with GWR standard boilers during the 1920s, yet all but three had been withdrawn by 1938. MSWJR 2-6-0 No 16 (GWR No 24) had been built by Beyer Peacock for a South American company but never actually left Britain. It was rebuilt in 1925 with a superheated Standard No 9 boiler – generous treatment for a solitary oddity whose duties were restricted to working pick-up goods. No 24 operated in this condition for only five years, being withdrawn mid-1930. *F. Moore's Railway Photographs*

significant effect on management thinking, although this information, coupled with a review of the previous period's financial performance, should have placed Collett and Swindon under searching interrogation during 1939. Of course, by then a host of new issues was emerging.

In retrospect, mechanical engineering policies of the 1920s and 1930s cost the company dear. For all his works management expertise, the far broader remit of CME was beyond Collett's competence. Despite the size of the enterprise, the GWR's character and quality rested on comparatively few key individuals. An alternative vision portrays Pole's foresight and dynamism continuing to reshape and modernise throughout the 1930s. An integral part of this reform would have been a Stanier-led Swindon,

supported by Hawksworth in the Churchward tradition of exploiting brilliant ideas from outside the company and outside the country (not least those of Chapelon). In such a world, the results of the 1937 survey for the company, and perhaps the industry generally, might have looked more encouraging.

# CHAPTER 3
# FUTURE DENIED

Every month the *Great Western Railway Magazine* recorded staff transfers, retirements, deaths and obituaries. During the war years there was also the grim catalogue of the sufferings by GWR men on military service, cogently providing a continuing reminder of the human cost. The names, military ranks and, where possible, their units, together with details of their last employment with the company, were faithfully recorded. Taken at random from the 'Killed in Action' list in the December 1943 issue is Private C. W. Downs, Lincolnshire Regiment, who was formerly a carriage cleaner in the Chief Mechanical Engineer's Department at Bristol.

That same issue listed individuals in the following categories:

| | |
|---|---|
| Killed in Action, or Died | 7 |
| Previously Reported Missing, now Reported Killed | 3 |
| Previously Reported Prisoner of War, now Reported Dead | 1 |
| Previously Reported Missing, now Presumed Killed | 2 |
| Reported Missing, Believed Drowned | 1 |
| Reported Missing, Presumed Killed | 1 |
| Reported Missing | 7 |
| Previously Reported Missing, now Reported Prisoner of War | 5 |
| Prisoner of War | 1 |

Thankfully, there were also listed nine employees who had been prisoners of war but were now safely repatriated. Most had been in captivity since 1940.

GWR personnel serving with the armed forces and in civil defence on the following dates totalled:

| Department | 30/6/43 | 16/9/44 |
|---|---|---|
| Traffic | 3,716 | 4,028 |
| Goods | 3,737 | 3,931 |
| Road Motor Engineering | 266 | 279 |
| Docks | 386 | 432 |
| Chief Mechanical Engineer | 3,885 | 4,203 |
| Engineering | 1,131 | 1,180 |
| Other departments | 1,244 | 1,324 |
| **Total** | **14,365** | **15,377** |

The conflict had a severe impact on the numbers of individuals lost or injured, and at company level in depletion of the workforce through mass absences on military service. The shortfall was made up by retention of employees past normal retirement age, by recruitment of large numbers of women from every walk of life

**LEFT** Wartime working brought many challenges and difficulties, not least in the enforcement of blackout regulations. 'Castle' Class No 4096 *Highclere Castle* was photographed at Swindon demonstrating the protective measures to prevent firebox glow from revealing a locomotive's position to enemy aircraft. The cab side window has been removed and the opening plated over. An all-over tarpaulin has been erected to cover the rear of the footplate; the loss of ventilation and resultant heat generated must have made footplate conditions intolerable. Further, night vision was a serious problem during the blackout and the restricted outlook would hardly have been conducive to safety. *BR*

**RIGHT** Class '2251' No 2227 in wartime state with cab side window removed. *P. Ransome Wallis*

**BELOW** Wartime 'Castle', wartime name. In 1940-41 'Castles' Nos 5071 to 5082 were given the names of aircraft that had become household names during the Battle of Britain. No 5071 *Spitfire* had been built originally as *Clifford Castle* in 1938. In this photograph, evidently for publicity purposes, the locomotive is shown in wartime condition with cab side window removed. The livery is still clearly pre-war as evidenced by the lining and the 'shirt button' monogram on the eight-wheeled 4,000-gallon tender No 2586. *Ian Allan Library*

to undertake a wide range of jobs including some that previously had been a solely male preserve, and by everyone working longer hours than would have been normal pre-war. In addition, many personnel served with voluntary organisations in their own time – Home Guard, Air Raid Precautions, etc.

By the start of 1945, more than 3,000 men aged over 65 years were at work, and 12 months later more than 6,000 employees were still awaiting release from military service. At the end of 1946 5,700 essential posts remained vacant and there were strenuous efforts to recruit and train new employees. The prolonged absence of experienced personnel was a serious problem for the CME's department, where operations were complicated by repairs arrears and poor-quality fuel.

The wear and tear upon infrastructure, track, rolling stock and equipment was enormous, and in ways not always immediately obvious. During the war emphasis was placed on expanding the locomotive fleet by continued new construction, deferment of scheduled withdrawals, and loans of freight locomotives built specifically for war service. Increased numbers of freight movements together with the burgeoning demands of the armed forces led to continued wagon construction. Also, passenger and troop trains were consistently filled to capacity and beyond.

No corner of the company's diverse activities was left untouched. Apart from overworked equipment, the GWR's assets suffered directly from enemy action. Many stations were bombed, on the locomotive front a 'Hall' and a pannier tank were destroyed, and

**ABOVE** Several vintage classes had been decimated by the renewal programme of the 1930s, but a smattering survived the war and some even made it into BR ownership. 'Aberdare' 2-6-0 No 2657 is at Southall in the late 1930s. This engine was withdrawn in July 1939 but, like a number of others taken out of service that year, was not scrapped. It was stored as a war reserve, then reinstated to service the following November. It worked through the conflict and was finally withdrawn in November 1946. *Lens of Sutton*

there was a long catalogue of items damaged beyond economic repair. A subject rarely covered in accounts about the company's activities was the shipping services, and Appendix J provides a brief synopsis of the price paid by the Great Western's vessels.

The restoration of peace in 1945 offered the hope of better times, but there was little easing of pressure. In certain respects the situation deteriorated further as optimistic expectations placed even greater demands upon a worn-out system, and upon a depleted, exhausted workforce. Senior managers faced difficult decisions over determination of priorities, mobilisation of limited resources, and deployment of scarce investment funds in refurbishment and new construction.

Measurement of the size and complexity of the issues that followed the return to peace is not easy, but some examples should help an understanding. VJ Day (15 August 1945) marked the end

of six years of conflict, and a population worn down by the monotony, deprivation and horror of war sought antidote by going on holiday. Travel restrictions had been lifted but the only means of covering any distance was by rail. Statistics for long-distance passenger departures from Paddington for the third week of that month give a measure of the demand:

| Week ended | Number |
|---|---|
| 20/8/38 | 105,000 |
| 23/8/41 | 178,000 |
| 25/8/45 | 256,000 |
| 24/8/46 | 202,000* |

\* Reduction largely as a result of measures to stagger the dates of paid annual holidays

Increases in passenger travel were not limited to holiday periods, and many trains were carrying around 70% greater loadings than had been usual pre-war. Twelve months after the war ended, the company was still providing 250 trains per week solely for governmental and military purposes. Between 1938 and 1945 there had been an 85% increase in the annual number of long-distance passenger journeys. With this growth in custom there was every incentive to restore services to normal standards of frequency and reliability.

In May 1946 the summer timetable was reintroduced, underlining the intent to return to normal conditions. The 'Cornish Riviera' was restored and, by running non-stop to Plymouth, achieved a 15-minute reduction in journey time, although it took 30 minutes longer to reach Penzance than in 1938. A total of 948 extra services, including the welcome return of slip coaches, increased total daily train mileage by 21,000. Restoration of catering facilities was another priority, and that summer 25 restaurant and four buffet car services were added, bringing the number of weekday trains offering food and drink to 53.

The position with coaching stock was particularly acute. The aggregate fleet size fell from 6,168 (with an average age of 18 years) in 1938 to 5,738 (an average age of 22 years) at the end of 1945. Several factors contributed to this fall: requisition of vehicles for military use; damage sustained in air raids; and withdrawal on grounds of age and condition. Of greater concern was that, in 1938, 349 coaches (5.7% of the total) on average were under or awaiting repair, whereas 1,297 (22.6%) were in this category in 1945. New coach construction recommenced in 1946, but shortages in materials delayed delivery, a situation that continued into the early 1950s. Passenger accommodation was the company's shop window, and sub-standard coaching stock adversely affected opinions on the attractions of rail travel.

Overcrowding of serviceable stock was inevitable as, despite timetable improvements, passenger train mileage in 1946 on the GWR was 17% below per-war levels (the average for the other companies was 27% down). Heavier trains adversely affected the performance of run-down locomotives and rolling stock. Before the war, passenger service failures had averaged one per 126,000 train miles, but in 1946 the rate had deteriorated to one in every 40,000.

Freight services brought a separate range of heightened demands. Reintroduction of vacuum-fitted fast services between London and principal provincial centres was given priority, and 75 such trains were running by the end of 1946. They were at full capacity because the company could not meet demand due to shortages of both suitable locomotives and vacuum-equipped wagons. In addition, there was a sharp increase in the need for special trains to handle perishable traffic from country locations. With food rationing still in force, it was important to find equipment to move agricultural produce – seasonal fruit and vegetables – from the West County, Wales, the West Midlands and the Channel Islands.

**BELOW** During the war 80 LMS Stanier 8F 2-8-0s were built at Swindon. They were used on loan to the GWR until 1946/47, when they were transferred to the LMS. Swindon-built No 48410 is seen on 5 July 1955. *B. Fletcher/R. K. Blencowe*

The wagon fleet was also afflicted with problems of age profile and repairs arrears. The average age had increased from 18 to 21 years over the war period, with an extra 10,000 wagons in the repair queue. The issue of wagon replacement presented an impending crisis as the total in the 30-40-year age band had grown during the war from 7,779 to 22,417.

Shortage of materials plagued the system at all levels. Before the war the Permanent Way Department had consumed approximately 19,000 new rail chairs in the annual cycle of track renewal. It was estimated that elimination of the replacement backlog would call for 25,000 new chairs per annum over a three-year period, whereas in 1946 the actual supply was around 12,000. This was one reason why a plethora of speed restrictions remained in place. For example, the journey time of the 8.00am Cardiff-Paddington service, an early candidate for acceleration, was 15 minutes longer than in 1938.

At the end of 1940, on the eve of Hawksworth's appointment as CME, the company's steam locomotive fleet totalled 3,688, a figure slightly down on the previous year as new construction had not yet fully offset the loss of 108 Dean Goods 0-6-0s sold to the British Government. Thereafter, wartime construction of new locomotives saw annual totals increase until 1944, when 3,889 were on the books – the largest in the company's history. In addition, there were still 0-6-0s on loan from the other companies

as substitutes for the Dean Goods, together with an armada of 2-8-0s built for war service (Stanier 8Fs, War Department 'Austerities' and US Army Transportation Corps 'S160s'), many of which departed for continental Europe as part of the liberation.

Improvement in motive power was necessary and, as demands associated with locomotives built for military use fell away, there were pressing decisions over whether to repair, rebuild or start afresh. Considerable effort had been made in the 1930s to modernise, but suspension of this programme during the war had yielded a heterogeneous collection of survivors from ageing classes that otherwise would have disappeared in the early 1940s. These remnants included older small and large pannier tanks; 'Duke' and 'Bulldog' 4-4-0s; 'Aberdare' 2-6-0s; 'Metro' 2-4-0Ts; Class '517' 0-4-2Ts; Class '2361' 0-6-0s; and life-expired 'Large Prairie' tanks of Classes '3150' and '51xx'.

**BELOW** Although widely considered a modification of the numerically large mixed-traffic 'Hall' Class, No 6959, built in March 1944, was a seminal locomotive in the GWR two-cylinder 4-6-0 story. Being fitted with plate frames throughout, it represented the first step away from Churchward's construction principles that had appeared with the 'Saint' Class in the early 1900s. Named *Peatling Hall* in December 1946, the prototype 'Modified Hall' is seen here at Swindon in BR days looking rather the worse for wear.

There were also broader issues of fleet management in need of attention. Many heavy freight locomotives built at government instigation during the war stayed on loan for the remainder of the company's existence, so the key need lay with new passenger and mixed-traffic locomotives. Again, a comparison with pre-war conditions was telling – at the end of 1944 there were 546 locomotives in service that were more than 40 years old compared with 450 in 1938.

During the latter stages of the war there were several changes in construction plans, reflecting uncertainty over future requirements. In July 1944 it was revealed that the following orders or parts of orders had been changed:

| Lot No | Class | Running numbers | Ultimate fate |
|---|---|---|---|
| 308 | 'Grange' | 6880-99 | Cancelled |
| 326 | 'Castle' | 7003-07 | Lot cancelled, and engines built as part of Lot 357 in 1946 |
| 331 | '2251' | 3229-39 | Cancelled |
| 332 | 'Castle' | 7008-27 | Lot cancelled, and engines built under Lot 367 in 1948/49 |
| 335 | '51xx' | 4140-49 | Lot cancelled then reinstated, completed in 1946 |
| 339 | '2251' | 2231-50 | Lot cancelled, and engines built under Lot 347 in 1944/45 |
| 344 | '57xx' | 4685-99 | Lot cancelled, and engines built as part of Lot 352 in 1944/45 |
| | | 7600-34 | Running numbers not used |

ABOVE Operating with US Army Transportation Corps Class 'S160' 2-8-0s had revealed the benefits of welded construction methods, and these principles were soon employed in the first new pattern of GWR tender for many years. Thirty, numbered 100 to 129, were constructed for exclusive use with the new 4-6-0 'County' Class. They were 8ft 6in wide, yielding a carrying capacity of 4,000 gallons of water and 7 tons of coal. No 1028 *County of Warwick* is on the up 'Merchant Venturer' at Thingley in May 1953. *Lens of Sutton*

The following orders were in doubt:

| Lot No | Class | Running numbers | Ultimate fate |
|---|---|---|---|
| 318 | '72xx' | 7254-89 | Cancelled |
| 319 | '31xx' | 3105-40 | Cancelled |
| 320 | '81xx' | 8110-49 | Cancelled |
| 324 | 'Castle' | 5098, 5099, 7000-02 | Cancelled, and engines built as part of Lot 357 in 1946 |
| 343 | '42xx' | 5275-94 | Cancelled |
| 350 | 'Modified Hall' | 6967-70 | Reinstated |

It was also necessary to resume replacement of obsolescent types. This programme was conducted on a like-for-like basis: 'Castles' for 'Saints' and 'Stars', Classes '57xx' and '74xx' for 19th-century pannier tanks, etc. There was also an emerging need for a new breed of tank locomotive, the rationale for which is reviewed in Chapter 7.

**ABOVE** No 5030 *Shirburn Castle*, at Ranelagh Bridge, is in original condition but attached to one of the new Hawksworth tenders, which complemented very well the traditional handsome appearance of this class. This view is undated but the livery is the last GWR style applied to large 4-6-0s. *Eric Treacy*

**LEFT** In October 1946 a second version of the Hawksworth tender appeared for general use by 4-6-0s. It differed from the 'County' version in being 6 inches narrower, reducing the nominal coal capacity by 1 ton. A total of 107 were built (together with a pair fitted with self-weighing equipment), and they were used with 'Modified Halls', 'Halls', 'Castles' and, very occasionally, 'Stars'. They first appeared with 'Modified Halls', as in this view of No 6992 *Aborfield Hall*.

Between 1941 and 1956, when construction of Swindon-designed locomotives finally ceased, 738 new locomotives were built at Swindon and another 200 by contractors. Fourteen different classes were included in this programme, of which nine were continuations of previously introduced types. Of the five new classes, the 'Modified Hall' and the 'County' introduced fresh features to the 4-6-0 fleet.

However energetically the GWR wished to restore normality, optimistic objectives were soon dashed by the harsh realities of austerity Britain, and reconstruction took much longer than had been originally anticipated. Regardless of compensation due to the company for its wartime contribution, fresh capital would be required and, based upon the poor trading results for the company's last year of normal operations (1938), the prospects for securing the requisite level of shareholder financial support were not encouraging.

These multiple challenges were set against doubts over the company's continued independence. Nationalisation had been contemplated following the First World War before imposition of the halfway-house solution of the 'Big Four'. By 1945 their financial condition was fragile, particularly so with the perennially impecunious LNER. The GWR might have been perceived to be in a stronger position but, as identified in the previous chapter, there were disquieting trends in the company's trading and investment policies that might not withstand rigorous scrutiny.

Uncertainty over the possibility of public ownership was quickly dispelled by political developments. Following dissolution of the wartime coalition government, the first general election for ten years saw the Labour Party win a landslide victory in July 1945, to international astonishment in view of Churchill's personal standing on the world stage. A key element of the Labour Party reform manifesto was extensive nationalisation of British industry, including the railways, and little time was wasted in pursuing that objective. A Bill to nationalise the 'Big Four' (and other transport undertakings) was published on 27 November 1946, and the Transport Act 1947 was passed into law by parliament on 6 August 1947. The newly formed British Railways took over with effect from 1 January 1948.

This rapid transformation did not invalidate implementation of post-war reconstruction plans, regardless of who owned the business. Until the legislation was passed there was no clarity over when the new organisation would be created, what form it would assume, and how long it would take to establish corporate policy. With these uncertainties, GWR management reacted in the best way it knew by adhering to the standards that had stood the company in good stead. This meant restoration of peacetime practices and, for locomotive policy, reversion (in simplified and more sensible form) to the asset management policies of the 1930s.

For a company with a long history, loss of independence was unwelcome at all levels. This was best demonstrated by the actions of the General Manager and the directors. Sir James Milne, by then aged 64, declined the appointment as Chairman of the newly created Railway Executive of British Railways, citing pressure of outside interests. As the most senior CEO of the 'Big Four', he had chaired the wartime Railway Executive, an experience that had apparently given him his fill of public sector intervention. The directors did their legal best for the shareholders by declaring a

ABOVE Suspension of carriage building during the war contributed to a severe shortage of operable stock in the late 1940s. The Hawksworth carriages were stylish and comfortable but their delivery was protracted and there were never enough of them. As more became available they were formed into sets for use with prestige trains. An unidentified 'Castle' is hauling the 'Torbay Express' in early BR days; the first three vehicles at least are Hawksworth coaches.

final dividend for 1947 of 5.282158% on GWR ordinary stock. Use of six decimal places ensured that there were no distributable funds left to pass to the government.

At the final general meetings of the other three companies, motions were tabled for the payment of compensation to directors for loss of office; shareholders of the LMS and Southern passed the respective motions, while that for the LNER board was defeated. The position with the GWR was quite different as the directors flatly rejected any idea of compensation, despite their not having been mere figureheads. They had been deeply committed to the railway's affairs, taking pains to be well-informed on important matters and knowledgeable about many practical issues. Their behaviour (of which certain 21st-century directors might care to take note) was reflective of their feelings, and of those of the employees, on the passing of a great institution.

\*

Setting up the new British Railways organisation with headquarters in 'the Kremlin' at 222 Marylebone Road was a massive task in itself, and in the initial months there was little or no visible evidence of change in ownership. On the now ex-GWR locomotive front, matters continued essentially as before. Construction and delivery

of engines already ordered proceeded, and further new building was sanctioned.

Plans included three entirely new classes, all additions to the legions of pannier tanks. One class, '94xx', which incorporated fresh features, had appeared in modest numbers during the old company's last year and its ranks were set to be multiplied with the aid of contractors. The remaining two classes of Swindon origin made their appearance during 1949, Hawksworth's last year in office. The Class '15xx' embraced new features that, at the 11th hour, yielded certain advantages long recognised elsewhere. In

BELOW Hawksworth coaches worked in matched sets for only a short period. No 4092 *Dunraven Castle* is at the head of an up express at Leamington Spa in 1952. The first two coaches are in smart condition but it is just discernible that the third is a pre-war vehicle. *Patrick Kingston*

**LEFT** The final style of diesel railcar, with the 'razor edge' cabs, appeared with No 19 in July 1940, and the second 'pair', Nos 37/38, completed the order in February 1942, by which time construction of steam-hauled carriage stock had been suspended for the duration. In the circumstances Hawksworth would have been quite entitled to curtail the order before completion. That he did not suggests that he had been engaged in the design and development work of these vehicles, and that he fully recognised their importance for the future of passenger trains. Single unit No W23W, built in September 1940, is in the 'blood and custard' BR livery.

**ABOVE** All-3rd No 786 was one of the first of the new style being built in mid-1946. After a spell in GWR livery, then BR 'blood and custard', it ended its days in the rather drab overall BR maroon. *J. H. Aston*

contrast, the other class, '16xx', was a reincarnation of Class '2021' of 1897, using modern construction methods

The latitude extended by the new masters in allowing delivery of locomotives to prenationalisation designs was entirely pragmatic. Reconstruction had to continue and it would be some time before production of a motive power breed suitable for use throughout the country would be possible. This forbearance also embraced work initiated by the 'Big Four' on new forms of traction. The LMS was developing two main-line diesels while concurrently building a pair of fine 'Pacifics' for comparison purposes; the name of one honoured of an old GWR man and long-time colleague of Hawksworth – *Sir William A. Stanier FRS*. The LNER was working on the introduction of overhead electric haulage. The most diverse experimentation was at the Southern Railway where, notwithstanding the commitment to third rail-electricity, main-line diesel power and a new style of steam engine (with typical Bulleid iconoclasm) were under development. Despite success with diesel-mechanical railcars, the GWR had initiated an entirely different field of enquiry by exploring a power source that had evolved from jet engine technology.

For the time being, steam power using indigenous coal, the quality and quantity of which was gradually improving, would remain the prime energy source, and BR policy focussed on locomotive standardisation. Historic sentiments aside, there could be little doubt that the LMS would provide the principal templates, as this company's fleet was the most modern. The corporate memory must have recalled how much damage had been wrought to that organisation by partisan prejudices in the 1920s, thus emphasising the practical and political benefits of taking other design schools into account.

An early step was the locomotive exchange trials held between April and September 1948. Several routes were selected whose differing characteristics were an important adjunct to comparative assessments under controlled conditions on the Rugby and Swindon stationary test plants. Three categories of locomotives were assessed – express passenger, general purpose (i.e. mixed-traffic) and heavy freight – representing the 'Big Four', together with two heavy freight types built for war service, although certain factors set the Swindon products apart from the rest.

The more generous loading gauge of the GWR engines precluded their presence on most 'foreign' routes, reducing the opportunities for objective comparison. Also, it was decided that only Yorkshire hard coal should be consumed, the most common type in use across the UK. This nominally placed the GWR contingent at some disadvantage as its boilers had been designed to burn Welsh coal with a higher calorific value. Regarding the locomotive types selected, it was immediately apparent that the GWR engines predated the others design-wise, if not necessarily in construction date (see Table 1).

The 'Modified Hall' embraced Hawksworth's improvements of 1944, while Class '2884' was effectively unchanged from the first production run of the Class '28xx'. The 'King' suffered the greatest penalty within its group by being in as-built condition with low degree superheat and original blastpipe arrangements. The other express passenger engines benefited from new ideas of the 1930s, i.e. double or multiple blastpipes plus high degree superheat.

Swindon's participation was distinctive for two other reasons. The Works was represented by only three locomotives – No 6018 *King Henry VI*, No 6990 *Witherslack Hall* and No 3803 – which contrasted with the other regions' representatives where, on several occasions, test locomotives were switched. This suggests that

Swindon took care to select locomotives in good condition with proven reliability. The other feature concerned identity. As the BR 'cycling lion' emblem had yet to appear, most participants were labelled 'BRITISH RAILWAYS', whereas the Swindon trio were smartly turned out in full GWR livery.

There was debate about the suitability of the types selected. Based on the locomotive categories, the GWR representation seemed reasonable, but there was regret about the exclusion of a 'Castle'. A high superheat engine would have provided an interesting comparison with the efforts of No 4079 on the LNER in 1925, and of No 5000 on the West Coast Main Line the following year.

Extensive data were collected and some conclusions drawn were contentious, perhaps inevitably so considering the partisan emotions in play, but there were real barriers to objective comparisons. There had been little consistency in briefing crews about how their locomotives were to be driven. Some went for maximum power output, as with the 'Royal Scot' and the 'West Country', which both produced brilliant performances at unexpected locations. Confusion was illustrated with the Bulleid heavy and light 'Pacifics', whose impressive hill-climbing was powered by boilers of seemingly inexhaustible capacity, but at the cost of heavy fuel and oil

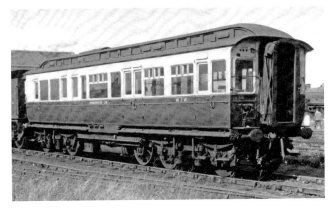

**ABOVE** In the formulation of BR's motive power policy, extensive interchange trials were conducted in 1948, which kept all available dynamometer cars and their crews busy. Dynamometer car No 7 played its part, and there is a story that Hawksworth had to ask the (non-GWR) personnel on board for permission to travel in this (i.e. his) vehicle on a test train starting from Paddington. Times were certainly changing. No 7 is seen outside Swindon stock shed on 20 September 1964. *R. S. Carpenter collection*

| TABLE 1 | | | | |
|---|---|---|---|---|
| **Category** | **Railway** | **Class** | **Type** | **Introduced** |
| **Express passenger** | | | | |
| | GWR | 'King' | 4-6-0 | 1927 |
| | LMS | 'Duchess' | 4-6-2 | 1937 |
| | | 'Royal Scot' | 4-6-0 | 1927/43* |
| | LNER | 'A4' | 4-6-2 | 1935 |
| | SR | 'Merchant Navy' | 4-6-2 | 1941 |
| **General purpose** | | | | |
| | GWR | 'Modified Hall' | 4-6-0 | 1928/44 |
| | LMS | Class 5 | 4-6-0 | 1934 |
| | LNER | 'B1' | 4-6-0 | 1942 |
| | SR | 'West Country' | 4-6-2 | 1945 |
| **Heavy freight** | | | | |
| | GWR | '28xx' | 2-8-0 | 1903 |
| | LMS | 8F | 2-8-0 | 1935 |
| | LNER | 'O1' | 2-8-0 | 1944** |
| | Ministry of Supply | 'WD' | 2-8-0 | 1943 |
| | | 'WD' | 2-10-0 | 1944 |
| * Introduced 1927 but rebuilt from 1943 onwards | | | | |
| ** 1944 rebuild of ex-GCR class O4 introduced 1911, retaining original frames | | | | |

consumption. The LMS 'Duchess' in contrast was disappointing, due to a driving style intended to save fuel.

To Swindon's chagrin, the GWR contingent showed little consistent distinction. Excuse was sought in the unsuitability of the coal, a rather spurious argument in view of *Pendennis Castle*'s exploits on the LNER in 1925. Also, engines in the company's northern reaches had habitually burned non-Welsh coal without marked disadvantage compared with their southern brethren. That the improvements applied to the 'Modified Hall' had not shown up more prominently must have caused genuine disappointment. Possibly the limited deployment of this engine beyond home territory (Marylebone-Leicester, Manchester-Sheffield and Marylebone-Nottingham only) counted against full assessment. The 'King' was at a definite disadvantage by virtue of it being an unimproved 20-year-old machine, which should have been a wake-up call to any remaining conservative elements at Swindon.

Claims of unfairness based on the fuel led to BR Western Region holding further tests with Welsh coal in November/December 1948. Sufficient credence was given to this exercise for inclusion of the results as an appendix to the official report of the Exchanges, although their value had to be discounted for several reasons. The intention had been to compare different types using the most common coal for evaluation of 'all lines' availability. Tests using selected coal for a specific locomotive group represented movement of the goal posts

that could have only marginal, if any, impact. Normal Welsh coking coal with an average of 15,100 British Thermal Units per lb compared favourably with the fuels used in the main tests – South Kirkby Hard (14,400 BTU/lb) and Blidworth Hard (13,940 BTU/lb).

The objective was to endorse the quality of Swindon's design traditions rather than to provide information, however imperfect, to help assess what would best meet the needs of a nationalised transport undertaking. The combination of indigenous crews with route knowledge, preferred fuel, a clear understanding of what was at stake, and a determination to prove something meant that an inevitable improvement would result (see Table 2).

To help set the context, coal consumption results in the main tests over the Western Region are shown in Table 3.

In respect of the GWR locomotives, the results for 2-8-0 No 3803 in the main trials were particularly impressive. This engine was overall fifth best performer in coal consumption and overall fourth in rate of water evaporation. The coal consumption at 2.64lb with a Class '2884' in the separate Western Region tests was the best achievement in all the tests combined, and its water evaporation rate at 9.15lb was the second best under the same criteria. The Class '2884' dated from 1938 with modifications that were cosmetic in the context of performance. Thus a 1903 design, when burning the fuel for which it was designed, outperformed all the much younger designs under scrutiny.

| TABLE 2 | | | | |
|---|---|---|---|---|
| | Coal consumption per drawbar horse power per hour | | Water evaporation per lb of coal | |
| | Yorkshire Hard | Welsh coking | Yorkshire Hard | Welsh coking |
| Ordinary 'King' | 3.74lb | 3.33lb | 7.41lb | 9.15lb |
| High superheat 'King' | n/a | 3.10lb* | n/a | 8.86lb* |
| 'Modified Hall' | 4.11lb | 3.22lb | 7.92lb | 9.84lb |
| '2884' | 3.54lb | 2.64lb | 7.42lb | 9.67lb |

* discussed in Chapter 5

| TABLE 3 | | |
|---|---|---|
| Category | Best | Worst |
| Express passenger | LNER 'A4', 3.19lb | GWR 'King', 3.74lb |
| General purpose | LMS Class 5, 3.39lb | SR 'West Country', 4.28lb |
| Heavy freight | LNER 'O1', 3.37lb | 'WD' 2-8-0, 4.02lb |

**LEFT** The company's second initiative with gas turbine traction resulted in No 18000, the construction contract for which was signed with Brown Boveri in September 1946. Eight months earlier the GWR had entered a joint venture with Metropolitan-Vickers to produce the gas turbine locomotive that eventually became No 18100. Neither were delivered until after nationalisation. *R.H.G. Simpson*

The results from both series of tests were peripheral to the broader objectives of British Railways, as it would not have been viable to produce a new locomotive generation specifically designed for Welsh coal. Also, beyond acknowledged advantages of better steaming capacity with tapered Belpaire boilers, there were no major GWR design features that lent themselves to adoption nationwide.

On the other hand, the tests were of particular value to Swindon in re-emphasising the obsolescence of its pre-war superheating policy. Here was validation, if any was by then still needed, that Stanier's message to Collett on this subject had been correct concerning an improvement that would have been self-funding in fuel economies. Going further back, it suggested what had possibly been lost following the cessation of the Stanier-Hawksworth investigation into compounding, an exercise so much in the spirit of enquiry and experimentation fostered by the great William Dean. In addition, the 2-8-0's performance reinforced the fundamental excellence of the original Churchward formulae, and supported the contention that, although Collett enlarged certain designs, on a 'pound-for-pound' basis he did not actually improve upon those created by the 'Old Man' at Newburn House.

For Hawksworth, the frustrations must have been palpable. The manner and style of the Collett regime had stymied potentially fruitful avenues of motive power improvement. When at last he did take control at Swindon, such ideas had to be subordinated to the demands of the national crisis. The window of opportunity offered by the arrival of peace was rigidly contained by prevailing shortages, then closed by the impending loss of corporate independence. The 1948 Exchanges validated many of his ideas, but by then the initiative was in the hands of others. The results of the subsidiary tests would have held little more than passing interest, as by then retirement was only a year away.

**ABOVE** Post-war reconstruction, fresh ideas and frustrated hopes for a new greater Great Western were best symbolised by the 4-6-0 'Counties'. Photographed on the left-hand (more tidy) side, No 1021 *County of Montgomery* shows a clean, purposeful simplicity that is matched by the neat lines of the new-style tender. The lined black neo-LNWR livery first used by British Railways for mixed-traffic types shows off the engine's lines well. No 1021 was fitted with a double chimney in October 1959, the last of the class to be so equipped. *R.C. Riley*

**BELOW** This group photograph was taken during a 1946 visit to the Severn Tunnel by directors and senior officials. Present (left to right) were K. W. C. Grand, K. J. Cook, Sir W. Reardon, Earl Baldwin, J. Rank, J. Codrington, Capt Vivian and F. W. Hawksworth. GWR directors made great efforts to remain well informed on practical aspects of the enterprise, and here they are demonstrating that commitment. They obviously knew all about the tunnel's damp interior.

# CHAPTER 4
# THE TWO-CYLINDER 4-6-0s

When the first 4-6-0 with two outside cylinders appeared in 1902, Hawksworth was midway through his apprenticeship. No 100, later named *William Dean*, was the fulcrum about which the Dean-Churchward transition pivoted, with Victorian elegance yielding to more austere functionality. This was the first clear indication of Churchward's intention to expand dramatically upon the experimental groundwork laid out for him by the GWR's finest Locomotive Superintendent.

Hawksworth saw at first hand the momentous changes presaged by No 100, yet was also responsible for that prototype's final descendant some 43 years later. As a working association with an iconic locomotive family, for longevity this was probably unique. By the time his 'Counties' appeared, it might be safely assumed that, from the conception and design standpoint, he knew more than any other about the development of Great Western two-cylinder 4-6-0s.

When No 100 entered service it was by no means certain that it would provide the template for further construction as Churchward was then engaged in numerous modifications and changes with the early 4-6-0s to determine the optimal way forward. The wisdom of this approach was proven by the comparative ease with which the production series of the next locomotive generation was introduced. On other railways, graduation from the traditional 4-4-0 to the 4-6-0 proved problematic and it is remarkable that other engineers took so long to acknowledge and be guided by Churchward's success.

The programme to assess alternatives must have been particularly instructive for the young apprentice. In a broad sense, the core issues were the preferred number of driving wheels and the merits of simple versus compound expansion. The stately Dean 'Singles' of the 'Achilles' Class were still at work and their smooth running was a reminder of the internal frictional resistance induced by coupled driving wheels. The issue of compound steam required assimilation of experiences beyond GWR territory. The history of the British compound locomotive had been chequered – especially in the case of the London & North Western Railway – but Churchward was neither hidebound nor parochial. His broad-mindedness regarding foreign practice was confirmed by the purchase of De Glehn compound 4-4-2s, a type that performed well on the French Nord system.

These factors influenced progressive thought elsewhere, as with J. G. Robinson on the Great Central Railway, who also compared

**LEFT** The start of it all: prototype two-cylinder 4-6-0 No 100 commenced work in February 1902, a few months before William Dean handed over to George Jackson Churchward. The successes and failures of Dean's experimental programmes had allowed accumulation of much empirical data that was of priceless value to his successor. It is unlikely that he had any direct involvement in the design and construction of this engine, but if Churchward had been the father of the genre, then Dean was unquestionably the grandfather. It must have been a source of quiet satisfaction that after years of unprecedented difficulties in building a reliable motive power fleet, he could see his efforts culminating in this exciting precursor of the new era. This engine was later regarded as a member of the 'Saint' Class, from which it differed in non-standard frames, cylinder and valve gear.

No 100 was unnamed when built, but the name *Dean* was added to the leading splashers, and soon changed to *William Dean*. A little later the nameplate was moved to what became the traditional position on the centre splasher. The naming was a timely and appropriate means of honouring the GWR's finest Locomotive Superintendent.

At the time No 100 appeared, Hawksworth had been with the company for four years; two-cylinder 4-6-0s were to remain a major part of his professional career right through to his retirement.

simple and compound expansion in four- and six-coupled engines. His conclusions favoured the simple arrangement, with a preference for 'Atlantics' in his graceful 'Jersey Lilies' of Class '8B' over the 4-6-0 equivalent (Class '8C'). This judgement was vindicated later when the 4-4-0 'Directors' were preferred over the 4-6-0 'Sir Sam Fays', and the complex four-cylinder 'Lord Faringdons'. The GCR 4-6-0 family eventually totalled 100, comprising two-cylinder (inside and outside) and four-cylinder engines, spread over nine classes with six different driving wheel sizes, but showing no particular distinction in performance. These results convincingly endorsed the superiority of contemporary GWR practice.

At Churchward's retirement the two-cylinder 4-6-0 was firmly established, although the small-wheeled version, the only omission from his 1901 Locomotive Scheme, had been deferred. This need had been largely filled by the mixed-traffic 2-6-0 Class '43xx', which derived from American practice and which from 1911 onwards proved its usefulness. More than 90 were built during the First World War alone, and 11 served with distinction in France. Also, Churchward grew the numbers of outside-framed 4-4-0s to fill a supporting role while the 4-6-0s were settling in. This was an early example of Swindon's penchant for concurrently building locomotives of different configurations to meet similar demands. There would be an operational need for engines of the 'Bulldog' breed for years to come, but the demand for some of the later, large-wheeled 4-4-0s was distinctly marginal, particularly the finely proportioned and beautifully named 'Flowers' of 1908.

This recurring Swindon practice was even to outlive the company, and another early case concerned the 4-4-0 'Counties'. Their main purpose was allegedly as a modern, prestige locomotive to work trains over the London & North Western route from Hereford to Shrewsbury, where the 'Saints' were prohibited. However, their performance was constrained by rough riding, and construction of ten more in 1911 was strange in view of the number of 4-6-0s by then in service. Similarly, there seemed little need for ten more Class '2221' 4-4-2Ts (the 'County Tanks') in 1912. This wheel arrangement might have been a suitable replacement for 19th-century 2-4-0Ts and 0-4-2Ts, but 6ft 8½in driving wheels were impractical for suburban work. 'Large Prairies'

**BELOW** The second large prototype 4-6-0 was No 98, which is considered the first standard Churchward locomotive. It was renumbered 2998 and named *Ernest Cunard* in 1907. *Ian Allan Library*

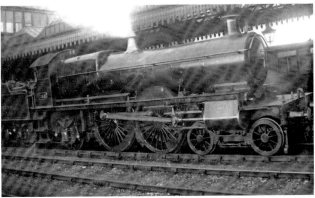

**ABOVE** The third 'Saint' (No 171 *Albion*) ran as a 4-4-2 between October 1904 and July 1907 for comparison with the French compounds. Nineteen more 'Saints' were built in 1905, six as 4-6-0s and 13 as 4-4-2s (numbered in the series 172-190, later Nos 2971-90). No 188 was photographed at Weston-super-Mare some time between 1905 and 1907. This engine was later renumbered 2988; it was named *Rob Roy* in 1907 and rebuilt as a 4-6-0 in May 1912.
*R. S. Carpenter collection*

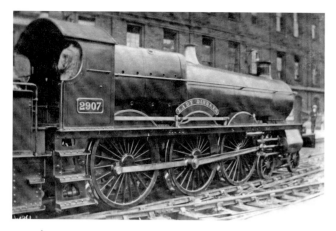

ABOVE The splendidly named *Lady Disdain* is seen in original saturated condition as built in 1906. No 2907 was one of the early withdrawals – in 1933. *Ian Allan Library*

ABOVE 'Saint' Class No 2937 *Clevedon Court* was one of the last batch, built late 1911. The right-angled front drop end and angular rear footsteps of the earlier engines upset contemporary ideas about styling. Commencing with No 2911 in August 1907, the lines were softened with curved drop ends, front and rear. No 2937 acquired new cylinders and outside steam pipes in June 1948 but survived for only five more years. She is seen at Hereford in September 1952 in BR lined black with a red background to the name and number plates, a livery ill-suited to this handsome class. *Lens of Sutton*

ABOVE The introduction of the 2-6-0 Class '43xx' in 1911 to fill a 'maid of all work' mixed-traffic role led to deferral of the 4-6-0 with 5ft 8in driving wheels, the remaining component of the 1901 Locomotive Scheme. The 'Moguls' could be uncomfortable at speed, with a pronounced roll, although not as extreme as with the similarly sized 4-4-0 'Counties'. A further drawback was severe flange wear on the leading driving wheels over curvaceous routes. To compensate, the weight borne by the pony wheels was increased to impart more side thrust to the main frames; this was achieved by mounting a heavy casting immediately behind the front buffer beam. Following initial tests with four of the '43xx' series, this makeshift arrangement was applied to 65 of the '53xx' series from 1928. The resultant 2-ton weight increase achieved the desired effect but moved the modified engines into the 'Red' route availability category; they were identified by being renumbered in the '83xx' series. From 1944 onwards a reduction in the numbers of 4-4-0s available for 'Blue' routes led to 53 reverting to their original condition, while the remaining 12 had already been withdrawn for rebuilding as 'Granges' and 'Manors'. No 8378 had been built as No 5378 in 1919 and ran in modified form from March 1928 until June 1944, when it reverted to its original condition and number. It survived until September 1959. *Stephenson Locomotive Society*

| TABLE 1 | | | | | |
|---------|------|-----------|---------------|-----------|------------|
| **Class** | **Type** | **Cylinders** | **No in service** | **Introduced** | **Last built** |
| 'Frenchmen' | 4-4-2 | 4 | 3 | 1903 | 1905 |
| 'Star' | 4-6-0 | 4 | 73 | 1906 | 1923 |
| 'The Great Bear' | 4-6-2 | 4 | 1 | 1908 | - |
| 'Saint' | 4-6-0 | 2 outside | 77 | 1902 | 1913 |
| 'County' | 4-4-0 | 2 outside | 40 | 1904 | 1912 |
| 'County Tank' | 4-4-2T | 2 outside | 30 | 1905 | 1912 |
| 'Armstrong' | 4-4-0 | 2 inside | 4 | 1894 | 1894 |
| 'Badminton' | 4-4-0 | 2 inside | 20 | 1897 | 1899 |
| 'Atbara' | 4-4-0 | 2 inside | 29 | 1900 | 1901 |
| 'Flower' | 4-4-0 | 2 inside | 20 | 1908 | 1908 |
| 'City' | 4-4-0 | 2 inside | 20* | 1903 | 1909 |

of Classes '31xx' and '3150' were by then appearing in significant numbers, making the 4-4-2Ts superfluous. Footplate crews made comparative judgements; the 'County Tanks' were disliked for their poorer accelerative and adhesive qualities.

By February 1923 the fleet of locomotives with 6ft 8½in driving wheels was large and diverse (see Table 1).

Contemporaneous construction of the 4-4-0s alongside the 'Saints' and 'Stars' led to a cascade of the smaller engines to secondary duties, but increasing loads were to revive the case for a mixed-traffic 4-6-0.

## 'Halls' – the lasting compromise

Design of the Class '43xx' was a straightforward exercise that would hardly have demanded Hawksworth's particular talents. However, his appointment as Assistant Chief Draughtsman in 1923, and his promotion two years later to Chief Draughtsman, drew him into the demands for a larger mixed-traffic machine. The Running Department had advised that a front bogie and a No 1 boiler would be ideal, i.e. a 4-6-0 with 5ft 8in driving wheels, as originally envisaged. In late 1924 No 2925 *Saint Martin* was rebuilt as a mixed-traffic machine to test the concept.

At this distance it is hard to be certain, but prevailing circumstances must have influenced the scale of the exercise. The works was busy processing locomotives absorbed at the Grouping,

**ABOVE** Prototype 'Hall' Class No 4900 *Saint Martin* was distinguishable from the production 'Halls' by the lower boiler pitch and by not receiving outside steam pipes and new cylinders until December 1948. *R. Blencowe collection*

**BELOW** The second production 'Hall' was No 4902 *Aldenham Hall*. This view dates from the early nationalisation period, as the number is still on the front buffer beam while the tender reads 'BRITISH RAILWAYS' in the standard GWR font.

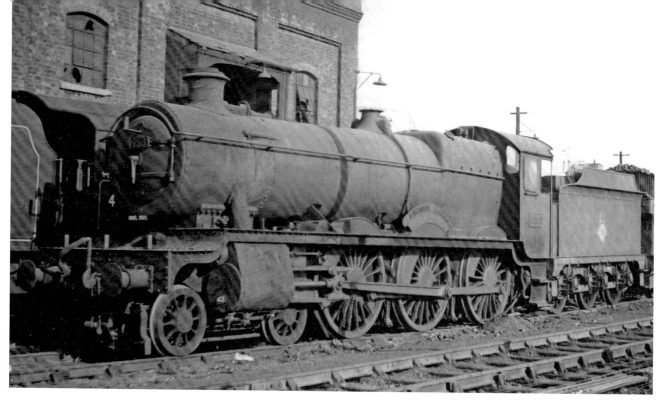

ABOVE The 'Halls' were attached to different tender types during their careers – 3,500-gallon of varying vintages, Collett 4,000-gallon, and Hawksworth 4,000-gallon. Late in its working life No 4958 *Priory Hall* is at Gloucester MPD on 3 October 1964, coupled, probably uniquely, to a tender of Great Central design. These 4,000-gallon tenders arrived with the famous ROD 2-8-0s (Class '30xx') purchased from the government in the 1920s, the last of which was withdrawn in 1958. Once declared surplus, the tenders were transferred to the 'Aberdare' 2-6-0s, then to the Class '2251' 0-6-0s. As the last 'Aberdare' was withdrawn in 1949, No 4958 must have acquired this tender from one of the 0-6-0s, few of which remained in service. Crews would have been annoyed to find that this tender had no water pick-up gear. *R. W. Norfolk*

as well as building 'Castles' and Class '56xx', and a quick-fix solution with minimal modification was preferred. Positioning of the frames and boiler relative to each other remained unchanged, while driving wheels of 6ft 0in diameter replaced the originals, thereby lowering the boiler centre line by 4¼ inches. The other distinctive feature was the provision of a side window cab similar to that inaugurated with No 4073; this improvement appeared thereafter with all new tender locomotives.

The treatment meted out to No 2925 proved popular. There was some irony as its interim status had a precedent in the enlarged 'Star', which was initially considered a stepping-stone to something bigger and more lasting. Thus two 'temporary' measures led to the two most common 4-6-0 classes – the 'Castles' and the 'Halls' – whose presence dominated GWR steam until the end. Nevertheless, there remained the notion that more enquiry and innovation might have yielded even better results, as was proven 12 years later with the 'Granges'.

With many of the large-wheeled 4-4-0s still comparatively young, there was no immediate pressure for their replacement, but when volume production started in 1928 the first Lot (No 254) comprised 80 locomotives. Minor changes were made with boiler mountings, but it was a pity that the driving wheel size and a thorough reassessment of the design was not then addressed. No 2925 (renumbered 4900 and absorbed into the 'Hall' Class proper in December 1928) remained readily distinguishable by its lower-pitched boiler.

## The splendid 'Granges'

The popularity of the 2-6-0 Class '43xx' resulted in there being 322 in service by 1925. Their versatility deferred the immediate need for mixed-traffic 4-6-0s, despite certain drawbacks. Most significantly, the pony truck exerted excessive flange wear on the leading coupled wheels, especially over curvaceous routes. To

ABOVE 'Grange' Class No 6866 *Morfa Grange* nearing completion in the erecting shops at Swindon on 26 February 1939. *Ian Allan Library*

RIGHT Newly completed No 6840 *Hazeley Grange* at Swindon in 1937. *Ian Allan Library*

increase side thrust on the pony truck and thereby even out flange wear, additional weight was added at the front by moving the buffer beam forward to make space for a heavy transverse casting. This makeshift arrangement improved riding but added 2 tons to the overall weight, elevating the modified engines to 'Red' category for route availability.

Collett added 20 more to the class in 1932, and it was typical of his caution that they mainly adhered to the Churchward format when something larger was overdue. Refinement with the '93xx' series took the form of screw reverse, outside steam pipes and side-window cabs, as well as minor dimensional changes. However, 'Red' category availability remained by virtue of the makeshift heavy front-end casting. Like the final batch of 'County Tanks', this small group of locomotives was obsolescent on introduction.

The Standard No 4 boiler enjoyed a proven reputation in service with such diverse types as the 'Cities', 4-4-0 'Counties', Class '3150' 'Prairies' and Class '42xx' 2-8-0Ts. Nonetheless, by the 1930s certain duties handled by the 'Moguls' were beginning to tax this boiler's capacity[2], and this factor, coupled with lively riding qualities, provided a case for a larger replacement. Collett stayed faithful to Churchward's principles in the resultant 'Granges', the earliest drawing for which was dated November 1935. The 'Halls' were a minimalistic diversion from the 'Saint' formula, while the 'Granges' precisely filled the remaining gap in the 1901 Scheme. The cost of the 'Granges' was mitigated by retention of wheels and motion from withdrawn 'Moguls', but the 5ft 8in-diameter driving wheels necessitated revision of the front end that had been circumvented with No 2925. Piston valves of

9-inch diameter were fitted, together with enlarged steam chest and steam ports. The latter two features are considered the key reasons why these engines were held in high regard, and considered superior to the 'Halls'.

Replacing the ageing Class '43xx' in this fashion reduced capital unit cost, but the saga was a roundabout means of providing a 4-6-0 that had been planned 35 years earlier. While other pressures on Swindon might had prevented more adventurous treatment of No 2925 in 1924, there was less excuse four years later to ignore the 'Grange' concept prior to starting volume production of mixed-traffic 4-6-0s. During this period Hawksworth was working with Stanier on an imaginative but doomed scheme to improve the four-cylinder engines, as discussed in the next chapter. Hawksworth could hardly have viewed the extended gestation of the 'Granges' with much enthusiasm.

BELOW A post-war view of No 6868 *Penrhos Grange*. *Ian Allan Library*

## The dismal 'Manors'

The first evidence of the 'Manor' project is a drawing of February 1936 that shows a 4-6-0 with a Standard No 4 boiler, but weight evidently remained an issue as, by April, a scheme using a modified Standard No 2 boiler was under consideration. Either combination should have eliminated the riding problem that plagued the 'Moguls', but not the matter of boiler capacity. The 'Manors' appeared in 1938 as a lightweight 'Grange' fitted with a new boiler (Standard No 14), which was a scaled-down version of the Standard No 1. The first 20 'Manors' also used material recovered from withdrawn 'Class 43xx' engines.

The unprecedented use of 4-6-0s over 'Blue' routes allowed replacement of ageing 4-4-0s. As would be expected, they enjoyed superior haulage capacity to engines whose origins lay in the Dean era, but there were signs of something amiss from observations during footplate journeys with Nos 7802 and 7803 when new. Everything was comfortably familiar except for surprising fluctuations in boiler pressure.[3]

There was apparently no effort objectively to test the new boiler's qualities, and in the difficult conditions from 1940 onwards the lacklustre performance of a 20-strong class on secondary work would have been regarded as a minor concern. Welsh duties that involved frequent stops and pilot work over the South Devon banks called for short periods of intense demand followed by respites during which the boiler could recover. Without sustained demands over long periods, the deficiency was less obvious than might otherwise have been the case.

Even so, there was inordinate delay before the shortcomings were addressed, and not before the error had been compounded. The decision to build ten more must have more or less coincided with Hawksworth's retirement, and presumably he had minimal interest in the matter. Nevertheless, construction of Nos 7820 to

7829 under Lot No 377 in 1950 was an odd episode. They differed in being completely new engines but were otherwise similar, including the indifferent steaming.

Following on from the final batch of 'Modified Halls', and notwithstanding the introduction of two 4-6-0 classes with plate frames throughout, these ten engines retained the earlier and more expensive Churchward bar/plate combination. Further, it is significant that there was no recourse to recycled 'Mogul' material, even though there were plenty of the '63xx' series available. Hawksworth's construction programmes were exclusively in new building, a major change from the practice of 1936-39, and significant in view of prevailing steel shortages. It might be concluded that he perceived little advantage in rebuilding/recycling on the scale that Collett had enacted, and that the benefits had been overestimated.

RIGHT A post-war view of No 7812 *Erlestoke Manor*. *Ian Allan Library*

ABOVE No 7818 *Granville Manor* is working a Cheltenham-Southampton service via Swindon Town and Andover at Millbrook. The engine is coupled to one of the few 'intermediate' 3,500-gallon tenders. *Frank F. Moss*

RIGHT No 7812 *Erlestoke Manor* is seen again in BR days following blastpipe modifications arising from the comparative trials between No 7818 and a 4-6-0 BR Class '75xxx' on the Swindon Stationary Testing Plant in 1952. Evidence for the alterations is found in the slimmer chimney than those carried by the engines depicted in the earlier photographs.

All 30 'Manors' were at work before their abilities were scientifically assessed, and then only when faced with immutable evidence of superiority in the comparable 4-6-0 BR Class '75xxx'. It had been long assumed that GWR boilers were better than anybody else's, justifying the extra expense in fashioning the tapered barrel and the complex curvature of the Belpaire firebox. The BR 4-6-0 (somewhat ironically designed and built at Swindon) convincingly reaffirmed these advantages in a maximum steaming rate of 19,600lb per hour on the Test Plant. A 'Manor' was then tested and found capable of barely achieving 10,000lb per hour.

At last, some 14 years after No 7800 had entered service, officialdom took notice. No 7818 was subjected to exhaustive examination on the Test Plant and on the road in 1951/52. It was established that the original blastpipe had been proportionally scaled down from that on the 'Grange' boiler when in fact a complete dimensional revision was needed. Based on test results, the jumper ring was removed and the blastpipe diameter reduced to 4¾ inches (the same as the BR engine). More testing led to a further reduction to 4⅝ inches and to a measured maximum steaming rate of 20,400lb per hour. Duly improved, the 'Manors' became excellent performers and were highly regarded, especially on the Welsh services for which they had been originally intended.

The first of the pre-war batch was withdrawn in April 1963 and the last in December 1965, right at the end of GWR steam, having enjoyed longer careers in sub-standard condition than they had as the efficient units they eventually became. The criticism occasionally directed at the 'Counties' diverts attention from the awkward fact that the last pure expression of the Churchward formula, and the very last 4-6-0s of GWR design to be built, were lamentable descendants of the ground-breaking No 100 of 1902.

RIGHT The poor steaming of the 'Manors' in original condition was exposed in stationary tests at Swindon when the similarly sized (and Swindon-designed) BR Class 4 4-6-0 raised steam at double the maximum rate of the GWR type. These Class 4s had quite a long association with Wales, as is apparent in this view of No 75055 at the head of the down 'Cambrian Coast Express' on 1 July 1966. By then routes to mid-Wales were under the control of BR's London Midland Region, but the GWR influence lingered on, as with the fourth coach, which is a Hawksworth vehicle. *Ifor Higgon*

**LEFT** 'Saint' Class No 2931 *Arlington Court* at rest on the Swindon Stationary Test Plant.

## The Stationary Testing Plant

The earliest stationary testing plants were established by a US university (1891) and by the Chicago & North Western RR (1895). The most significant development, however, was the plant set up by the Pennsylvania RR at Altoona in 1904, and work started on Europe's first plant at Swindon the same year. Yet another example of Churchward's interest in contemporary US practice, this facility was intended both to test and to run in locomotives. In practice it was little used and, with a capacity to absorb power outputs of up to about 500hp, it had long been inadequate for testing modern motive power.

The value of stationary testing of large locomotives first came to prominence in the UK through a report in *The Locomotive* for January 1929, which referred to comparative assessment in the United States of a 2-8-2 freight locomotive type, 150 of which had been constructed. Assumptions had been made that the front-end design was satisfactory and that the maximum estimated water consumption rate was 59,000lb per hour. Stationary testing under controlled conditions then revealed that not only was the locomotive difficult to fire, but also that the maximum measured consumption rate was 48,000lb per hour. For a large group of locomotives, this was a cogent example of substantial waste

Although dynamometer cars had been used for many years, the data collected could be doubtful where journeys were interrupted by station or unscheduled stops and speed restrictions, making it necessary to estimate constant steaming rates. In the US case cited above, the stationary plant revealed unsatisfactory features that had not been exposed by testing on the road. Gresley had already recognised the advantages, having proposed in 1927 a national testing facility as an adjunct to the traditional dynamometer car. The following year a committee representing all the 'Big Four' was formed to investigate, but there was little progress and the idea was shelved.

In May 1934 Gresley's prototype 2-8-2 Class 'P2' express locomotive was assessed at the French locomotive testing centre at Vitry-sur-Seine, and this exercise reignited discussion about creating something similar in Britain. The French facility was built on land owned by the Paris-Orleans Railway and close to electrified routes, in anticipation that testing would not be confined to steam engines. The plant was significantly more powerful than Churchward's, being able to absorb power outputs up to 3,000hp and to cope with speeds up to 170kmph.

By then the Southern Railway, heavily absorbed with its electrification programme, had no further interest in the idea. Further discussions were held between the LMS and LNER, and it is unclear whether the GWR was consulted. The obvious forum for joint consideration of the project was the ARLE, but Collett was not by then participating in the affairs of that body. By early 1938 a committee had been formed with the intention of establishing a facility at Rugby under joint LMS/LNER sponsorship, following study of testing stations at Vitry-sur-Seine and Grunewald, near Berlin.

Regardless of any interest shown by the GWR, Collett commissioned refurbishment and overhaul of the Swindon plant in late 1935, but it was soon apparent that more extensive upgrading would be necessary, involving new equipment. The work was completed by the end of 1937 at a cost of about £7,000, evidently in secret. 'Saint' No 2931 *Arlington Court* was used as the guinea pig for testing the equipment during installation. This locomotive was in place and going nowhere at 70mph in 'A' Shop for a visit by senior representatives of the LMS and LNER. The date has not been determined, but the invitation seems to have been extended in early 1938, apparently to coincide with the start of the Rugby project.

This episode reflected the complexity and duplicitous nature of Collett's character. The visitors' astonishment must have appealed to his sense of humour, but it was an expensive and rather pointless joke. The project as a joint venture in which the other companies could have shared investment cost and access would have been financially sensible. Alternatively, part of the expense could have been recovered by renting out the facility for use by the other companies. Records are incomplete, but there seem to have been few cases of the GWR making use of the upgraded plant. It was remarkable that there was no effort to test (and thus expose) the new boiler that had been developed for the 'Manors', or to measure a 'King' in the context of ideas à la Chapelon (see Chapter 5).

It has been suggested that use of the 20-year-old 'Saint' in the demonstration was to give the impression that this was an everyday event, which it certainly was not. *Arlington Court*'s presence as the test locomotive was convenient, but there could have been another motive. Other CMEs might have wished to show off a 'King' or a 'Castle', but observers would have naturally asked about the indicated power output. Presumably in anticipation, use of an engine attributed to his predecessor would have deflected scrutiny of Collett's own work.

Although the plant played a valuable role after nationalisation, the GWR derived little benefit. The refurbishment looked like an expensive exercise in one-upmanship and a tangible example of Swindon's isolationist attitudes. Perhaps most acutely, it demonstrated Collett's lack of commercial acumen.

## Change of direction

Wartime conditions increased the need for freight engines, exacerbated by the sale of 108 Dean Goods, and motive power was borrowed from the other companies:

| | |
|---|---|
| **0-6-0** | 2Fs and 3Fs from the LMS, Class 'J25' from the LNER |
| **2-8-0** | Stanier 8Fs from the LMS, Class 'O4' from the LNER |
| **4-6-0** | Classes 'H15'/'S15'/'N15X' from the Southern Railway |
| **4-4-2T** | Class 'I3' from the Southern Railway |

By GWR standards, these were outdated types except for the LMS 2-8-0s. The loan of 25 was comparatively short-lived, commencing in September 1940 and ending with the return home of the final example in October 1941. However, this transaction elevated debate from theoretical discussion that Collett had discouraged into confrontation with progress achieved beyond the company's borders. Although Swindon was later to build Stanier 8Fs, this initial temporary attachment was also influential in a policy revision concerning two-cylinder 4-6-0s. The last two GWR 4-6-0 classes – the 'Modified Halls' and the 'Counties' – owed much to experience gained with the 8Fs, and there was a clear association between the three types. The design process went through a number of iterations (Schemes 1 to 13 mentioned below, leading to the 'Counties') before the first change took physical form with 'Modified Hall' No 6959.[4] The timeline was as shown in Table 2.

| TABLE 2 | | | |
|---|---|---|---|
| Date | Event | Boiler type | Design details |
| Sep 40 | Commencement of Stanier 8F loans | | |
| Jul 41 | Hawksworth appointed CME | | |
| Oct 41 | Final Stanier 8F on loan returned to LMS | | |
| Oct 42 | Scheme 1 | LMS | 'Hall' with LMS boiler, 6ft 0in driving wheels |
| Mar 43 | Schemes 2 & 3 | LMS, modified | 6ft 0in driving wheels |
| Mar 43 | Scheme 4 | LMS, modified | BP 280lb per sq in, 6ft 3in driving wheels |
| Apr 43 | Scheme 5 | LMS, modified | BP 280lb per sq in; first scheme with plate frames throughout |
| Unclear | Scheme 6 | Standard No 15 | Outside Walschaerts valve gear, raised footplate, drawing notes 'rough scheme' |
| Apr 43 | Last ordinary 'Hall' into service | Standard No 1 | |
| May 43 | First Swindon-built Stanier 8F into service | | |
| Jan 44 | Scheme 7 | Standard No 15 | Outside Walschaerts valve gear, raised footplate |
| Feb 44 | Scheme 8 | Standard No 15 | Inside valve gear, splashers |
| Feb 44 | Scheme 9 | Standard No 15 | Outside valve gear, raised footplate, new tender |
| Mar 44 | First 'Modified Hall' into service | Standard No 1 | Plate frames |
| Apr 44 | Scheme 10 | Standard No 15 | Inside valve gear, single continuous splasher |
| Apr 44 | Scheme 11 | Standard No 15 | Outside valve gear, raised footplate, new tender |
| May 44 | Scheme 12 | Standard No 15 | Inside valve gear, splashers, straight-sided tender |
| Sep 44 | Last of first 12 'Modified Halls' into service | | |
| Dec 44 | Scheme 13 | Standard No 15 | Lot No 354 issued for 20 'Counties' |
| Apr 47 | Last 'County' into service | | |
| Oct 47 | First of 2nd batch of 'Modified Halls' into service | Standard No 1 | |

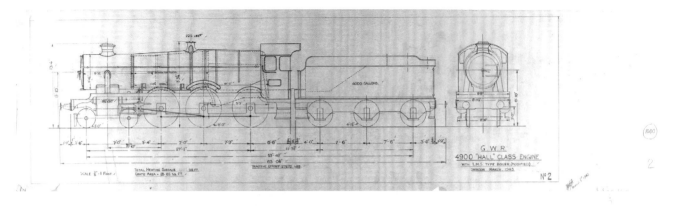

**ABOVE** The second effort in the use of the 8F boiler (Scheme 2) involved the proposal to fit a cut-down version on a standard 'Hall' chassis. This was the first stage towards the creation of the Standard No 15 boiler, although at this point the usual boiler pressure at 225lb per sq in was planned. *NRM*

**LEFT** No 6995 *Bentham Hall* at Swindon.

## The 'Modified Halls'

The first attempt to revise the 'Halls' dated from October 1942, but construction of the class in unchanged form totalled 73 between November 1939 and April 1943. Differences from the 186 built pre-war followed the pattern of alterations introduced to 4-6-0s generally – a more austere livery, removal of cab-side windows, and attachments for mounting canvas blackout screens. With effect from No 6916, locomotives were not named until after the war. The first fruits of outside influence, and of Hawksworth's determination to effect change, appeared with No 6959 in March 1944. The class designation of 'Modified Hall' heralded a more profound transformation than had been applied to 'Saint' No 2925, with revision of key features undisturbed since Churchward's day. Previously required to toe his predecessor's reactionary line, he was now prepared to break new ground.

Revision of the 'Halls' started with investigation into fitting an 8F boiler, an approach that echoed the attempt to marry a '47xx' (Standard No 7) boiler with the 'Star'/'Saint'/'28xx' chassis in the early 1920s. In this later exercise, the Standard No 1 was retained while the cut-down 8F boiler eventually appeared as the Standard No 15 with the 'Counties'. The 'Modified Halls' were principally distinguished by a major departure from the Churchward format in frame design, and higher degree superheat.

No 98, the second two-cylinder 4-6-0 of the Churchward era, had set the pattern of front-end frame construction for the 'Saints', and continued with the original 'Halls', 'Granges' and 'Manors'.

The cylinder block was cast in two halves that were bolted together, back-to-back along the centre line of the frames. Each casting incorporated one driving cylinder below its corresponding 10-inch-diameter piston valve, and the co-joined blocks formed the supporting saddle for the smokebox. Such was the driving cylinder alignment that the outer faces of the blocks had to be bolted to bar frames installed between there and the rear of the buffer beam. These bar frames at the rear overlapped the main (plate) frames to which they were bolted at that point.

The result was a cylinder block that was strong, corrosion-free, and which avoided the risk of leaks in joints between smokebox and cylinders. Normally, the thrust exerted by the motion was most acute around the cylinder area, but the strength imparted by the solid structure comfortably absorbed these stresses. Also, as uneven wear developed in the cylinders, the entire assembly could be dismantled and reversed for further use.

A disadvantage lay in the inherent weakness of the fabricated frame structure, which risked disproportionate damage arising from quite moderate front-end collisions. In larger-wheeled engines there was adequate space for the bar frames to be set horizontally and to clear the cylinder centre line. As a precaution, a rigidly braced stay plate was fitted vertically in line with the slide bar brackets and extended upwards close to (but not quite touching) the underside of the boiler. Thus, in the event of unusual shock upon the buffer beam the stay plate would move upwards and the weight of the boiler would absorb the thrust.

The 'Modified Halls' used plate frames throughout with a new design of cylinders and smokebox saddle. Operating demands favoured simplicity with resultant speed and lower cost in construction, which was achieved in a significant step away from Churchward's principles. A regressive aspect was plate frame

| TABLE 3 | | | | | | |
|---|---|---|---|---|---|---|
| Built | Number | No of 2in tubes | No of 5⅛in tubes | Heating surfaces (sq ft) | | |
| | | | | Tubes | Superheater | Firebox |
| 1922-44 | 599 | 176 | 14 | 1,687 | 263 | 155 |
| 1944-60 | 136 | 145 | 21 | 1,583 | 315 | 155 |

construction for the bogie, which could be subject to cracking; the De Glehn/Churchward bogie frame was considered stronger, with this shortcoming virtually unknown.

No 6959 heralded an important change in superheater policy showing that Hawksworth had heeded Stanier's message on that subject. Before the war Stanier had vainly tried to draw to Collett's attention his reservations about low degree superheat, but Hawksworth had obviously heeded the message. The Swindon Standard No 1 boiler before 1922 had been produced with several variations in tube numbers and diameters with resultant variations in heating surfaces. Construction from then was simpler, with two basic variants (see Table 3).

The later type was fitted with a three-row superheater and a header regulator. There were minor reductions in heating surfaces later, but the key dimensional changes marked a break with tradition as significant as the revised front-end frame construction. Other fresh ideas included a welded tender of normal flared-top profile (No 6959, March 1944), a hopper grate (No 6965, July 1944), and a welded steel firebox (No 6967, August 1944). In October 1947 No 6971 appeared with a welded straight-sided tender that was visually similar that used with the 'Counties'. The promise of better times took shape in March 1946 with naming those engines that had been labelled 'Hall Class' only on the

**ABOVE** 'Modified Hall' No 6970 *Whaddon Hall* at Hayes in 1947. *Ian Allan Library*

centre splashers. Then in late 1947 No 6974 entered service as the first in post-war lined green livery.

The spirit of innovation heralded by the 'Modified Halls' was broadcast by their wide initial distribution:

| No | First shed | Comments |
|---|---|---|
| 6959 | Swindon | After trials on Swindon Test Plant |
| 6960 | Paddington | |
| 6961 | Westbury | Transferred to Hereford in October 1944 |
| 6962 | Bristol | |
| 6963 | Stafford Road | |
| 6964 | Stafford Road | |
| 6965 | Hereford | |
| 6966 | Swindon | Transferred to Westbury in October 1944 |
| 6967 | Oxley | |
| 6968 | Paddington | |
| 6969 | Newport | |
| 6970 | Oxley | December 1947 |

Nos 6959-65 were fitted with a modified lubrication system to cope with the higher degree of superheat, while Nos 6966-70 had the same modification but appeared with older-type, lower superheat boilers. This was supposedly for comparison purposes, but perhaps material for the new boilers was in short supply (No 6966 was actually in service before No 6965 was completed). Nos 6959-61/65/66/70 were fitted with automatic feed drifting gear, which allowed a mix of steam and oil to be fed to the cylinders while running with the regulator closed; a small single-feed mechanical oil pump mounted below the left-hand footplate and driven by the left-hand rocking shaft actuated this gear.

The new engines were well received, with a judgement passed at Stafford Road on No 6963 as a 'super engine'. Their smooth absorption into the motive power fleet was achieved without specific explanation or guidance, and might have engendered confidence that the same would be possible with the next new 4-6-0 class.

## The enigmatic 'Counties'

Despite their early success, the 'Modified Halls' were only a step towards further changes, and in many respects the 4-6-0 'Counties' were a direct evolution. Plate frames were again used, but new features were 6ft 3in driving wheels, a larger boiler with a 280lb per sq in working pressure, a hopper-type ashpan as standard, a full-width cab, and a double chimney (on the first example only). The single straight-topped driving wheel splashers had been seen pre-war with the streamlined 'King' and 'Castle'. The boiler was a cut-down version of the LMS design produced at Swindon for the Stanier 8F. The 4,000-gallon tender was entirely new, with a revised underframe and an all-welded reprofiled flat-sided body. The width matched that of the cab, helping increase the coal capacity to 7 tons.

The design combined fresh thinking with the traditional, particularly in the retention of inside Stephenson link motion. Outside valve gear had been considered in preceding design iterations, but apparently only of the Walschaerts type. Until then, Stephenson's motion had been virtually exclusively fitted between the frames by the GWR and other companies. It was not until 1947 that outside motion was tried by H. G. Ivatt on LMS 'Black 5' No 4767 – an experiment that resulted in a highly effective locomotive.

Uncertainty about future needs led to a number of changes in proposed locomotive Lots in the mid-1940s, and the new Class '99xx' (changed shortly before introduction to Class '10xx') was no exception:

| Lot No | Date | Running numbers | |
|---|---|---|---|
| | | Original | Actual |
| 354 | ? | 9900-9909 | - |
| 354 (revised) | ? | 9900-19 | 1000-19 |
| 358 | Feb 45 | 9920-34 | - |
| 358 (revised) | Dec 45 | 9920-29 | 1020-29 |
| 359 | ? | 1030-34 | Lot cancelled |

Sixty-five 'Counties' were originally planned, but their failure to meet expectations was borne out by cancellation of Lot 359 and cessation of construction with No 1029 in April 1947. Introduction of more mixed-traffic 4-6-0s resumed the following October with 59 'Modified Halls', the last appearing in November 1950.

The large boiler, high working pressure and No 1000's double chimney suggested that the 'Counties' offered something special. This was compounded by Hawksworth's statement that they were to be driven like 'Castles', unsupported by empirical evidence and open to misinterpretation. It has been suggested that failure in the normally close communication between the drawing office and the running inspectors also had an effect.[4] Without clear definition of their prospective duties, they were rostered alongside 'Kings', 'Castles' and 'Stars', making comparisons inevitable, to the disadvantage of the new locomotives.

Unusually for the period, No 1000 was given a dedicated senior crew on allocation when new to Old Oak Common, and difficulties were soon experienced. The novel draughting arrangements proved unsatisfactory as at early cut-off the steaming rate fell alarmingly while adjustment towards full forward gear sharpened the exhaust, tearing the fire to pieces. The double chimney was soon labelled as 'experimental', but there was no attempt at modification until early 1954.

The single-chimney engines also acquired a reputation for indifferent steaming, but here the explanation might have been simpler. Continuing absence of many experienced footplate personnel on military service and poor-quality fuel would have made it that much harder to sustain pressure at a level 55lb per sq in higher than was normal for a two-cylinder 4-6-0. They were widely spread throughout the system with a bias towards the West Country (Appendix C shows allocations when new, and at December 1947 and 1950). Distribution among so many running sheds reduced opportunities for crews to familiarise themselves and share experiences with colleagues. By comparison, before the

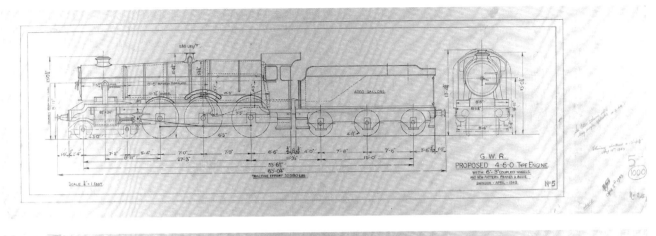

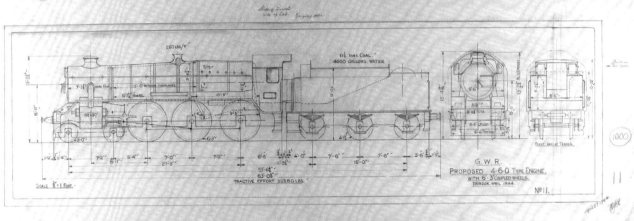

**TOP** The fifth iteration (April 1943) in the development of the 'County' Class was the first to see the new standard No 15 boiler carried on plate frames. *NRM*

**ABOVE** The 11th version in this design saga had a pronounced austerity flavour. Plate frames and a high running plate remained, but the outside valve motion has been discarded. The cab and tender were clearly influenced by the Ministry of Supply 2-8-0s. *NRM*

Second World War the 30-strong 'King' Class had been allocated to only four sheds, allowing familiarity to accumulate with these large engines and their demanding boilers. (A similar phenomenon occurred with the BR 'Britannias', which only became fully accepted following their concentration on South Wales services.)

The tender, unusually dedicated solely for use with the class, heralded the first substantial design change for many years as, despite variations in wheelbase, height and carrying capacities, these vehicles had basically remained unchanged since the days of William Dean. The body was 9 feet wide, which yielded a coal capacity of 7 tons as compared with the nominal 6 tons of the preceding flared-top type, and with the visually similar but

**ABOVE** Hawksworth (left) aboard No 1000. It is thought that this view might have been taken immediately prior to this engine's maiden run, although the condition of the cab-side paintwork suggests previous service.

It has been suggested that poppet valve gear was considered, but there is no firm evidence to support this contention, and certainly experience with 'Saint' No 2935 would have offered no incentive. The new driving wheel size and the high boiler pressure suggested an intent to maximise the hill-climbing capabilities imparted by the Stephenson motion. This implied concentration west of Exeter on services demanding more power and speed than a 'Hall' could deliver, and a speciality that hardly accorded with the standardised, utilitarian needs of the times. Alternatively, it might simply have been an effort to exploit the maxima permitted under the dimensional precedents set in 1941 by Oliver Bulleid.

The 'Counties' are immutably linked with Hawksworth's professional reputation, unreasonably drawing attention away from his other achievements. They were evidently intended as a new strain of more powerful mixed-traffic locomotive for which there was logic in the marriage of the plate-frame variant of the 'Hall' chassis with the larger boiler derived from the 8F. It was a shame that the draughting of No 1000 was not investigated and rectified sooner, as otherwise application of double chimneys to 'Kings' and 'Castles' might have accompanied introduction of higher degree superheating. The selection of a 280lb per sq in boiler pressure, evidently for no reason other than to equal Bulleid's 'Pacifics', was their biggest shortcoming, for reasons discussed below.

Although the 'Counties' were regarded as not quite fitting within the GWR 4-6-0 family, they were simpler and cheaper to build than the 'Castles'. These factors also applied when measuring them within their peer group, as other organisations had also recognised the need for a more powerful mixed-traffic machine (see Table 4).

The increase in weight was modest over that of the 'Modified Halls' (75 tons 16 cwt) and the original 'Halls' (75 tons), but negatively the maximum axle loading combined with two-cylinder drive yielded a significant increase in hammer blow. This was acceptable over GWR routes but denied availability over some of the other companies' lines – particularly the LMS between Standish Junction and Yate.

Despite the expectation of concentration in the West Country, a report from the winter of 1945/46 indicates that they were working on all the principal routes from Paddington, with the following quoted:

**ABOVE** 'County' Class No 1000 *County of Middlesex* was photographed at Old Oak Common on 25 August 1947. It is easy to see why these engines impressed on first acquaintance. Anyone familiar with the pre-war streamlined 4-6-0s would have immediately recognised the design origin of the straight splashers and nameplates, while the boiler looked larger than the traditional Standard No 1. The hulking double chimney, despite imparting the notion of super power, was soon associated with steaming difficulties and did much to undermine the engines' reputation in the early years. *P. C. Wheeler collection*

narrower flat-bodied type that followed, and found use with 'Star', 'Castle', 'Hall' and 'Modified Hall' locomotives.

The increased coal capacity was presumably in response to the deepening supply crisis, and in expectation of the engines' use on heavy duties over long distances. The matching wider cab almost eliminated the running plate below. In the absence of front footsteps, access to the smokebox was usually along this narrow ledge (about 3 inches wide), aided by the cab-side handrail. Almost as an afterthought it was realised that with the 'Counties' the smokebox would be virtually inaccessible without a ladder. A footstep was therefore fitted below the buffer beam on the right-hand side – a feature that revealed lack of practical input in the design.

| TABLE 4 | | | | | | | |
|---|---|---|---|---|---|---|---|
| Class | Introduced | Cylinders | Locomotive weight (full) | Maximum axle loading | Driving wheels | Boiler pressure | Tractive effort |
| 'V2' (LNER) | 1936 | 3, 18.5in x 26in | 93 tons 2 cwt | 22 tons 0 cwt | 6ft 2in | 220lb/sq in | 33,730lb |
| 'West Country' (SR) | 1945 | 3, 16.375in x 24in | 86 tons 0 cwt | 18 tons 15 cwt | 6ft 2in | 280 lb/sq in | 31,040lb |
| 'County' | 1945 | 2, 18.5in x 30in | 76 tons 17 cwt | 19 tons 14 cwt | 6ft 3in | 280lb/sq in | 32,580lb |
| 'Britannia' (BR) | 1951 | 2, 20in x 28in | 94 tons 0 cwt | 20 tons 5 cwt | 6ft 2in | 250lb/sq in | 32,150lb |

| No | Date | Service |
|---|---|---|
| 1002 | 9, 10, 24 Jan 46 | Paddington-Weston-super-Mare |
| 1003 | 10 & 12 Jan 45 | Paddington-Birkenhead |
| 1004 | 26 Dec 45 | Paddington-Cheltenham |
| 1006 | 11 Feb 45 | Penzance-Paddington |
| 1007 | 30 Jan 46 | Paddington-Bristol |
| 1008 | 27 Dec 45 | Paddington-Taunton |
| 1008 | 5 Feb 46 | Paddington-Bristol |
| 1008 | 7 Feb 46 | Paddington-Cheltenham |
| 1012 | 20 Feb 46 | Paddington-Birkenhead |

They were seen regularly on Paddington-Birmingham/ Wolverhampton trains, while Nos 1008, 1009 and 1011 appeared on Reading-Swindon local services. By the end of January Nos 1001, 1004 and 1006 were frequently reaching Penzance. Nos 1003 and 1011 were seen on 13 and 18 February respectively at Tiverton Junction on a service from Plymouth to the North of England. Also on 18 February, No 1013 was at Taunton bound for

**ABOVE** No 1011 *County of Chester* in BR lined black livery at Bristol on 5 March 1950. *R. H. G. Simpson*

**ABOVE RIGHT** No 1004 *County of Somerset* in lined black BR livery… *Brian Morrison*

**BELOW RIGHT** …and the same engine from the other side, at Shrewsbury with livery indeterminate beneath the grime.

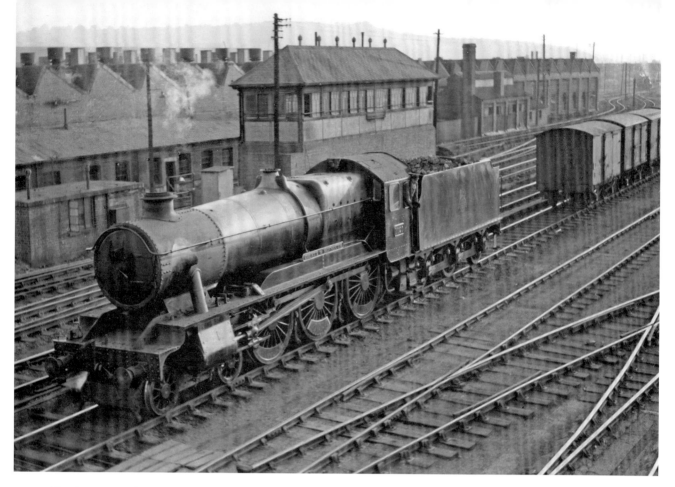

**ABOVE** No 1020 *County of Monmouth*, then of Neyland shed, comes off the fish train in the early evening of 25 July 1955 in front of Cardiff Canton Signal Box. It was normal practice to change engines at this point. *R. O. Tuck*

**BELOW** No 1022 *County of Northampton* at Reading in August 1954. *G. Wheeler*

**ABOVE** No 1009 *County of Carmarthen* at Swindon with temporary fabricated single stovepipe chimney and indicator shelter installed. This engine entered Swindon Works for testing in July 1954 and did not resume ordinary duties until early 1955. No 1007 had been subject to scrutiny on the Swindon Test Plant in October 1953, then No 1000, still with original double chimney, was tested at the beginning of 1954. The extended trials with No 1009 seem to have been the conclusive exercise to determine how the draughting could be improved, in due course leading to the fitting of a new squat double chimney to the entire class. Even then the conversion exercise was protracted, commencing with No 1022 in May 1956 and concluding with No 1021 in October 1959. The latter was converted a little more than four years before withdrawal.

| Passenger 4-6-0 | Boiler type | Cost | Mixed-traffic 4-6-0 | Boiler type | Cost | Freight 2-8-0 | Boiler type | Cost |
|---|---|---|---|---|---|---|---|---|
| **TABLE 5** | | | | | | | | |
| LMS 'Jubilee' | 3A | 0.94* | LMS Class 5 | 3B | 1.20** | LMS Stanier 8F | 3C | 1.51 |
| LMS 'Royal Scot' | 2A | 1.00 | LMS Class 5 | 3B | 1.24* | LNER 'O1' | 100A | 2.24 |
| GWR 'King' | Standard No 12 | 1.32 | LNER 'B1' | 100A | 1.95 | GWR '28xx' | Standard No 1 | 2.56 |
| LMS 'Jubilee' | 3A | 1.52** | GWR 'Hall' | Standard No 1 | 2.48 | 'WD' | BR10 | 3.24 |
| GWR 'Castle' | Standard No 8 | 1.80 | GWR 'Grange' | Standard No 1 | 2.49 | | | |
| SR 'Lord Nelson' | - | 1.80 | GWR 'County' | Standard No 15 | 4.90 | | | |

\* Crewe
\*\* St Rollox

Bristol and Paddington. The most remarkable working occurred the same day when No 1009 hauled the up 'Cornish Riviera' from Penzance to Plymouth, where No 1012 took over for the remainder of the journey.

By early 1947 the 'Counties' were settling down to regular working patterns. No 1027, a Westbury engine, often hauled the 8.40am to Paddington, returning home on the 12.30pm from the capital. Nos 1022 and 1023, Laira engines from new, were working exclusively into Cornwall, and around March they were transferred to Penzance and Truro respectively. No 1019 was a regular on Newton Abbot-Penzance duties. On the other hand, almost all of the class seem to have appeared at some stage at Paddington in the first two years or so; this might have been connected with an alleged arrangement to ensure that engines could be observed regularly passing Hawksworth's office window at Swindon!

Later in their careers allocations were more stable. As at 31 December 1959, 19 had resided at the same shed for periods between four and 14 years, while several of the others had recently changed sheds on a local basis. The allocation was nevertheless still diverse: Bath Road had eight, Exeter two, Hereford one, Laira two, Neyland three, Penzance three, Swindon six, and Shrewsbury five.

Performance was later improved, but not until after Hawksworth's retirement. No 1000 was road-tested in early 1954 between Swindon and Reading, fitted with an indicator shelter and hauling a dynamometer car and train. Then between July and November 1954 No 1009 was subjected to more intensive trials on the Test Plant and on the road, included hauling 20 coaches and the dynamometer car. This exercise was managed by S. O. Ell, who had sorted out the 'Manors', and saw No 1009 carrying a fabricated double stovepipe chimney. This enabled easy adjustments to identify the optimal draughting dimensions. The result was a new double chimney of squatter profile, which was applied to the entire class between 1956 and 1959. Strangely, No 1000 was not modified until May 1958.

**RIGHT** No 1009 at work on a test train; the fabricated stove-pipe double chimney is prominent.

While the revised double chimney was visually prominent, a more significant change stemmed from a survey conducted in 1954 to compare the repair costs of selected classes. One analysis considered boiler repair costs, defined as expenditure per class in pence per engine mile (see Table 5).

Several factors had an impact – boiler age and effectiveness of water treatment facilities were two – and it was clear that there were other causes of distortions (e.g. there was no convincing explanation for the disparity between Crewe and St Rollox with the 'Jubilees'). The Southern Railway had invested heavily in water treatment facilities and, combined with relative boiler youth, the 'Merchant Navy' costs at 0.63 and the 'West Country' at 0.42 (in the 'Pacific'/2-6-2 category where the GWR was not represented) were by far the best of any group.

Due to what was regarded as an inferior water treatment regime, the GWR contingent performed poorly, especially in

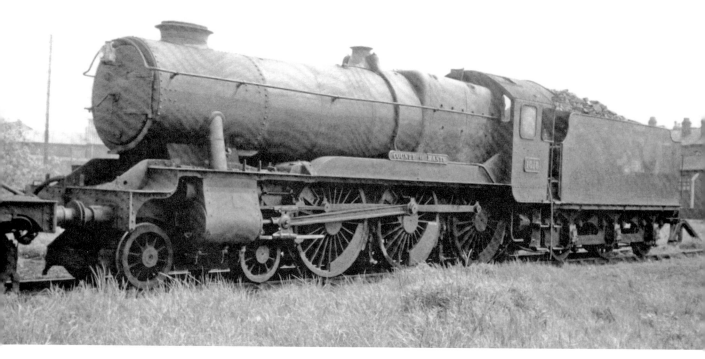

**ABOVE** No 1016 *County of Hants* with double chimney. The new design was held by some to give these engines a hunch-back look, but this seems to have been a matter of the viewing angle. No 1016 has lost its smokebox number plate, a warning sign that withdrawal may not be far away. *Kidderminster Railway Museum*

**BELOW** No 1010 *County of Caernarvon* at Swindon MPD, fitted with the new form of double chimney. *M. Edwards*

ABOVE The cut connecting rod of No 1013 standing in Swindon roundhouse on 26 July 1964 leaves no doubt about the status of this engine. No 1000 is standing behind, while withdrawn No 1010 was also present. *J. C. Haydon*

RIGHT The right-hand nameplate of No 1017 showing the mounting independent of the splasher to clear the reversing rod. *I. Simpson*

comparison with the Southern, but variations among GWR classes rendered reasonable explanations. The 'Kings' all had relatively new boilers whereas most 'Castles' still carried the original (and older) two-row superheater version. The Standard No 1 boilers' results showed acceptable consistency between the 'Halls', 'Granges' and '28xxs'. On these bases, allowing for possible errors, the results could be construed as a reasonably authentic portrayal.

This brought the Standard No 15 boiler into focus, as the repair costs for these young boilers, at double those of the Standard No 1, were extraordinary. Even worse was its relationship to the Stanier 8F boiler, of which it was a cut-down version. While differing water treatment and construction methods might have been influential, clearly the high working pressure had serious impact. The pressure was therefore reduced to 250lb per sq in, thus lowering the notional tractive effort to 29,090lb. This was still high compared with other two-cylinder 4-6-0s engaged on broadly similar work.

No 1012 (built in February 1946 and withdrawn in December 1963) achieved the highest mileage, at 794,555, while the lowest was No 1029, at 555,216 (built in April 1947 and withdrawn December 1962). In the period to 31 December 1963, when recording of steam mileages was abandoned, the annual average

across the entire class was 39,500. By comparison, the clearly defined express passenger role of the 5098 'Castle' series yielded an annual average mileage of 47,200.

The 'Counties' suffered from poor communication regarding their intended duties and resultant misunderstandings, and from Hawksworth's shortage of operating experience. The factors that yielded a tractive effort higher than that of the 'Castles' pointed out the weakness of using that notional figure as an indicator of power potential. Poor fuel and inexperienced crews did not help their cause. The idea behind the class seems to have been as replacements for the 'Saints', which were good hill-climbers by virtue of the punch delivered by their Stephenson link motion.

Finally, they were high-profile locomotives and their uncertain start meant that, rather like the LMS 'Jubilees', initial doubts were never totally extinguished by later improvements. Nonetheless, to give some perspective it should be noted that some nine years after introduction the tests with No 1009 effectively solved the problems compared with the 14 years it took to rectify the 'Manors'.

# CHAPTER 5
# LARGE ENGINE POLICY

At the core of Churchward's achievements stood his work on boiler design, of which the Standard No 1 was its most potent symbol. The early examples, the very first of which slightly preceded his appointment, went through several iterations before the optimal version was agreed. So far as the two-cylinder 4-6-0s were concerned, it was never dislodged from its pre-eminence, but there was less certainty with the boilers needed for conditions that demanded more than a 'Saint' or '28xx' could comfortably deliver.

William Dean had entered the large locomotive field through an exercise that combined innovation with caution in considering the challenge of working mineral trains through the Severn Tunnel. The convenience of the new route generated intense traffic flows, but underpowered locomotives risked substantial disruption in the event of stalling or failure while traversing the tunnel. A reliable, large locomotive was needed, resulting in the experimental double-framed 4-6-0 No 36 (the 'Crocodile') of 1896. Boiler and firebox were the largest to date, carried by a robust chassis that conformed with prevailing standards, except for the unprecedented wheel arrangement. No 36 proved its competence by handling greater loads through the tunnel than pairs of 0-6-0s could manage.

While this pioneer locomotive was pure Dean in style, variations in the form of the 'Kruger' Class 4-6-0s/2-6-0s, the 'Aberdare' 2-6-0s and the early 4-4-0s (the 'Badmintons') showed evidence of collaborative exploration through that inter-generational partnership whereby G. J. Churchward exploited the fruits of his predecessor's work. The result was the seminal Locomotive Scheme of 1901, which as a statement of intent was remarkable for its visionary quality, and for the speed of its implementation.

Before this programme was proven, an alternative approach to boiler design was aired, which Churchward obligingly considered. He was renowned for his open debates with drawing office personnel and for considering subordinates' views, even when they might contradict his own. In the early 1900s the advantages of the Belpaire firebox had been confirmed, but variations of parallel, short cone and long cone barrels were still being assessed when an assistant by the name of Wright queried this line of thought.

He suggested that a large parallel boiler with a round-topped firebox would be better at maintaining steam pressure over undulating routes, the reasoning being based on the greater reserve capacity over the slimmer Churchward-style vessel. It speaks

**ABOVE** The GWR's first 4-6-0 was No 36, nicknamed the 'Crocodile'. Much of the design below the running plate reflected the contemporary practice of William Dean, but the boiler incorporated some novel features and was the largest to date. Intended as a heavy freight engine, this was the first recognisable step towards significantly larger motive power to cope with new traffic patterns. It provided a significant advance in haulage power over the traditional 0-6-0 types.

**FACING PAGE** Regarded as a product of the Dean-Churchward transition, No 2601 was the company's second 4-6-0. It embraced further fresh ideas that were theoretically sound but previously untried in practice. The type could not be considered successful and the engine had a career of five years, having been completed in December 1899. Lacking the rakish elegance of No 36, the high-pitched boiler included a combustion chamber, and the appearance was not improved by the massive saddle sandbox. Generally an unpopular design, it was known colloquially as 'Kruger', after Public Enemy No 1 in the Boer War then being fought in South Africa.

**ABOVE RIGHT** The modification of 'Badminton' Class No 3297 *Earl Cawdor* graphically demonstrated Churchward's broadmindedness and willingness to entertain ideas contrary to his own. Responding to proposals from Mr Wright, a junior member of his design team, this engine was experimentally fitted in July 1903 with a boiler that differed completely from the Belpaire tapered model then under development. The addition of the commodious side-window cab was also out of step with the Churchward style. The result was an engine that resembled North Eastern Railway types, an organisation with which the GWR maintained friendly relations.

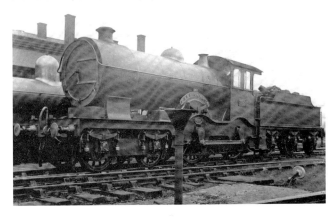

volumes for the great man's broad-mindedness that he took up the challenge by rebuilding 'Badminton' Class 4-4-0 No 3297 *Earl Cawdor* in 1903, while going even further by adding a large side-window cab. The engine reverted to normal three years later, after no appreciable benefit had been discerned, but the episode foreshadowed issues relating to larger boilers.

**ABOVE** No 3297's spacious cab did not last long, being replaced in November 1904 with a standard GWR type. No measurable advantage was achieved with the alternative boiler and it was replaced in October 1906 with a more conventional type. The large unique boiler was not used again but cut up soon after removal. *Locomotive & General Railway Photographs*

## The Great Bear

This locomotive, not included in the 1901 Scheme, marked the conclusion of the first stage of Churchward's restocking programme, and provided the first encounter with a substantially enlarged boiler. No 111 arrived after a hectic period of change, as only six years had elapsed between the 'Crocodile' and No 100, the first 4-6-0 demonstrably of the modern era. When *The Great Bear* entered traffic, a cadre of modern express engines was already in service (see Table 1).

Their performances validated Churchward's views, placing the fleet well in the van of British steam development, and No 111 was thus a prestigious venture within a high-profile success story. The policy of cutting through the hierarchy and giving challenging tasks to promising young men had already served the company well. In this case, responsibility for the general arrangement drawings was passed to a young draughtsman who had recently completed his apprenticeship – Frederick Hawksworth.

The need for the 'Pacific' has been endlessly debated, partially fuelled by Churchward's evident ambivalence. The engine later benefited from standard improvements (superheating and top feed), but was never stretched to establish its full potential. On the other hand, Churchward appeared genuinely sorry when No 111 was withdrawn. It is certain, though, that its design process was a notable accolade for an able young man.

Discounting its unprecedented size, No 111 was essentially conservative, being a modified 'Star' chassis, stretched at the back end to accommodate a long boiler and wide firebox. Comparison of the leading dimensions with those of a saturated 'Star' illustrates the enlargement (see Table 2).

**RIGHT** The GWR's only 'Pacific' – No 111 *The Great Bear* – in original condition with no top feed or superheating, and with the awkwardly placed footsteps immediately in front of the cylinders. Going one better than a single celestial body, the larger engine was named after a constellation. *Pamlin Prints*

**ABOVE** The GWR's only 'Pacific' was an enlargement of the successful 'Star' Class 4-6-0. This post-1935 view shows No 4044 *Prince George* hauling a mixed goods train with horseboxes and cattle wagons coupled, as was the normal operating custom, immediately behind the tender. This later member of the class was built with the stylish dished inside cylinder cover, and has acquired a top feed and a top lamp bracket mounted on the smokebox door; a 4,000-gallon Collett tender is attached. It would have been a tough proposition for the young Hawksworth to improve upon the 'Star' in looks or performance. This was the best proportioned and best looking of the GWR four-cylinder types, and pound-for-pound they outperformed the others. No class of engine was ever more fittingly titled – they truly were stars. *National Railway Museum*

Despite his purportedly dismissive attitude, Churchward was sensitive to certain details. His early locomotives had been criticised for stark, angular lines that conflicted with preceding Victorian ideas on styling, and No 111 was an uneasy compromise between these expectations and operational efficiency. The cabs of the 'Stars' and 'Saints' were not commodious, but that on No 111 was positively spartan. On the other hand, aesthetics took precedence over practicality with the inside radial trailing axle boxes set below the firebox, uncomfortably close to the ashpan. Although a point of visual disharmony, outside boxes would have been more practical, as was later normal with other 'Pacifics'.

| TABLE 1 | | | |
|---|---|---|---|
| Engine Nos | Wheel arrangement | No of cylinders | Comments |
| 98/100/171/173-178 | 4-6-0 | 2 | No 171 ran as 4-4-2 October 1904 to July 1907 |
| 2901-30 | 4-6-0 | 2 | Production series 'Saints' |
| 172/179-190 | 4-4-2 | 2 | Rebuilt as 4-6-0s in 1912/13 |
| 102-104 | 4-4-2 | 4* | The 'Frenchmen' |
| 40 | 4-4-2 | 4 | Rebuilt as 4-6-0 in November 1909 |
| 4001-10 | 4-6-0 | 4 | Production series 'Stars' |
| * 4-cylinder compound | | | |

| TABLE 2 | | |
|---|---|---|
|  | 'Star' | The Great Bear |
| Cylinders | 14.25in x 26in | 15in x 26in |
| - barrel length | 14ft 10in | 23ft 0in |
| - outside diameter | 4ft 10.75in to 5ft 6in ft | 5ft 6in to 6ft 0in |
| - pitch | 8ft 6in | 9ft 0in |
| Firebox outside length | 9ft 0in | 8ft 0in |
| Tubes (length x diameter) | | |
| - fire | 250 x 2in | 141 x 2.5in |
| - arch | n/a | 4 x 3.375in |
| - flue | n/a | 21 x 4.75in |
| - element | n/a | 84 x 1.375in |
| Heating surfaces | | |
| - tubes | 1,988.7 sq ft | 2,673.5 sq ft |
| - arch tubes | n/a | 24.2 sq ft |
| - firebox | 154.3 sq ft | 158.1 sq ft |
| - superheater | n/a | 545 sq ft |
| Grate area | 27.1 sq ft | 41.8 sq ft |
| Total engine weight | 75 tons 12 cwt | 97 tons 0 cwt |
| Max axle loading | 18 tons 12 cwt | 20 tons 0 cwt |
| Engine wheelbase | 7ft 0in + 5ft 6in + 7ft 0in + 8ft 3in | 7ft 0in + 5ft 6in + 7ft 0in + 7ft 0in + 8ft 0in |

Something more imposing than the standard 3,500-gallon tender was deemed necessary, and a unique vehicle was provided (No 1755). This had a taller body carried on two bogies with inside bearings to match the locomotive, and the result resembled the London & South Western's 'water cart' type. The weight was 5¾ tons greater than standard, but coal and water capacities were unchanged. Use of bogies led to an incident that must have chastened the young, ambitious Hawksworth. The layout prevented location of the water pick-up gear in the usual place towards the rear, so it was placed equidistant between the bogie centres with the tank filled by means of a hinged hatch set in the dome, which sat in the middle of the coal space. It was only a matter of time before the hatch door was left insecurely fastened, and at the next 'dip', when passing over troughs, intense water pressure up the inlet pipe forced open the hatch. The water cascaded over the tender and crashed through the vestibule door in the leading

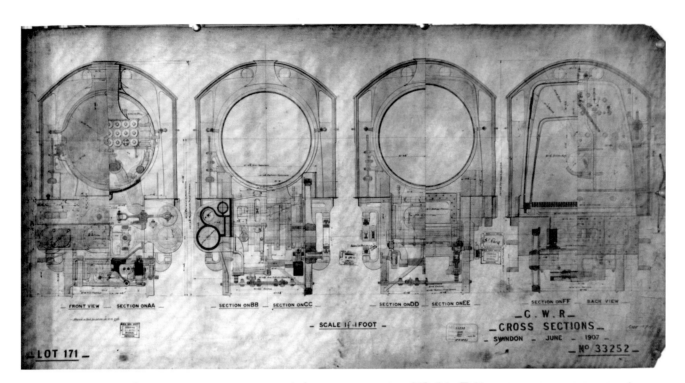

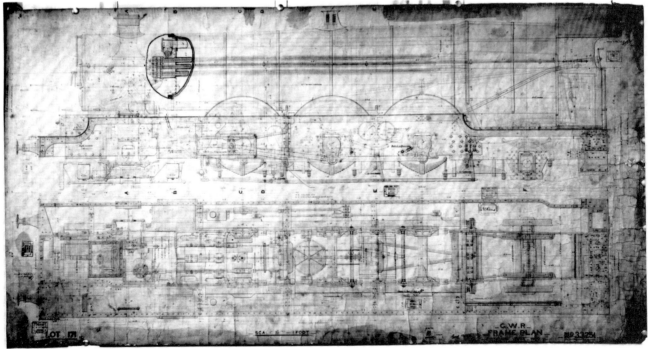

carriage, flooding that and the next vehicle to a depth of around 2 feet. The incident proved expensive in compensation and 'hush money' to keep the affair quiet. The tank filler was immediately relocated in the normal position behind the coal space, well away from the pick-up apparatus. The incident reflected lack of practical experience in the design process.

Despite it's size, *The Great Bear* was mainly confined to relatively mundane work. Always allocated to Old Oak Common, it was restricted to Paddington-Bristol services, usually departing at 11.00am or 6.40pm and returning to London on fast fitted freight workings, duties that were not demanding. However, a report of an illicit footplate ride non-stop between London and Bath

ABOVE No 111 on an up train from Weston-super-Mare and Bristol in Twyford cutting. *Ian Allan Library*

RIGHT By 1919 No 111, seen here at Old Oak Common, was in final condition with superheating and top feed. *Ian Allan Library*

LEFT Some of Hawksworth's original drawings of *The Great Bear*.

provided an indication of its potential. The fire was built up with a prodigious amount of coal soon after leaving Paddington, and no more was added before arrival 1 minute early at Bath. Progress was steady and unexciting, with pressure holding constant at around 200lb per sq in until after passing Didcot, when it started to rise as the fire burned through. The observer left the footplate at Bath but speculated that Bristol might have been reached without the need for further fuel.

Churchward joked about selling No 111 to Gresley, on learning of the new 'A1' 'Pacific' for the Great Northern, but there was another new design around that time that had more in common with the GWR's machine. Shortly before the North Eastern Railway lost its independence, Sir Vincent Raven introduced a pair of 'Pacifics' (later LNER Class 'A2'), and three more appeared after the Grouping. They were designed and built in a hurry, adopting methods reminiscent of No 111's origins. Based on the successful, superheated 4-4-2 Class 'Z', the new type was effectively achieved by 'stretching' the 'Atlantic', in similar vein to the 'Star' chassis lengthening. The NER engines looked ungainly, whereas the 'A1' had been largely designed from scratch and its graceful appearance was complemented by performance that was superior to Raven's 'Pacific'.

Comparisons with other companies' 'Pacifics' were not really necessary in assessing *The Great Bear*, as Churchward's 'Stars' persistently outshone the lonely giant. The exercise should have reminded that a successful, larger locomotive could demand more than mere tinkering with an existing proven concept.

ABOVE This official photograph of No 111 shows its reincarnation as a 'Castle' named *Viscount Churchill* and attached to the infamous eight-wheel tender No 1755, although it is believed that they never worked together in ordinary service. The tender later served with other 'Castles', 4-4-0 'Counties', 'Stars' and 'Saints', and was withdrawn in 1936. *Ian Allan Library*

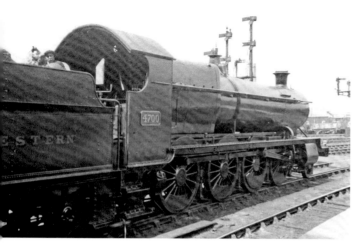

**LEFT** Class '47xx' 2-8-0 No 4700 at Bristol Temple Meads some time between 1919 and 1921. Its original condition is apparent from the Standard No 1 boiler and absence of outside steam pipes. *R. S. Carpenter collection*

## Class '47xx'

The risks of enlargement were realised in 1921 with the failure of Churchward's final design, 2-8-0 No 4700. Hawksworth had been promoted in August 1919 as Assistant to the Chief Draughtsman and, while the nature of his involvement in the new 'Consolidation' is unknown, he would inevitably have been aware of its early problems. This engine was intended to cope with heavy vacuum-fitted express freight services, coincidentally the type of work given to *The Great Bear* during the night hours. This specialised need had not been covered in Churchward's original plans, and experience had shown that the 'Saints' lacked the requisite adhesion, while the Class '28xxs' were best at slow, heavy freight work.

The only absentee from the 1901 Scheme had been the 4-6-0 with 5ft 8in driving wheels, which was rendered unnecessary for more than 20 years by the Class '43xx' 2-6-0s. The latter wheel arrangement had an honourable history as a maid-of-all-work type in the United States, and such was Swindon's progress in standardisation that the 'Mogul' was effectively a fusion of existing components. Its instant success suggested that a larger mixed-traffic machine would be possible by stretching a '43xx' chassis to add an extra driving axle, and to accommodate a Standard No 1 boiler.

No 4700 appeared in May 1919, but no more of the type were added until January 1922. This was rather different from the 'Moguls', where the first 50 had been delivered in about 30 months. In October 1921 the *Great Western Railway Magazine* coyly advised that:

'…the locomotive was given an exhaustive trial and it did thoroughly good work in semi-fast passenger services, among which were the following trains:

| | |
|---|---|
| 6.30am | Swindon-Paddington |
| 5.30am | Paddington-Bristol |
| 10.52am | Paddington-Swindon |
| 9.40am | Bristol-Paddington |
| 11.45pm | Parcels, Swindon-Carmarthen |
| 6.20am | Bristol-Plymouth (non-stop from Exeter) |
| 5.55 pm | Parcels, Carmarthen-Swindon |
| 12.30pm | 'Riviera', Plymouth-Exeter (non-stop) |

At the time the engine was put into service the proper boiler was not ready, and it was sent out fitted temporarily with a No 1 standard boiler. A short time ago the engine was withdrawn from traffic and sent into the Swindon factory to receive her proper boiler, which is larger than that first placed upon the frames…'

**ABOVE** No 4707 passes Sonning signal box in 1945 on a down freight. By then 4,000-gallon tenders were normal for this class. *Ian Allan Library*

The magazine again referred to the matter in January 1922:

> 'In the case of the locomotive works at Swindon, probably the leading item of interest was the bringing up to date of mixed-traffic engine No 4700, 2-8-0 type. This engine was originally set to work in May 1919, fitted temporarily with a standard No 1 boiler. In July last a No 7 standard boiler was substituted. The steam admission pipes to the cylinders are now taken through the smokebox and coupled externally to the cylinders. A number of similar engines are under course of construction. The fleet of 2-6-0s has been considerably augmented and there has been an increase also in the 2-8-0 type.'

The disingenuous flavour is obvious. Why should 'thoroughly good work' so soon demand a larger boiler, and why should 'bringing up to date' be necessary after only two years? Political 'spin' is not a modern invention.

The assumption that existing major components would meet the need suggests overreaching confidence, and it must have been a shock that the redoubtable No 1 boiler was not up to the task. The corollary was to ask what would be needed next, not only for the

**LEFT** No 4700 is seen again as rebuilt with a Standard No 7 boiler and outside steam pipes. Snifting valves were also fitted to the steam chests during the process, a feature that was repeated only with Nos 4701-04. This side view amply demonstrates the size and proportions of these fine engines. *Ian Allan Library*

**ABOVE** No 4700 in BR lined green livery on a daytime passenger working at Exeter, circa 1961. *Ian Allan Library*

production series of '47xxs', but also for any enlargement of the 'Saint'/'Star' format. The purpose-designed Standard No 7 boiler solved the immediate problem in May 1921, and a handsome machine resulted that for 40 years handled its duties with ease, and occasionally served with distinction on passenger expresses.

Confirmation of the regard the '47xxs' enjoyed led to discussions in 1924 between Collett and Felix Pole about naming them, before the chairman stated that this practice should be limited to express passenger types. The Class '47xx' certainly deserved the honour, and 12 names had been selected, all from GWR engines of the past. *Behemoth, Bellerophon, Champion, Dreadnought, Gladiator, Hercules, Mammoth, Plutarch, Romulus, Tantalus, Thunderer* and *Trafalgar* would have provided a welcome change from the monotony then infiltrating GWR passenger classes.

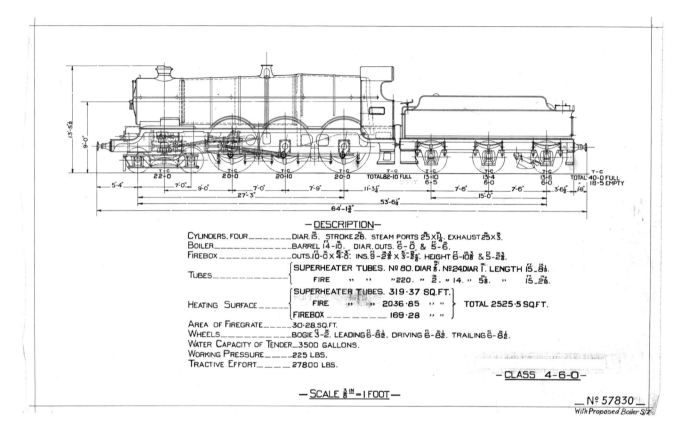

— DESCRIPTION —

CYLINDERS, FOUR _____ DIAR. 15. STROKE 28. STEAM PORTS 25×1½. EXHAUST 25×3.
BOILER _____ BARREL 14-10. DIAR. OUTS. 6-0 & 5-6.
FIREBOX _____ OUTS.10-0 × 4-0. INS. 9-2¾ × 3-2⅝. HEIGHT 6-10⅞ & 5-2⅛.
TUBES _____ { SUPERHEATER TUBES. № 80. DIAR ⅝. №24 DIAR 1. LENGTH 15-8¼.
                     { FIRE " " " 220. " 2. " 14. " 5½. " 15-2⅛.
HEATING SURFACE _____ { SUPERHEATER TUBES. 319·37 SQ.FT. }
                     { FIRE " " 2036·85 " " } TOTAL 2525·5 SQ.FT.
                     { FIREBOX _____ 169·28 " " }
AREA OF FIREGRATE _____ 30·28. SQ.FT.
WHEELS _____ BOGIE 3-2. LEADING 6-8½. DRIVING 6-8½. TRAILING 6-8½.
WATER CAPACITY OF TENDER _3500 GALLONS.
WORKING PRESSURE _____ 225 LBS.
TRACTIVE EFFORT _____ 27800 LBS.

— CLASS 4-6-0 —

— SCALE ⅜ IN = 1 FOOT —

№ 57830
With Proposed Boiler S/7

## The Standard No 7 boiler

Satisfaction with No 4700's larger boiler led to consideration of its use with other classes – 'Stars', 'Saints' and '28xxs'. Consecutively numbered drawings were prepared, evidently forming the one exercise. In each case the chassis was unchanged, so the key question was acceptability of the increased weight. A comparison of these proposals with actual locomotives is shown in Table 2.

The drawings are undated but presumably followed closely upon proving the new boiler in service, which suggests late 1921 or early 1922. The concept did not proceed far as the Chief Civil Engineer rejected the modified 'Star', so there was no point in

**ABOVE AND RIGHT** The success of the Standard No 7 boiler on Class '47xx' 2-8-0s led to consideration of its use with the 'Star', 'Saint' and '28xx' classes. *NRM*

pursuing the enlarged 'Saint'. It would seem that the Class '28xx' with a No 7 boiler would have been acceptable, but the need for more 2-8-0s was covered by the purchase of 100 war-surplus engines of Great Central design origin at attractive prices. The first 20 were virtually unused, while the remainder were a distinctly mixed bag. The best 30 of the latter were retained for the long term, and this covered needs until the late 1930s. By then the idea

| TABLE 2 | | | |
|---|---|---|---|
| | **Drawing No** | **Max axle loading** | **Weight full** |
| Production 'Star' | | 18 tons 12 cwt | 75 tons 12 cwt |
| 'Star' with No 7 boiler | 57830 | 20 tons 10 cwt | 82 tons 10 cwt |
| 'Castle' (No 8 boiler) | | 19 tons 14 cwt | 79 tons 17 cwt |
| Production 'Saint' | | 18 tons 8 cwt | 72 tons 0 cwt |
| 'Saint' with No 7 boiler | 57831 | 20 tons 10 cwt | 80 tons 0 cwt |
| Production '28xx' | | 17 tons 5 cwt | 75 tons 10 cwt |
| '28xx' with No 7 boiler | 58832 | 18 tons 5 cwt | 80 tons 0 cwt |
| NB Weights quoted for production versions are indicative, as there were variances in the early days pending design finalisation | | | |

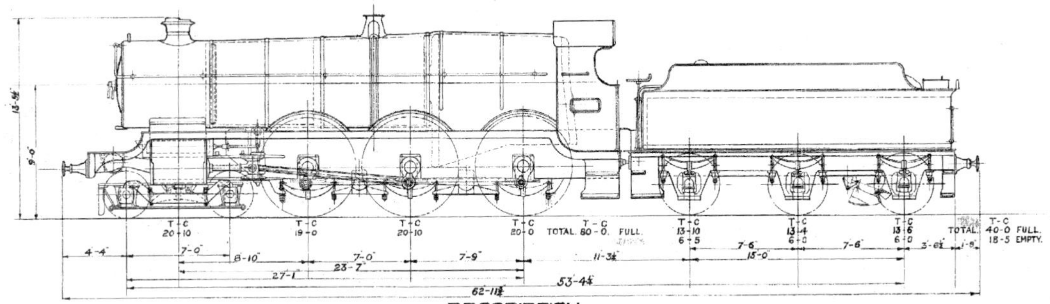

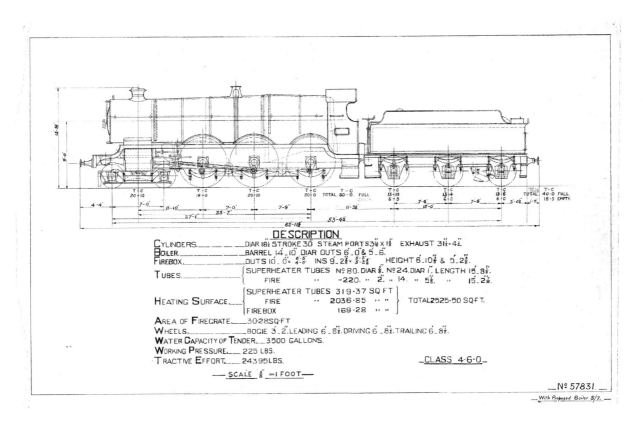

## DESCRIPTION

| | |
|---|---|
| CYLINDERS | DIAR 18½" STROKE 30" STEAM PORTS 3¼" x 1¾" EXHAUST 3½" x 4¼". |
| BOILER | BARREL 14'-10" DIAR OUTS 6'-0" & 5'-6". |
| FIREBOX | OUTS 10'-0" x 6'-3"/4'-0" INS 9'-2⅝" x 5'-2⅝"/3'-2⅝" HEIGHT 6'-10⅞" & 5'-2⅜". |
| TUBES | SUPERHEATER TUBES Nº 80. DIAR ⅞". Nº 24. DIAR 1". LENGTH 15'-8⅛". |
| | FIRE " " 220. " 2". " 14. " 5⅛". " 15'-2 7/16". |
| HEATING SURFACE | SUPERHEATER TUBES 319·37 SQ FT |
| | FIRE " 2036·85 " " |
| | FIREBOX 169·28 " " — TOTAL 2525·50 SQ FT. |
| AREA OF FIREGRATE | 30·28 SQ FT |
| WHEELS | BOGIE 3'-2". LEADING 6'-8½". DRIVING 6'-8½". TRAILING 6'-8½". |
| WATER CAPACITY OF TENDER | 3500 GALLONS. |
| WORKING PRESSURE | 225 LBS. |
| TRACTIVE EFFORT | 24395 LBS. |

CLASS 4-6-0

SCALE ⅜" = 1 FOOT

Nº 57831.

With Proposed Boiler S/7.

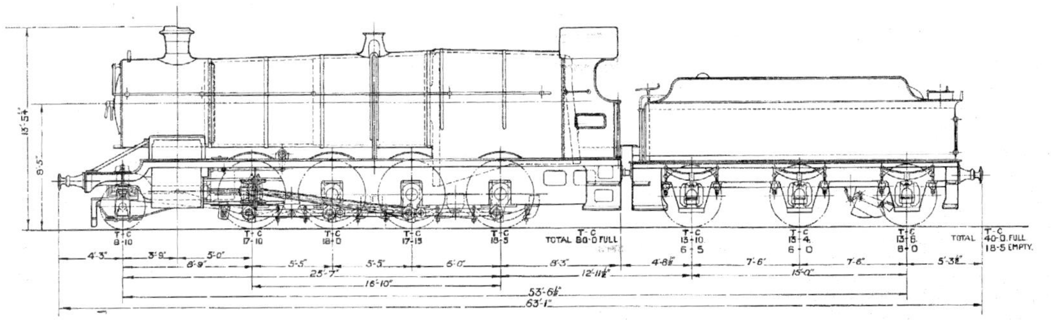

## DESCRIPTION

| | |
|---|---|
| CYLINDERS | DIAR. 18½". STROKE 30". STEAM PORTS 3¼" X 1¾". EXHAUST 3½" X 4¼". |
| BOILER | BARREL 14'-10". DIAR. OUTS: 6'-0" & 5'-6" |
| FIREBOX | OUTS: 10'-0" X 6'-3"/4'-0". INS: 9'-2⅝" X 5'-2⅝"/3'-2⅝". HEIGHT 6'-10⅞" & 5'-2⅜". |
| TUBES | SUPERHEATER TUBES Nº 80. DIAR. ⅞". Nº 24. DIAR 1". LENGTH 15'-8⅛". |
| | FIRE " " 220. " 2". " 14. " 5⅛". " 15'-2 7/16". |
| HEATING SURFACE | SUPERHEATER TUBES 319·37 SQ. FT. |
| | FIRE " 2036·85 " " |
| | FIREBOX 169·28 " " — TOTAL 2525·50 SQ. FT. |
| AREA OF FIREGRATE | 30·28. SQ. FT. |
| WHEELS | PONY 3'-2". LEADING 4'-7½". INTERMEDIATE 4'-7½". DRIVING 4'-7½". TRAILING 4'-7½". |
| WATER CAPACITY OF TENDER | 3500 GALLONS. |
| WORKING PRESSURE | 225 LBS. |
| TRACTIVE EFFORT | 35380 LBS. |

CLASS 2-8-0

SCALE ⅜" = 1 FOOT

Nº 57832

With Proposed Boiler S/7.

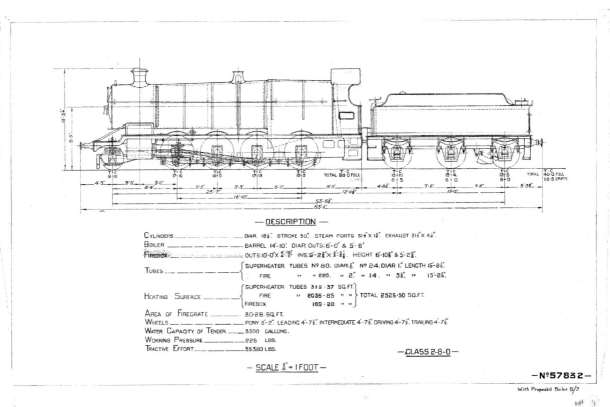

of a Class '28xx' with a No 7 boiler had been discarded. (The only other sign that the No 7 boiler might be put to another use was in connection with a 2-10-2T for South Wales mineral traffic, as proposed in 1937. The 2-8-2T Class '72xx' had by then developed a reputation for being rather curve-shy, so the idea of a 14-wheeled large tank engine weighing well over 100 tons and intended for specialised duties hardly seemed a practical proposition.)

It is striking how unlucky timing and seemingly modest corporate misjudgements can have significant repercussions. Felix Pole's crucial management reorganisation was being implemented but had yet to be honoured in practice. The CCE thus vetoed the enlarged 'Star' without revealing the extent to which his bridge-strengthening programme had progressed. Had Pole been fully informed, he could have arbitrated between CME and CCE, applying simple cost comparisons to identify the financial merits of reordering departmental budgets to accommodate the heavier locomotives. The No 7 boiler was thus a casualty of an inefficient management structure and poor communication, shortcomings that Pole was striving to correct.

The issue resurfaced and was swiftly resolved five years later in planning for the 'Kings', providing belated confirmation of Pole's foresight. There is a persuasive argument that, but for the outdated management attitudes of 1921, the boiler restricted to nine specialised locomotives might have become central to large engine policy.

## The original 'Castles'

The CCE's objections to an enlarged 4-6-0 apparently stimulated thoughts of rebuilding *The Great Bear* to circumvent the weight issue. Collett had only recently been appointed CME, was innately cautious and, being from a workshop background, had little experience in design practice. More investment in a wheel arrangement that so far had not brought any improvement over the 'Stars', and which was as yet unproven elsewhere, would have offered little attraction. He thus compromised with an improved 'Star' 4-6-0 that met the CCE's criteria through a 3-inch reduction in the No 7 boiler diameter to create the Standard No 8 version. The interim nature of the measure was underlined by initial references to the 'enlarged Star', but soon the 'Castle' Class title took hold. In tractive effort terms it was the most powerful passenger type to date, and its effectiveness extinguished interest in improving *The Great Bear*.

With its unique boiler reaching the end of its working life, the 'Pacific' entered Swindon Works for radical treatment in early 1924 and was reincarnated as 'Castle' Class No 111 *Viscount Churchill*. Although not taken out of stock, little else remained apart from the front end of the frames, the number plates and possibly the driving wheels. Collett's fetish for accounting minutiae resulted officially in a rebuild that was manifestly a new engine. In 'Castle' form, No 111 was photographed in company with tender No 1755, but then the pair parted company. Whatever emotions Hawksworth might have

felt about the demise of the 'Pacific', his work on the 'Castle' design stimulated thought about how to generate more power in the face of the restrictions placed upon the No 7 boiler.

Unfortunately, this was an inopportune period for promotion of innovative ideas. The prototype 'Castle' appeared in August 1923 and its presence at the 1924 Empire Exhibition at Wembley generated competitive interest versus the visually larger LNER 'Pacific' displayed nearby. The resultant 1925 Exchange trials validated the GWR's claims of the superiority of the 'Castle', forming the core of Collett's conviction that there was little need for more development of top-line motive power.

## The compound question

By early 1926 the company's needs were well-served by a four-cylinder 4-6-0 fleet comprising 71 'Stars', 20 production series 'Castles' and No 111, two rebuilt 'Stars' (Nos 4009 and 4016), and yet more 'Castles' in the offing. Nonetheless, there was a lingering recognition that No 4073 et al existed through disqualification of the No 7 boiler, and that *The Great Bear*, while hinting at extra potential, had graphically shown the limitations that size could impose.

Anticipating that something more would be needed, Hawksworth and Stanier collaborated on a proposal whose seeds were traceable back to Churchward's early days, and to an omission in the comparisons undertaken with the 1901 Scheme. Assessment of express passenger types covered simple versus compound expansion, and four- versus six-coupled wheels in both two- and four-cylinder forms, but a multi-cylindered compound 4-6-0 had been omitted.

In 1926, with the three French De Glehn compound 4-4-2s still at work on the GWR but near the end of their careers, drawings were prepared for a compound 'Castle'. The arguments in favour were quite persuasive as, although Churchward had preferred simple expansion engines, the 'Frenchmen' had done well and were much liked. Weight estimates for the proposed compound have not been traced, but it would have been heavier than the conventional 'Castle'. Divided drive was retained but the outside cylinders were set further forward. This required lengthening of the wheelbase at the front end, which would have precluded the traditional rocking levers to actuate the outside valves. Details of what alternative was intended are not clear, but presumably the issue could be surmounted, rather as the North British Locomotive Co had found a solution to the cluttered front end of the LNER Class 'B17' 4-6-0. The idea had merit in circumventing weight restrictions that disqualified a larger boiler.

In contrast to Churchward's receptive attitude in indulging Wright's views in the modification of 4-4-0 *Earl Cawdor*, Collett briefly considered the proposal before dismissing it out of hand. He was not being asked to consider an iconoclastic view from a junior officer, but to review a reasoned proposal from two senior lieutenants to satisfy an emerging need when other options

**ABOVE** Acquisition of foreign-built locomotives for use in Britain was quite rare, usually as an interim measure driven by lack of spare capacity among domestic manufacturers. Churchward's purchase of No 102 *La France* from Société Alsacienne des Constructions Méchaniques at Belfort (works No 5409) was therefore most unusual. The engine was a copy of two compound 'Atlantics' then very successfully at work on the Nord Railway of France, but with minor modifications for GWR running conditions. The purchase demonstrated Churchward's willingness to step outside the confines of the parochial UK railway community, and was a financially efficient means of assessing new ideas in preference to extensive experiments with a home-grown product. No 102 entered traffic with a standard 4,000-gallon tender and in lined black livery, broadly similar to that of the LNWR. Modifications were made to the tubes in 1909, and in September the original boiler was superheated and top feed added. This view (either late 1913 or 1914) was taken at Leamington Spa, with the engine on a Wolverhampton-Bournemouth service comprising LSWR stock. By this time it was in standard lined green livery. *R. S. Carpenter collection*

**ABOVE** In September 1916 No 102 was rebuilt with a Standard No 1 boiler, which was pitched higher than the original necessitating a shorter chimney and safety valve bonnet. Around 1923 the copper-capped chimney was replaced with the plain cast-iron type; the absence of a garter on the tender suggests that this view was taken shortly before withdrawal in October 1926. *F. G. Cockman collection*

impressive results. The compound 'Castle' was rejected in 1926 and the last De Glehn compound was withdrawn in 1928. By 1930 Chapelon's work was gaining recognition at a time when the GWR had the resources to make a serious effort in this arena. If Collett had matched his predecessor's interest in foreign practice, an alternative sequence of events might have seen GWR motive power on a profoundly different course in the 1930s.

The relationship between Stanier and Hawksworth was both professional and personal, and they remained friends into retirement. Together they formed a formidable and possibly intimidating combination that might have alerted Collett to the threat presented by dynamic, creative subordinates. It also seems probable that Hawksworth was fully briefed about Stanier's later findings on the LMS, contributing to the empirical data from those sources that Swindon exploited from 1941 onwards.

Further, by peremptorily rejecting the compound idea, Collett terminated a development strand that could have met a need that emerged sooner than he might have anticipated. Expanding traffic demands called for a small group of locomotives to handle heavier trains than a 'Castle' could comfortably manage. Rather than pursue a second enlargement of the 'Star' format, as took shape in 1927 with the 'Kings', a more imaginative approach could have embraced the ideas of Stanier and Hawksworth. Estimated power increases available through compounding were naturally theoretical, and needed validation by road testing. Nevertheless, it seems reasonable to assume that more could be extracted from the 'Castle' format while avoiding the weight increase and reduction in operating availability that attended the 'Kings'. Even if the compound did not meet all the expected criteria, an increase in boiler pressure and/or a reduction in driving wheel diameter could have taken the nominal tractive effort above the apparently significant 40,000 milestone.

appeared closed. Once again, his caution seems to have been decisive, although other elements might have supported his view. Compounding had acquired a tarnished reputation in Britain from the erratic behaviour of Webb's locomotives on the LNWR in the late 19th century. 'Midlandisation' on the LMS in the 1920s saw extensive construction of compound 4-4-0s, but growing disenchantment with this type's abilities led in 1926 to the loan of No 5000 *Launceston Castle* for trials over the West Coast Main Line. Reservations about the Midland engines stemmed more from their modest size than from their cylinder arrangements, but it would have been typical of Collett to cite this as evidence against compound expansion.

However, the concept was far from a lost cause as in 1925 André Chapelon joined Chemin de Fer de Paris à Orléans and in cooperation with Finnish Engineer Kyösti Kylälä designed the Kylchap exhaust system. Then in 1929 Chapelon started rebuilding of De Glehn compounds based on scientific analysis that was superior to the British trial-and-error approach, leading to

**ABOVE** No 103 is on an up service from Cheltenham with the superheated Standard No 1 boiler fitted in January 1914. This type was carried until withdrawal in March 1928. Between February 1910 and January 1912 this engine had carried the spare saturated Standard No 1 boiler first fitted to No 104 (see the second photograph of that locomotive right), then No 104's original boiler from January 1912 until January 1914. *Railway Photographs*

| TABLE 3 | | | | | |
|---------|---|---|---|---|---|
| **Type** | **Inside cylinders** | **Outside cylinders** | **T/E lb** | **Weight** | **Max axle loading** |
| 102 | 2 x low pressure: 22 1/16" x 25 3/16" | 2 x high pressure: 13 3/8" x 25 3/16" | 23,710 | 68t 9c | 17t 9c |
| 103/ 4 | 2 x low pressure: 23 5/8" x 25 3/16" | 2 x high pressure: 14 3/16" x 25 3/16" | 27,174 | 70t 14c | 19t 0c |
| 4073 | (2) 16" x 26" | (2) 16" x 26" | 32,625 | 79t 16c | 19t 14c |
| Compound Castle | 2 x low pressure: 25" x 26" | 2 x high pressure: 17" x 26" | 35,700 § | ? | ? |
| 6000 | (2) 16 1/4" x 28" | (2) 16 1/4" x 28" | 40,300 | 89t 0c | 22t 10c |
| § Boiler pressure at 250 lb/sq would have raised T/E to 39,667 lbs | | | | | |

**ABOVE** No 104 was the final member of the French trio, seen here soon after delivery and before a GWR copper-capped chimney was fitted and the name *Alliance* added. *Ian Allan Library*

**RIGHT** To provide a spare for Nos 103 and 104, a specially adapted saturated long cone Standard No 1 boiler was carried by No 104 from August 1907 to June 1909, as shown. The original boiler was then restored, and swapped with No 103's original boiler in October 1911. A superheated, top feed Standard No 1 boiler was carried from July 1915 until withdrawal in September 1928, in which condition it looked like the second photograph of No 103 above. *Ian Allan Library*

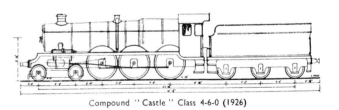

Compound " Castle " Class 4-6-0 (1926)

**RIGHT BELOW** A drawing of the proposed compound 'Castle'. *Reproduced from official diagrams*

This objective might have almost been achieved with just the first of these measures, as is evident in Table 3.

Interest in compounds was not totally extinguished, as late in the 1930s the Board queried the lack of progress in locomotive development and suggested that Chapelon's achievements should be studied. The task was given to a university-educated French-speaking draughtsman who translated the seminal work *La Locomotive à Vapeur* (1938) and wrote comparative reports. The inefficiency of the 'Kings' was highlighted by the performance of Chapelon's most advanced design (specifically Paris-Orleans compound 'Pacific' No 231.726), which at 70mph produced 60% of its nominal tractive effort as compared with just over 20% for the 'King'. The poor performance of the GWR engine was attributed to higher back pressure, and substantial pressure drop between boiler and steam chest when maximum power output was sought.

The French engine was nominally 13.5% heavier, with a tractive effort rating of only 30,000lb, yet at 80mph it developed double the drawbar pull. It was concluded that the root causes of the inferiority of the 'King' were low degree superheat, undersized steam passages and ports (which unduly restricted the flow on both inlet and exhaust sides of the cycle), undersized steam chests for the outside cylinders, and inefficient draughting. The French engine had none of these constraints and was also assisted by its Kylchap double chimney.

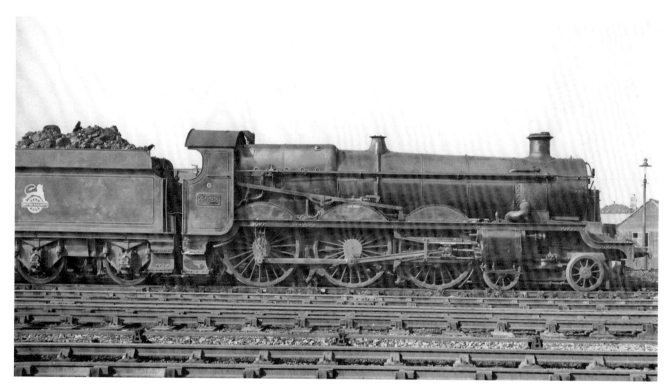

The efficiency of the Chapelon layout was such that, at normal operating speeds, the minimal pressure drop in the steam cycle allowed a greater constancy in available tractive effort. Tests with a 'King' in 1931 had shown that at 56mph only 64% of the boiler pressure was actually converted into work, i.e. before condensation and leakages took their toll. Hypothetically, a 'King' using Chapelon's principles would have generated 2.3 times the drawbar pull.

Yet again there was misfortune in timing. With policies now in a petrified state, these findings must have been so revolutionary to Collett (and others) as to be unbelievable. Nonetheless, the author of the investigation was rewarded (and neutralised) with promotion to the wagon works, and doubtless Collett was prepared to deploy his well-honed skills at inactivity. In this instance, not only was the Churchward legacy under threat but also the pattern of four-cylinder development that had supported his own and the company's prestige since 1923. Equally, any reminder of his dismissal of the Stanier/Hawksworth proposal of 1926 would not have sat well. However, the investigation's findings were only available in the second half of 1939, by which time his customary role of prevaricator was not necessary.

On the other hand, any triumph that Hawksworth might have felt over the validation of ideas developed with Stanier would have been muted by opportunity frustrated through Collett's obduracy. Budgetary and other constraints in the 1940s were to stymie exploitation of all the exciting possibilities identified. Such low-cost improvements as were possible opened only a limited window on the potential of a Chapelon-Hawksworth 4-6-0.

## Hawksworth's 'Castles'

Changes with express passenger engines were suspended during the war, and the fleet at the end of 1940 comprised:

| Type | Introduced | No in service |
|---|---|---|
| 'Saints' | 1906-13 | 54 |
| 'Stars' | 1907-22 | 48 |
| 'Castles' built new | 1923-39 | 115 |
| 'Castles' rebuilt from 'Stars' and 'Pacific' | 1924-29 | 6 |
| 'Castles' rebuilt from 'Stars' | 1938-40 | 10 |
| 'Kings' | 1927-30 | 30 |

The pre-Grouping contingent proved resilient, with the last example surviving until 1957. Only 40 purpose-designed express engines – the 5098 sub-series of 'Castles' – were provided in the replacement programme, and the balance was made up by 'Counties' in a quasi-express role, together with the introduction of BR Standard types.

The first of the new 'Castles' appeared in April 1946, bringing further changes to Swindon practice. The standard two-row superheater hitherto used was estimated to yield steam temperatures up to 525°F. Stanier had advocated the three-row type, estimated to raise the final temperature to 580°F, and this was used on No 5098. A further stage was reached in September 1947 when one of the earlier 5013 series received a four-row superheater, taking the final steam temperature to 660°F. The original type boilers, with a

**LEFT** Veteran 4-6-0s were still on front line work when the GWR ceased to exist. 'Star' Class No 4022, built in 1909, is in reasonably clean, early BR livery, but with no brass beading (which had been removed during the First World War). 'Elbow' outside steam pipes have been fitted, indicating a modern No 1 boiler married to a chassis with an old-style cylinder block. This was an interim arrangement between the original inside steam pipe layout and the later 'Castle'-type pattern – only two 'Stars' (Nos 4048 and 4060) actually carried all three combinations during their career. The last 'Star' in service, No 4056 *Princess Margaret*, was all the more distinctive in retaining the 'elbow'-pattern pipes.

No 4022 carries the painted legend 'Star Class' on the centre splasher. It was named *King William* until the arrival of the 'King' Class in 1927, when it was renamed *Belgian Monarch* in June of that year. Following the fall of Belgium, this name was removed in May 1940, and the engine was unnamed for the remainder of its life. *Ian Allan Library*

superheater surface of 262 sq ft, totalled 150 by 1940. Fifty-four three-row boilers (313 sq ft) were built in 1946-50, and 46 four-row boilers (393 sq ft) appeared up to 1960. As surpluses became available, it was possible to rotate improved boilers among the earlier series, but upgrade across the entire class was never completed. Hawksworth's 'Castles' introduced other new features, including mechanical lubricators for cylinders, valves and regulator. The sum of these changes wrought little visual modification, but performance was greatly improved, especially in the face of declining coal quality. Here was further evidence of enthusiasm for new ideas and willingness to reverse aspects of Churchward policy that Collett had dogmatically sustained.

Although the new boilers enhanced the performance of the 'Castles', the process of improvement was incomplete at the time of Hawksworth's retirement, as No 1000's double chimney awaited

corrective attention. It was a pity that he did not tackle this problem, as a solution could have provided the template much earlier for application to the 'Castles'. As it was, this final measure did not happen until 1956, by which time fitting the 'Kings' with double chimneys was already under way. Under a programme supervised by S. O. Ell, No 7018 *Drysllwyn Castle* was fitted with a double chimney and extensively road-tested. This three-row-superheater engine, reputedly a poor performer, was transformed, and modification of a further 65 'Castles' followed. The Indian Summer of GWR steam was at its most potent in the 1956/57 period when the last 'Star' could be seen at work alongside a double-chimney 'Castle', while small Churchward 'Prairies' were appearing resplendent in lined chrome green, and chocolate and cream coaching livery was being reinstated.

The first 'Castle' (No 100A1) had been withdrawn in March 1950, prior to construction of the final ten of the class (between May and August 1950). The disposition of superheater types and double chimneys at their respective withdrawal dates is shown in Table 4 overleaf.

Identities of locomotives in each category and dates of modifications appear in Appendix D.

After the frustrations and disappointments since the Grouping, and following the tribulations of the war years, the successful refinements in the 5098 sub-class must have given Hawksworth

**BELOW** The sense of tradition with the four-cylinder 4-6-0s was strong. No 4000 *North Star* had been the 'Star' Class and the family prototype. It was rebuilt as a 'Castle' in 1929 but always differed from the 'Castles' proper in the deeper front and rear curved fall plates and shallower splashers. No 4000 has the modified form of outside steam pipe, while No 4091 *Dudley Castle* retains the original shape. *Ian Allan Library*

**ABOVE** This view is recorded as 'No 4097 *Kenilworth Castle* on up Ilfracombe', – a reference to the regular Paddington-Ilfracombe *via* Barnstaple service. The prestige service over this route was courtesy of the 'Cornish Riviera' which slipped coaches at Taunton. The first three vehicles of this train are a 'Concertina' Brake Composite, a double-ended 'Concertina' Tri-composite Slip (both of 1906/07 vintage), and a 'Siphon G'. The presence of the 'Concertinas' suggests that they are from the 'Cornish Riviera' and are on the return working. *Ian Allan Library*

**TOP RIGHT** No 7029 *Clun Castle* with a double chimney is a familiar sight on the preservation scene. Here is this engine in as-built condition. *Ian Allan Library*

**BOTTOM RIGHT** Some of the final 40 'Castles' were blessed with evocative and nostalgic names associated with the Old Company. A good example was No 7017 *G. J. Churchward*, standing here at Honeybourne in July 1956. *P. Ransome-Wallis*

| TABLE 4 | | | | | |
|---|---|---|---|---|---|
| **Series** | **2-row** | **3-row** | **4-row** | **3-row with double chimney** | **4-row with double chimney** |
| 4073-5012 | 24 | 6 | 1 | - | 9 |
| 5013-82/5093-97 | 23 | 24 | 1 | - | 27 |
| 5098-7037 | - | 12 | 1 | 1 | 26 |
| Rebuilt 'Stars' and No 111 | 10 | 3 | - | - | 3 |
| **Total** | **57** | **45** | **3** | **1** | **65** |

**ABOVE** Fictitious 'Castle'? The GWR did not stray far from home turf in selecting castle names (unlike the 'Halls'), but there appears to be no certainty about the location of the building represented by No 7010 *Avondale Castle*, although there is apparently such a place in Scotland. This engine received a double chimney in October 1960 and was a late survivor, not being withdrawn until March 1964. Here it is beginning to look tired and travel-stained. *A. Swain*

**BELOW** No 7021 *Haverfordwest Castle* poses at Old Oak Common. This engine was appropriately allocated to Welsh sheds throughout its career. All the 'Castles' were handsome and great to look at, and almost as charismatic as the splendid old 'Stars'. Double chimneys gave them a particular impression of power, purpose and presence – especially in the class's final years. *D. P. Williams*

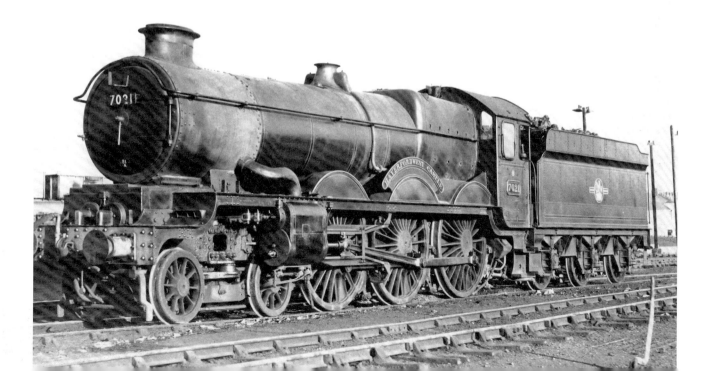

**ABOVE** No 7004 *Eastnor Castle* (double chimney) together with No 7011 *Banbury Castle* (single chimney) are seen at Worcester Shrub Hill on 14 July 1962. *Patrick Kingston*

**BELOW** Brand-new, unnamed 'Castle' No 7037 in August 1950. It was named *Swindon* by HRH Princess Elizabeth at the Works on 15 November 1950. *Ian Allan Library*

quiet satisfaction. As an apprentice he had prepared the general arrangement drawings for *The Great Bear*, and as Assistant Chief Draughtsman had been engaged in the design of the first series of 'Castles'. Now he was responsible for the first improvements that took the genre into its final and finest evolutionary stage. Hawksworth is remembered mainly for the 'Counties', but the last 40 GWR four-cylinder 4-6-0s were really his masterpiece.

Renaming of the 'Castles', which had started in 1936, gained widespread resonance with the adoption of well-known aircraft names during the war. Several of the 5098 series were distinguished in more esoteric vein by names that reflected warm sentiments for the Old Company: No 7000 *Viscount Portal*, No 7001 *Sir James Milne*, No 7007 *Great Western* (the last 'Castle' built by the GWR and so renamed in January 1948), and No 7017 *G. J. Churchward*. In 1957 No 7005 *Lamphey Castle* became *Sir Edward Elgar* (a name that had previously adorned a 'Bulldog'). There was even a sense of fulfilment that peripatetic names *Denbigh Castle* and *Ogmore Castle* eventually gained their last resting places with Nos 7032 and 7035. Personalities notable by their absence were C. B. Collett and F. W. Hawksworth. The very last 'Castle' was named *Swindon*, a choice none could dispute.

**ABOVE** In conjunction with the installation of four-row superheaters, mechanical lubricators were fitted. This unidentified 'King' heading the up 'Cornish Riviera' along the sea wall has been so equipped, but the original-shaped steam pipes are retained. The first five coaches are Hawksworth vehicles. The picture is undated but is thought to have been taken in about 1951-52.

## Improving the 'Kings'

The improvements started with the third 'Castle' series led to similar treatment of the 'Kings'. Prevailing operating conditions presumably made it less imperative to consider the performance of the largest members of the 4-6-0 family. Passenger loads were heavy but schedules were still relaxed, so there was no immediate need for trains that demanded the sustained high levels of power output for which the 'Kings' had been built.

In February 1948 No 6022 *King Edward III* received a new boiler with a four-row superheater that increased the heating surface from 313 sq ft to 489 sq ft. A leading commentator remarked that the 'King' that represented ex-GWR interests in the 1948 Locomotive Exchanges (No 6018) was fitted with little more than a 'steam dryer'.

Experience thus far with the 'Castle' had obviously endorsed the advantages and it was unfortunate that No 6022 was not selected for use in the Exchanges. Nonetheless, it was available for the subsidiary tests conducted by BR Western Region later in 1948, and the results more than justified the modification. Coal consumption with an original 'King' was reduced from 3.74lb per drawbar horsepower hour when using Yorkshire Hard coal in the main tests to 3.33lb burning Welsh coal, while No 6022 did even better with an average consumption rate of 3.10lb. These figures were adjusted to take into account the higher consumption level during the winter months, to provide train heating.

**BELOW** When high degree superheat was installed, mechanical lubricators were fitted immediately behind the right-hand outside steam pipe, but this impeded access to the valve motion. No 6025 *King Henry III* was one of three that retained this arrangement until after receiving a double chimney. This engine is at Newton Abbot double-heading a 'Castle' on a down train bound for Plymouth. No4949 *Packwood Hall* is at an adjacent platform. *Transport Treasury*

The following year a second element of the improvements that had been identified as desirable in 1939 commenced with modifications to the draughting. This involved replacement of the existing chimney liner with one that was longer and of slightly smaller diameter, and substitution of a slightly smaller blastpipe without a jumper top. This measure was not totally successful as there was an increase in exhaust pressure with a resultant diminution in power output. To correct this problem, the class started to assume its final form with the fitting of double chimneys in 1955, after a period of experimentation.

### The second 'Pacific'

The final element of Hawksworth's association with large engine policy concerned the alleged proposal to build a new 'Pacific' after the war. This notion has gained some credibility, fired by the ardency of enthusiasts wishing to believe that the GWR was determined to 'catch up' with the other companies, but there is no evidence that it was ever a formal proposition.

F. C. Mattingly, Chief Draughtsman, evidently instructed a subordinate to commence drawings for a new 'Pacific', more or less

**ABOVE** This view of No 6028 *King George VI* shows the condition in which it was withdrawn in November 1962. *Lens of Sutton*

**TOP LEFT** No 6002 *King William IV* is in final condition awaiting departure from Paddington on 'The Royal Duchy'. Approximate dating is possible as the 'King' received its double chimney in March 1956, whereas single-chimney No 1004 *County of Somerset*, standing alongside, was not so modified until April 1957.

**BOTTOM LEFT** No 6008 *King James II* displays its final condition before receiving a double chimney in December 1958. The mechanical lubricator is located forward of the revised-shape right-hand steam pipe.

concurrent with several other ideas then being floated that never took physical form. These included a 2-6-0PT, a 4-4-0 with outside valve gear, and varying combinations of 'Halls' with different boilers and types of valve gear. Theoretical design exercises were useful for generating technical debate without constituting firm propositions, as with the 'Pacific' idea, which appeared to emanate from Mattingly himself. Some drawings had been completed before Hawksworth became aware of what was afoot. He instantly ordered that this work should cease, took personal charge of the papers, placed them under lock and key, and stipulated that their availability was subject to his personal approval.

The drawings' existence became well known, and in retirement Hawksworth was so exasperated by requests for details that he returned to the works and personally destroyed the relevant documentation. A profile drawing exists that is broadly similar to

an LMS 'Princess Royal' with a dome, but also with the 'inside/outside' 'King'-type bogie frame that by the 1940s was known to be unnecessary. The provenance of this drawing is considered doubtful, and possibly the result of wishful thinking.

There were several factors that supported Hawksworth's stance. He was familiar with the hazards of enlargement from experience with Nos 111 and 4700. Collaboration with Stanier and the results of the 1939 study of Chapelon's work had reinforced the contention that there was much more to be extracted from the 'Kings' and 'Castles', as was partially proven. There was a lingering doubt whether there had ever been sufficient work to justify the extra ten 'Kings' built in 1930. Prevailing traffic patterns and relaxed schedules caused by overdue infrastructural renewal obviated any immediate need for a larger, high-speed steam engine. The company's financial condition placed a higher priority on improving the fleet's operating core rather than any expensive diversion into large, prestige locomotives. Alternative technology (gas turbines and possibly a new DMU generation) was then regarded as a more prudent course for future development.

There is a final factor that argues persuasively against any adventures with a new 'Pacific'. As has been proven with the mixed-traffic and express locomotives, Hawksworth had an enterprising streak and was not afraid of risking new ideas. Nevertheless his (largely under-acknowledged) successes were won with a frugality that matched the austerity of the times. The improvements wrought through the 'Modified Halls' and the 5098 series 'Castles' were at minimal cost and in stark contrast to extravagance exercised elsewhere.

# CHAPTER 6
# DIVERSIONS

Collett's adherence to the Churchward format and the advantages of standardisation sustained a familial resemblance throughout the motive power fleet, so divergences from the norm were especially interesting. Hawksworth participated in three such exercises – two as a senior member of the Swindon team and the third during his tenure as CME.

Considering Collett's reactionary nature, two projects were intriguing in their iconoclasm, suggesting instances where he was unsuccessful in circumventing initiatives emanating from his superiors. The third was a response to economic imperatives under difficult post-war conditions. All three left no lasting impact on Swindon practice but held considerable intrinsic interest.

### The poppet valve project

In contrast to the minimalist rebuilding of 'Saint' Class No 2925 that had widespread impact in providing the forerunner of the 'Halls', the next 'Saint' modification was more radical, but confined to a single locomotive. The treatment given to No 2935 *Caynham Court* was an exploration of alternative means of valve actuation, a subject that had stimulated much interest during the 1920s.

Most 20th-century British locomotives used either Walschaerts or Stephenson valve gear, both of which relied on piston (previously slide) valves to admit and exhaust steam into and from the driving cylinders. Because of this dual role, there is an inherent weakness resulting from steam's expansive property, as each port and its corresponding valve must exhaust a greater volume than was admitted, thus naturally throttling the steam flow. Where poppet valves are used, this problem is avoided by making the exhaust ports larger than the inlet ports.

Towards the end of the 19th century, poppet valves were introduced to marine and stationary steam engines, and in about 1905 Dr Hugo Lentz (an Austrian who had been born in South Africa) applied his system to steam locomotives. Link motion connected with the driving axle actuated oscillating or rotating cams that in turn opened and closed the poppet valves that were set vertically to the driving cylinder. In the following years this arrangement was applied quite widely by continental European railways, although development was checked by the First World War.

Apart from better steam flow, it was argued that there were other advantages over the traditional piston valve. The overall weight of the complete assembly could be significantly reduced,

**LEFT** An official photograph of 'Saint' Class No 2935 *Caynham Court* as rebuilt with Lentz rotary cam valve gear in 1931.
*Ian Allan Library*

**ABOVE RIGHT** A three-quarter view of No 2935, apparently on the same occasion. *Ian Allan Library*

**BELOW RIGHT** The cylinder casting with rotary camshaft layout for No 2935. *Railway Gazette*

there was less chance of wiredrawing (with piston valves, the leakage of steam past the valve head), there were fewer non-productive movements of mechanical parts, wider cut-off adjustment was possible, and there was less exposure to the violent temperature changes that might induce metal fatigue. Also, use of superheated (i.e. dry) steam demanded efficient, constant lubrication of piston valves, whereas this need was substantially reduced with the poppet system. Further, careful shaping of the cams was held to improve overall efficiency by allowing a sharp opening of the valve then gentle closing, to reduce impact.

Interest in poppet valves was boosted by the work of Arturo Caprotti who, from 1915 onwards, sought to exploit motor car technology to improve the efficiency of steam locomotives. By 1921 his system, a competitive alternative to that of Lentz, was considered superior to that generally used in contemporary internal combustion engines. With the style of Caprotti valve gear then in use, a gearbox mounted on the driving axle was connected by shaft to a rotating camshaft adjacent to and in parallel with the driving cylinder. These camshafts actuated a pair of poppet valves for each cylinder.

Davey Paxman acquired the UK marketing rights (later transferred to Associated Locomotive Equipment Co) for the Lentz system and some success was achieved in its promotion to the LNER in the 1920s. This system was also tried by the LMS, which appeared to favour the Caprotti system, the rights for which were held by William Beardmore & Co. The GWR was late on the scene, with a single locomotive modified with Lentz gear in 1931, whereas the Southern did not try poppet valves at all. It would appear that these efforts did not achieve the hoped-for response as the proponents of the two systems later appeared to combine forces by operating from the same London address.

The factors that justified installation of poppet valves in existing locomotives were complex. Promoters typically promised fuel savings of the order of 20%, and there were instances in other countries where impressive improvements were achieved. However, these claims were gross figures that took no account of contingent elements. Amortisation of the additional capital cost militated against modification of a locomotive in mid-life. Less maintenance was involved with poppet valves but, when in need of attention, specialised skills were required; traditional valves and motion demanded more frequent servicing but simplicity made this less technically onerous. Importantly, poppet valves required a different

driving style, including very early cut-offs to maximise fuel savings, but habits built up over many years were not easily changed.

Perhaps the biggest drawback was the capital expense. In 1930 Beardmore rebuilt two four-cylinder 4-6-0s of the Great Southern Railways Class '400' with two cylinders and Caprotti gear at a cost of £7,000 per locomotive. This would have stretched the resources of the cash-strapped Irish company, and it is believed that the manufacturer bore all or most of the cost as a sales promotion. Presumably the GWR was induced to modify No 2935 on the premise that Associated Locomotive Equipment Co (ALE) paid the bill. In view of his typically hostile attitude to commercial manufacturers, it seems unlikely that Collett would have agreed to the project otherwise. However, this raises questions over who supervised the design and installation work. It might be significant that so far the Lentz drawings have not been traced, suggesting a protective attitude towards control of the intellectual property rights and a reluctance to release too much commercially sensitive information about dimensions, etc.

A report appeared in *The Railway Gazette* for 12 June 1931, which described the gear as a standard ALE product except that, instead of the usual outside drive, a gearbox was mounted between the frames on the driving axle. From this a shaft extended forward to a

**ABOVE** No 2935 in Swindon Works in conjunction with road-testing. The condition of the paintwork suggests that the locomotive has seen some service. An indicator shelter is in course of being assembled and the dynamometer car is on the right. This photograph is undated and the side sheeting obscures the smokebox side, so it is not possible to determine whether this view depicts the engine in its original poppet valve state, or following later modifications. It is in company with a 4,000-gallon tender, which appears to have been modified, perhaps in connection with the testing programme. Most early views of No 2935 show it with a 3,500-gallon tender. *R. S. Carpenter collection*

totally enclosed transverse shaft that ran in double-purpose ball bearings. At either end of this transverse shaft, gears drove short shafts on either side of the engine forward to the cam boxes. Thus drive was delivered through a series of bevel gearbox connections between the driving axle and the rotating camshafts. Universal joints were inserted in the main drive shaft and in the short camshafts. An obvious expense in setting up this arrangement lay in the number of bevel gears, which had to be specially machined as such components were not then in normal railway use.

Standard ALE valves were used except that those for exhaust were placed on the outside and those for admission on the inside. This reversal of the usual arrangement was adopted to permit specially enlarged exhaust ports and passages. The diameter of the

inlet ports was $6\frac{3}{16}$ inches and that of the exhaust ports was 8 inches. In forward gear the cam mechanism allowed for nine different rates of steam admission through cut-offs ranging from 10% to 85%. To alter the cut-off or to engage reverse gear, the camshafts moved transversely by means of a system of levers that connected with ball-thrust boxes fitted to the inner ends of the camshafts. The outside extremities of these levers engaged with a rack and pinion actuated by a worm and wheel gear, in turn connected to a rotary shaft extending from the front of the engine along the right-hand side of the boiler back to the cab. This shaft connected with a hand-operated reversing wheel similar to the normal type. Contrary to the promoters' claims, the conversion added about 2 tons to the overall weight, although this might have been due to conversion of an existing locomotive, i.e. weight savings might still have been possible with an engine designed from scratch to use rotary cam poppet valves.

Modification of No 2935 was completed in May 1931 and road trials were conducted over about an 18-month period. Although little information is available on this work, S. O. Ell prepared a paper in 1933 that summarised some of the findings. Broadly speaking, it was concluded that the potential benefits were not realised. Wiredrawing was not eliminated and leaks of steam and water (arising from condensation) were experienced. Double-beat valves had originally been fitted, and during the testing period a number of modifications were tried to reduce leakage. The most significant change was a unique arrangement of each valve having one standard poppet valve seating and one piston ring seating of a valve pattern patented by Corliss (an American valve manufacturer). The date of this modification and further details of this arrangement have not been traced, but its presence is indicated by the different shape of the cam box housings above the running plate. The engine ran most of its post-1931 career in this condition.

Under the Collett regime that might well have been the end of the story, but research[5] has revealed fragments of correspondence that appear to have been exchanged between ALE and Hawksworth in 1938/39. The timing appears significant as, with the untimely demise of Hannington, Hawksworth would by then have recognised the probability that he would be the next CME. Investigative efforts had ceased with No 2935 about five years earlier, but he seems to have believed that the potential for poppet valves had not been fully explored. It has been suggested that the incomplete records indicate that private discussions/exchanges were held to avoid Collett becoming aware. This is feasible in view of his autocratic style, apparent disinterest in the 1931/33 exercise, and hostility towards outside contractors. It would also accord with Hawksworth's evident open attitude to innovation from the 1920s, and with his later enthusiasm for trying new ideas. There are suggestions that he considered fitting a new two-cylinder 4-6-0, probably a 'County', with poppet valves, but no drawing to support this logical contention has been found.

The pre-war discussions appeared to focus on fitting higher-lift cams to improve the steam flow, and that this simple, relatively low-cost modification had not been tried earlier speaks volumes for Collett's attitude. This idea was revived soon after nationalisation; with continuing reliance on steam power but with fuel of uncertain quality, British Railways reviewed the innovations of the 'Big Four', including alternative valve systems.

The proposal was quickly abandoned when it was calculated that the cross-sectional area of the admission ports at 19 square inches was unduly small in relation to the driving cylinder dimensions. With steam flow restricted at the start of the piston cycle, it seemed unlikely that new cams could offset the key problem of port size, let alone negate issues related to leakage. Accordingly, nothing could be achieved without provision of new cylinders, which was hardly feasible with a 37-year-old member of a class in process of withdrawal.

Reportedly this conclusion was drawn in 1948, but it is inconceivable that an engineer of Hawksworth's calibre was not already aware of the problem. The fitting of a modern 4-6-0 with poppet valves that took into account these factors would have been a worthwhile experiment, providing an objective basis for comparison with the traditional Stephenson Link arrangement. It was notable that No 2935 had been modified concurrently with the construction of 40 'Halls' (Lot Nos 268 and 275), and the use of one of them, rather than a 20-year-old 'Saint', as the guinea pig

**ABOVE** No 2935 at Swindon on 16 August 1936, by which time cladding above the running plate around the steam pipes has been modified, indicating that Corliss valves have been fitted. *H. C. Casserley*

**BELOW** *Caynham Court* on 26 March 1946 at Swindon, working a slow train to Paddington. *B. W. L. Brooksbank*

**ABOVE** A close-up view of No 2935 dated July 1947 showing the left-hand cylinder and valve cladding. *R. H. G. Simpson*

would have been more sensible. As with *Arlington Court*, which was later displayed on the upgraded stationary plant, Collett might also have been reluctant to have a design for which he was responsible placed under comparative scrutiny.

Finally, if the issue of port size had been known from the start then the question of financial responsibility for the project and how the modifications were monitored was relevant. Collett might have insisted on just enough to ensure failure. Given that he was later to spend a considerable sum on the stationary testing plant, then make little use of the upgraded facility, he might equally have been unconcerned about the expense of this project. No 2935's weaker performance led to it being the first of the 25 'Court' series to be withdrawn (in December 1948). All the others had gone by mid-1953.

## Streamliners

There can be few exercises in engineering futility that match attempts to improve steam locomotives by adorning them with streamlining. Nevertheless, in the 1930s this particular nonsense seized the imaginations of elements in the engineering community (who should have known better), and of the public at large.

Streamlining had first appeared on the LNER in 1929 with experimental 4-6-4 No 10000, by coincidence rather than specific intent. The shrouding that enveloped this locomotive was there to cover the unusually shaped Yarrow-type boiler rather than to pursue aerodynamic advantage. Rather surprisingly, the first entrant into the field of steam locomotive streamlining for its own sake was the GWR.

The company had already adopted streamlining with its diesel railcars, where some correlation could be drawn between air

**ABOVE** 'King' Class No 6014 *King Henry VII* as released from the Works and before entering traffic in streamlined condition. If the 'plasticine' method had indeed been applied to design the shrouding and fairing, it is easy to see how the clay must have been applied to cover nooks and crannies that might have contributed to drag. Equally, later removal of much of the offending sheeting should not have proved too difficult. *Ian Allan Library*

resistance, power efficiency and payload economy. Further, public relations were aided by the implication of speed and efficiency through styling techniques that conformed with contemporary tastes in Art Deco. The favourable impact encouraged the message of modernity in the programme of celebrations for the company's 100th anniversary in 1935. Other themes included the GWR's presence at the birth of the railway network, continuity, and sustained progress. Commitment to passenger comfort was epitomised in the sumptuous 'Centenary' coaching stock, whose pedigree was traceable back to the short-lived 'Torbay Pullman Limited' of 1929, and the conclusion that it was preferable to build, rather than hire, luxury coaches. Love it or hate it, the most persistent Art Deco statement was the GWR 'shirt button' totem, which spread like a plague, appearing on tanks and tenders, coaches and brown vehicles, station frontages, labels, delivery vans, timetables and menus. Even in the 21st century the end supports of some platform seats reveal that Art Deco GWR has yet to be extinguished.

In this groundswell of enthusiasm for what the modern era offered, locomotives looked out of place. To the untrained eye little seem to have changed since the 1900s, appearing old-fashioned compared with the styling trend unleashed in other

RIGHT A three-quarter view of No 6014 before its return to traffic.
*Ian Allan Library*

BELOW No 6014 is seen in the early stages of having the streamlining fitted. Working from the rear, a transverse framing had been installed to support the fairing at the front of the tender. The wedge-front cab, new splashers and sheeting sweeping up to the side of the firebox are in place, as is also the sheeting in front of the firebox shoulders. There is a hint that the fairing might be in place behind the chimney. Some mounting brackets are in place to accept the sheeting over the space in front of the cylinders and over the front running plate before the drop end. The handrail on the front of the smokebox has been reduced to a quarter arc and hinge brackets have been fitted to hang the bullet nose. A footplate has been welded on the front left lower quadrant of the smokebox. Obviously the intention was to open the bullet nose and use this footplate and the quarter handrail to reach the top lamp bracket.
*Stephenson Locomotive Society*

quarters to recognise the Centenary. It was almost inevitable that Swindon locomotives had to be brought on board, and there was no better way than by streamlining – or so it was believed by some of Collett's superiors.

A streamlined steam locomotive enjoys little aerodynamic advantage except in still air or when facing into a headwind, although even then any benefit might be negated by drag exerted by the rolling stock. In other conditions, the treatment is of no benefit whatsoever, other than for the sake of appearance. Add the inconvenience of inhibited access to moving parts and any gain is trifling, as was highlighted by the LNER's programme. The wedge front of the semi-streamlined 'P2' 2-8-2s was effective in steam lifting, while the same feature combined with full streamlining of the Class 'B17/5' 4-6-0s on routes with moderate line speeds bestowed no advantage. Collett clearly appreciated the drawbacks, his attitude amply demonstrating his disinterest.

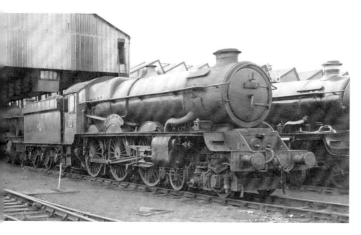

**LEFT** No 6014 *King Henry VII*, late in its career, has been restored almost to normal, displaying a double chimney and the final version of the outside steam pipes. The V-shape of the cab can just be discerned. *P. J. Sharpe*

Having received orders to decorate a couple of engines, it is famously recounted that he reluctantly set about the task by sticking lumps of plasticine onto a silver locomotive desk model, then passing this on as the template for preparation of suitable drawings. It has been alleged that this story is apocryphal, but the image conjured engenders a certain poignancy – the middle-aged, lonely, childless widower playing with a child's toy, then passing the result to Hawksworth, a middle-aged bachelor, for implementation.

If true, Collett subconsciously adopted a method from the pre-CAD era used to fashion the subtle curves found in modern motor cars and in aeronautics. For the most part, there was nothing subtle in this exercise, but at least the cost of shape optimisation by use of wind tunnels was avoided. Two locomotives were selected for 'improvement' – No 5005 *Manorbier Castle* and No 6014 *King*

**LEFT** 'Castle' Class No 5005 *Manorbier Castle* is seen in service with all streamlining still in place, about to leave Gloucester on the up 'Cheltenham Flyer' in 1935. There is an anonymous note on the reverse of this image: 'This was surely C. B. Collett's effort at pulling the leg of the GW Directors.'

**BELOW** No 5005 with the front end sheeting over the cylinders and footplate, and the tender fairing removed. *Stephenson Locomotive Society*

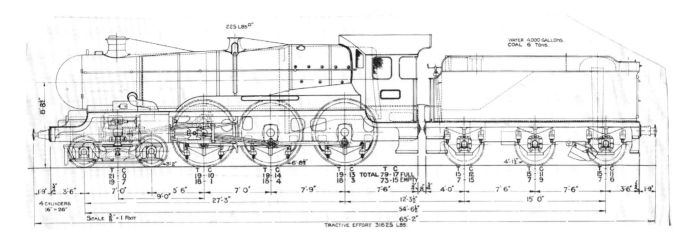

*Henry VII*. The result met with criticism and ridicule, with suggestions that King Henry VII was not such a bad monarch and that No 6013 would have been a more suitable choice. Collett was presumably as unhappy with the results as he had been reluctant to take on the task, but there is evidence to suggest that his deft hand limited the impact.

Fairing was installed behind the chimney and safety valve bonnet, and in front of the upper part of the firebox to smooth out the prominent shoulders of the throat plate. Shrouding was fitted to the front of the tender to harmonise with the cab roof profile, which practically speaking acted as an impediment. The cab was wedge-fronted, providing the most useful feature of the whole ensemble as the diagonal slant in the vertical plane eliminated reflection and improved the view through the spectacle plates. Single continuous driving wheel splashers with straight nameplates replaced the normal variety, and fairing covered an air pocket between the upper face of the splasher and the firebox side from just forward of the throat plate back to the cab face.

At the front end, the running plate area before the drop end was encased in convex sheeting, and the space between the lower arc of the smokebox and the leading face of the outside steam pipes was also encased. These coverings were complemented by cladding below footplate level that extended back from the rear of the buffer beam to the leading edge of the outside cylinders. There were no mechanical modifications to chassis, valve gear or motion.

The semi-spherical proboscis mounted on the smokebox front dominated the entire ensemble, drawing attention away from the front-end sheeting below. The convex covering of the front footplate in wet or frosty weather, or under a thin coating of oil or grease, threatened to make lethal such mundane tasks as opening the smokebox door or mounting a lamp on the top bracket. The sheeting over the cylinders without any form of ventilation was a technical oversight so blatant as surely to have been premeditated. It is doubtful that either Collett or Hawksworth would have been mentally equipped to argue the nuances of styling, Art Deco and

so forth, but mechanical failure drew the debate into an arena they understood.

The sheeting did its job, leading to overheating of the cylinders and providing the precedent for its removal. Other unsightly elements quietly disappeared piecemeal; a report dated early 1943 noted that the bullet nose from No 6014 had recently been removed, leaving only the straight splashers (and presumably the cab) as evidence of the defacement the engine had suffered. In May of that year, No 5005 was seen at Swindon with newly restored curved splashers; all other streamline body features had been removed except for the wedge-shape cab. Only the special snifting valve on the 'Castle' and the special cab on the 'King' remained in place at withdrawal.

The company's conclusions on steam locomotive streamlining were published in the book *Next Station* of 1947. Reference was made to Nos 5005 and 6014 in the mid-1930s, and to their '... improvised streamlined casings so that their efficiency might be tested under normal running conditions'. Arguments were then presented that centred on the impact of train length, asserting that side winds had more effect on a steam train 900 to 1,000 feet long than on a (single) diesel railcar that was 62 feet long, and that therefore the latter had more to gain by a streamlined front. The section ended in pithy fashion: 'The Great Western has always been an intensely practical railway. A streamlined locomotive might be good to look at, but the train went no faster because of it and the coal bill remained the same.'

The exercise was brilliantly executed, making the GWR's essay into steam streamlining far and away the most successful among the 'Big Four'. Collett's tactical masterstroke quickly extinguished the impetus, allowing the stupidity to wither without regret. The other companies were less fortunate.

OIL BURNING ENGINE. No. 2872.

## Oil-burning conversions

Before the war it had been the practice carefully to monitor locomotive coal, and the company wielded formidable buying power in obtaining appropriate quality. Purchases were made only from collieries capable of handling the company's purpose-designed 20-ton and 40-ton loco coal wagons, after screening and grading at the pithead. These disciplines fell away under the stresses of wartime, and quality became variable. The situation became even worse in 1945 with crisis conditions in mining compounding supply difficulties. Locomotive coal comprised three basic component materials:

**Volatile content:** the gaseous element that is important in lighting up, and in meeting sudden demands for more power when running.

**Carbon content:** the combustible element that does not burn as gas, but which reduces to coke on the firebars, thereby creating the fire bed, which generates steady continuous heat at a slower rate.

**Ash:** the remainder, which is always present in varying degrees, consisting of sundry non-combustible material.

An excess of volatile content renders a faster combustion rate and the need to replenish the fire more frequently. At the other extreme, too much ash limits airflow to the combustible elements. In excessive quantities ash, with its lower melting point, coalesces into solid clinker that at worst necessitates the cleaning out of the firebox and reconstruction of the fire from scratch. Analysis established that Welsh coal in 1938 averaged 14,960 heat units per ton, but by 1945 fuel from the same area averaged 13,840 heat units per ton (a 7½% deterioration), while yielding a greater accumulation of clinker and ash. The other companies faced similar difficulties, but the GWR was acutely affected as its narrow fireboxes had been designed specifically for good-quality Welsh

**ABOVE** The first oil-burner was Class '28xx' No 2872, later renumbered 4800 (which led to the 0-4-2T Class '48xx' engines being renumbered in the '14xx' series). *Ian Allan Library*

coal. This situation was even more unwelcome at a time when efforts were being made to restore service quality.

In addition to erratic quality, there had been substantial cost escalation:

| Per engine mile: | lb coal consumed | cost (old pence) |
| --- | --- | --- |
| 1938 | 43.32 | 4.23 |
| 1939 | 44.21 | 4.44 |
| 1940 | 46.58 | 5.60 |
| 1941 | 50.03 | 7.38 |
| 1942 | 51.68 | 8.51 |
| 1943 | 52.47 | 9.47 |
| 1944 | 55.18 | 10.78 |
| 1945 | 53.86 | 11.88 |
| **1938/1945% increase** | **19.60** | **180.90** |

Conditions therefore favoured experimentation with oil as a substitute for coal. Oil-firing had been tried before in the UK, most prominently by James Holden (a former assistant to William Dean) on the Great Eastern Railway. He modified approximately 50 engines to burn (primarily) spent oil from the plant at Stratford that produced gas for carriage lighting. When insufficient volume was available from this source, market purchases were necessary that ultimately became too expensive. In other cases conversions were short-term, usually during crises such as the 1926 coal strike. Imported oil was generally uneconomic, but by 1945 the mining situation was such that cost convergence made it feasible to switch energy sources.

Experimental work in collaboration with the Anglo-Persian Oil Company culminated in fitting Class '28xx' No 2872 with the weir system in October 1945. Technical viability was established following inevitable teething problems, using heavy Bunker C-type oil. Two Class '2884' 2-8-0s (Nos 2888 and 3865) had been modified by year-end, concurrent with the announcement that ten 2-8-0s of Classes '28xx'/'2884' and eight Class '42xx' 2-8-0Ts would be converted to haul heavy coal trains from the collieries of South Wales. Tenders of 3,500-gallon water capacity were to have 1,800-gallon oil tanks installed in the coal space; the tank engines were to have 850-gallon oil tanks fitted in their bunkers.

In the first half of 1946 a further announcement revealed expanded plans to include one 'Hall' and 25 'Castles' in addition to the eight-coupled engines. Then in August 1946 the Ministry of Transport officially endorsed the initiative by stating that oil-firing using the weir system was to be adopted nationwide by conversion of approximately 1,200 locomotives (including 110 on the Southern Railway, 485 on the LMS and 450 on the LNER), mainly focussing on heavy freight types. The GWR's participation was to be 25 'Castles', 73 2-8-0s and 86 mixed-traffic engines. The intention to convert tank engines was dropped, presumably on the grounds that tender locomotives had a greater operating range.

By early 1946 the first two refuelling stations had been commissioned at Llanelly and Severn Tunnel Junction, and it was found that about 400 gallons of oil were consumed working between these two points. The 2-8-0s, the focus of local pride and maintained in smart condition, regularly made return journeys as far as Gloucester or Swindon without becoming stranded for want of fuel. At the Ministry's instigation, refuelling points were to be established at Old Oak Common, Reading, Didcot, Swindon, Bristol (both Bath Road and St Phillip's Marsh), Newton Abbot, Newport (Ebbw Junction), Cardiff, Landore, Gloucester, Westbury, Banbury, and Plymouth (Laira). By the autumn of 1947 a 352,000-gallon storage plant for heavy oil had been brought into use at Old Oak Common. This facility, which included two tanks 34 feet in diameter and 30 feet high, could be filled at the rate of 20,000 gallons per hour and could refuel three locomotives concurrently. Another 15 refuelling stations were then either planned or being constructed, but it is understood that only those at Old Oak Common, Swindon and Laira were commissioned before the project was cancelled.

Engines to be selected were those used on the heaviest duties, thereby yielding the greatest savings. It was estimated that coal

**BELOW** A cut-away illustration of a tender for an oil-burning Class '28xx' 2-8-0. *Trains Annual 1948, Ian Allan Ltd*

**BELOW** A cut-away illustration of an oil-burning '28xx'. *Trains Annual 1948, Ian Allan Ltd*

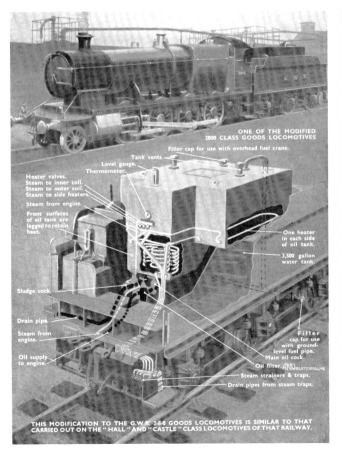

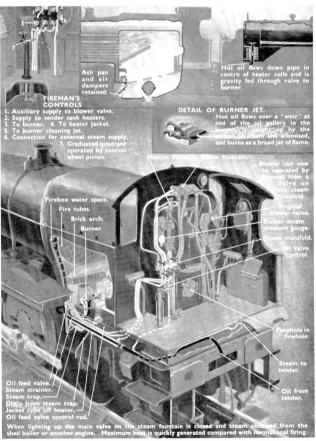

reductions of 22,000 tons per day, or approximately 1 million tons per annum, would be possible nationwide – although these levels suggested rather more locomotive conversions than were identified in the published plans. The railway companies would bear the capital expense in return for a subsidy of £1 per ton of oil consumed. Early experience on the GWR showed that the equivalent consumption of a locomotive burning 75lb of coal per mile was approximately 6 gallons of oil.

The locomotive modification programme had to be preceded by provision of strategically located refuelling stations. Apart from the Old Oak Common facility, each was to comprise three 12,000-gallon storage tanks replenished from specially adapted 3,000-gallon oil tank wagons. Oil was pumped by steam-driven duplex pumps from the wagons through flexible hoses at the rate of 10,000 gallons per hour. The viscosity of the oil was reduced by the wagons having carriage

steam heating equipment that fed internal heating coils; the storage tanks and the hoses were also steam-heated. To refuel a locomotive the process was reversed and, as tenders had oil capacities of 1,800 or 1,950 gallons, this task took around 15 minutes.

Tenders were equipped with tanks that were inserted snugly into the coal space. Each tank front was lagged with asbestos composition material and other precautions were taken to minimise the circulation of air around the sides and back. A filler cap was located centrally towards the rear of the tank to accept gantry-mounted overhead hoses. The tank could also be replenished at ground level by hoses coupled to additional fillers fitted on either side below solebar height just forward of the rear tender wheels. A T-junction in the transverse pipe connecting these fillers took oil up a 4-inch-diameter pipe through the water space and looped over the rear of the oil tank.

The oil then flowed into a partially sealed chamber approximately 3ft 6in by 2ft 4in by 1ft 8in by means of holes in the back partition plate. This chamber contained two steam heating coils with a surface area of 29½ square feet, which were linked to a Rototherm thermometer, the dial of which was fitted to the front of the tank. Two auxiliary heating loops with a surface area of 8½ square feet were fitted in the main section of the oil tank. The steam supply to the heating coils was controlled by three manifold-mounted valves on the front of the tender, fed by a flexible hose from the engine's steam manifold.

Oil flowed through a standpipe fitted with a shut-off cock and a filter, then by flexible hose connected to a 1½-inch-diameter pipe fitted under the left-hand locomotive footplate. From there it passed through an auxiliary heater in the form of a steam jacket 5ft 3in long, next to which was located the oil regulating cock that controlled admission to the burner. The cock was linked to a graduated quadrant and operated by pinion drive connected with a horizontal control wheel mounted in the front left-hand corner of the cab. The steam manifold was installed immediately to the right of the wheel and consisted of five valves that regulated saturated steam from the boiler fountain. These valves controlled steam supply to the burner in the firebox, the burner cleaner, the blower in the smokebox, the heating steam jacket on the engine, and the heating coils in the tender tank. A further valve in the manifold controlled admission of steam from an outside source (i.e. another locomotive or boiler wash-out steam line) to start the process of lighting up. This auxiliary steam could be tapped into the normal blower valve through the manifold so that the blower could also help this process.

The burner was mounted at foundation-ring level in a small chamber at the front of the firebox and was fed by oil that flowed over a weir on to a ribbon of steam. Interaction with the steam atomised the oil and projected it towards the back of the firebox at an upward inclination to the horizontal. The oil orifice was initially 2 inches by half an inch and the steam orifice immediately underneath was 2½ inches by 0.018 inches, but it is understood that several dimensional variations were tried to establish the optimal combination. The chamber containing the burner had a small damper that could be pre-set to a suitable opening. The floor of the firebox was a steel plate into which were cut six rectangular holes giving a total air inlet of 2¼ square feet.

The ashpan was modified to form a fire pan, and the original damper gear was retained. Air supply to the firebox was adjusted using the settings of the damper doors in the fire pan. The floor and lower areas of the firebox walls, where the heat was most intense, were lined with special firebricks with a high alumina content, manufactured by the firm of Pearson at Stourbridge. A standard brick arch was used, although this might have been modified later. The firehole door was redesigned to improve the seal and, while it could be easily opened, it remained locked during operating. A peephole with cover was inserted in the door.

**BELOW** 'Hall' Class No 5955 (later No 3950) *Garth Hall* was the first 4-6-0 to be converted, and is depicted ex-works in July 1946. The livery is plain green, but relieved by the polished brass beading on the splashers. The 3,500-gallon (water) tender was replaced by the larger type in early 1948. *Ian Allan Library*

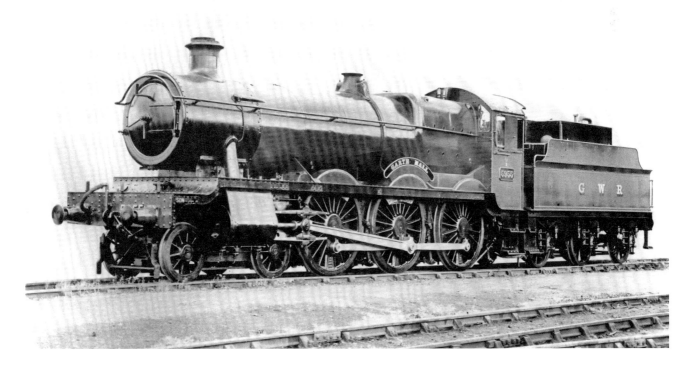

Spark-arresting measures in the smokebox were no longer needed and experiments were conducted to find the most suitable diameter for the blastpipe orifice.

It was anticipated that tender locomotives with an 1,800-gallon oil tank capacity would have an operating range of 250 miles, which might have been slightly optimistic. Córas Iompair Eireann (whose fuel supply problems during the 1940s were more extreme than anything facing the British companies) proportionately converted more of its fleet to oil burning around the same time. CIE's experience suggested that 180-200 miles was a safe operating range, although the situation with its Woolwich 'Moguls' (Classes '372' and '393', derived from the SECR Class 'N') was markedly less favourable. These engines, with their Swindon-inspired narrow fireboxes, averaged 11½ gallons per mile, and their 1,400-gallon oil tanks gave a range of little more than 100 miles. The comparison may not be entirely fair as oil type was relevant to consumption levels – CIE used only light grades.

In addition to the financial advantages, oil yielded several operating benefits once the different firing techniques had been mastered. Steaming was rock steady under varying conditions, the fireman was relieved of much heavy labour, boiler tubes remained comparatively clear, and spark emission at the blastpipe was eliminated. Preparation (and disposal) of an oil burner is simpler – for example, with the ex-South African Railways 2-6-2 +2-6-2 Class 'NGG16' Garratts on the Welsh Highland Railway, with the help of compressed air it is possible to raise full working pressure from cold in 1½ hours.

It is doubtful whether the advantages of oil-firing were ever fully identified. This is understandable in view of the short period

ABOVE Five 'Halls' were converted in April 1947. Two from the 49xx series were renumbered 3900 upwards, while those in the 59xx and 69xx series adopted 3950 upwards; the purpose for this differentiation was unclear, as they were to all intents and purposes identical. No 3951 (formerly No 5976) *Ashwick Hall* is ex-works and in similar condition to No 5955 (3950) *Garth Hall* except that it has a polished chimney rim and safety valve bonnet. By then 4,000-gallon (water) tenders were available with a larger oil capacity at 1,950 gallons, necessitating the shaping of the upper part inwards to clear the loading gauge. *Ian Allan Library*

that the system was in use compared with the preceding 100-plus years of development with coal burners. Early evidence from Ireland suggested that conversion did not necessarily improve maximum steaming rates and that more refinement was needed in setting blastpipe and damper dimensions. It was also suspected that oil was more effective where the firebox provided a greater proportion of the total heating surface. This contention was supported by faster response in steaming rates through adjustment of the firebox controls, and because of the relative lack of heat storage in the firebox and boiler.

Firebox maintenance costs were allegedly greater. Closing down the burner completely saved fuel, but subsequent lighting up concentrated heat on a cooled area with resultant cracking of seams and weeping of stays. This was the reported experience on the Southern Railway, and it may be assumed that the GWR was similarly affected. Also, if the valve that controlled oil admission was not completely closed, seepage into the ashpan could render a near explosive atmosphere in the firebox. The process of relighting the burner could thus be hazardous, with the outside of the firebox momentarily enveloped in flame.

Steaming was not fully effective until the brick firebox lining had thoroughly warmed up, this being the only means of heat retention when the oil admission was at minimal level or closed off. Damper control was thus critical when the oil supply to the burner was reduced, as excessive air admission rapidly cooled the firebox. It followed that the optimal rate of fuel consumption occurred under load, and that lacking the residual constant heat emanating from a coal fire bed the burner had to remain in use to keep the firebox hot. Thus it was wasteful for a locomotive to be stationary for prolonged periods as fuel was still consumed at a comparatively high rate.

On disposal, it was found advisable to use a chimney cover and to close all the dampers to slow the pace at which the boiler cooled down. These factors favoured the employment of specially trained crews on oil-fired engines. The biggest unanswered question perhaps was what impact oil burning had on overall boiler life.

To some degree the benefits of shorter lighting-up and disposal times were offset by the drawback that the system was not self-contained. It relied on steam supplied from an outside source to heat oil tank wagons, hoses and storage tanks, and for lighting up. The processes using coal were more time-consuming and dirtier, but oil-burning prevented the ability to light up a cold firebox

starting with oily cotton waste, and also removed the convenience of leaving a locomotive simmering in light steam with minimal fuel consumption ready for the next duty. Thus an oil-burner's fuel consumption rate rose exponentially with an engine in steam but not under load.

The programme initially focussed on 2-8-0 heavy freight engines together with the solitary 4-6-0 No 5955 *Garth Hall* (later renumbered 3950), the latter to assess the potential for passenger train working. More tenders than locomotives were converted, and the freight orientation was evident in the first three 4-6-0s (No 5955 and 'Castles' Nos 5039 and 5091) being equipped with 3,500-gallon (water) tenders. As the only type then available, these seem to have been the last cases of 'Castles' with small tenders in regular service. Following conversion of 16 4-6-0s between October 1946 and May 1947, the programme reverted to 2-8-0s. Summarised by quarters, the conversions were:

| Quarter | '28xx' | '2884' | 'Hall' | 'Castle' | '63xx' |
|---|---|---|---|---|---|
| Oct to Dec 45 | 2 | 2 | - | - | - |
| Jan to Mar 46 | 1 | 1 | - | - | - |
| Apr to Jun 46 | 4 | - | 1 | - | - |
| Jul to Sep 46 | - | - | - | - | - |
| Oct to Dec 46 | - | - | - | 1 | - |
| Jan to Mar 47 | - | - | - | 2 | 1 |
| Apr to Jun 47 | 1 | 1 | 11 | 2 | - |
| Jul to Sep 47 | 4 | 3 | - | - | - |
| **Total** | **12** | **7** | **12** | **5** | **1** |

BELOW 'Hall' Class No 3953 *Leighton Hall* at work on a passenger train. *C. Leigh Jones*

Details of conversion/re-conversion/renumbering dates and tender numbers appear in Appendix E.

Oil-burners were heavier than their conventional counterparts, as shown by the following weights of locomotives when full:

| Class | Coal-burner | Oil-burner |
|-------|-------------|------------|
| 'Castle' | 79 tons 17 cwt | 80 tons 18 cwt |
| 'Hall' | 75 tons 0 cwt | 75 tons 11 cwt |
| '28xx' | 75 tons 10 cwt | 76 tons 1 cwt |
| '2884' | 76 tons 5 cwt | 76 tons 16 cwt |
| '63xx' | 62 tons 0 cwt | 62 tons 6 cwt |

Increased tender weights when full were proportionately greater (see Table 1).

Renumbering commenced in November/December 1946 with 2-8-0s Nos 4800-06/4850-52, and 'Hall' No 3950. Distinctive numbers were useful for freight engines that habitually wandered from their home sheds for extended periods. There was little point in sending an oil-burner to a destination without refuelling facilities to enable a return home. The Class '28xx'/'2884' conversions covered almost the complete age spectrum. There was speculation that 'Modified Halls' and the higher superheat 'Castle' 5098 sub-class might be included, but engines with less efficient boilers had more to gain.

The equipping of No 6320 was interesting as its size ostensibly made it an unlikely candidate for the demanding duties associated with oil-burners, although the 'Mogul' performed well. The evident objective was to evaluate the economics with secondary motive power, which is borne out by Swindon drawing No 125692 dated November 1947. This provides a useful descriptive layout of the Laidlaw Drew apparatus, but the most intriguing aspect is that the locomotive type depicted is the 2-6-2T Class '4575'.

Although Class '42xx' locomotives had been originally earmarked, no tank locomotives were actually converted, presumably because the greater operating range of a tender locomotive would be more beneficial to the scheme's objectives. Following the last conversion in September 1947 (No 2847/4811), there was a hiatus during which preparation of this drawing suggested that the next phase would have broader application. No reference has been traced regarding the area where an oil-burning 'Small Prairie' might be used, but the type was popular in the West Country. Perhaps the objective was to evaluate the running of remote branch services with oil-burners, to reduce coal movements over long distances. (Eventually there was an oil-burning tank engine of GWR origin; Robert Stephenson & Hawthorn converted 0-6-0PT Class '57xx' No 3711 in April 1958 and it worked as a shunter at Paddington and Swindon before withdrawal in May 1963).

The first evidence of operations beyond the Llanelly-Severn Tunnel Junction axis was the use in June 1946 of No 5955 (3950) on Swindon-Gloucester local trains, before becoming a regular performer on the 1.18pm Paddington-Bristol semi-fast and the 8.25pm Bristol-Swindon, covering about 1,440 miles per week. On 27 August 1946 this engine was tested on the 10.30am Bristol-Newton Abbot service. On 18 October, following use on Swindon-Reading local trains, No 5091 took over No 3950's regular duties and the latter was transferred to Bristol. The programme's second 'Castle', No 5039, was allocated immediately to Bristol Bath Road. The third, No 5083, started work on the original roster of the 'Hall' in December 1946; this was the first oil-burning 4-6-0 with a 4,000-gallon (water) tender (No 2827).

By February 1947 work was well advanced on the refuelling station at Plymouth, but no oil-burners had yet been seen that far west, although Nos 5083 and 5091 were frequently reaching Newton Abbot on the 'North Mail', which departed from Bristol at 6.45am. There was a report dated March 1947 that No 5083 was on loan to the Southern Railway, presumably in conjunction with that company's conversion programme, but no other details have been traced.

It is uncertain whether the Plymouth facilities had by then been commissioned, but Nos 4852 (STJ) and 5079 (LA) were stranded there in March during a period of severe weather conditions. The

**LEFT** 'Castle' Class No 5083 *Bath Abbey* was the third of its class to be converted and the first to appear with a 4,000-gallon (water) tender. It was apparently deemed unnecessary to renumber the 'Castles', as it was also with the solitary 'Mogul', No 6320. *Ian Allan Library*

| TABLE 1 | | | | |
|---------|---|---|---|---|
| **Water capacity** | **Standard** | **Oil-burner** | **Fuel capacity (coal)*** | **Fuel capacity (oil)** |
| 3,500 gallons | 40 tons 0 cwt | 45 tons 6 cwt | 7 tons | 1,800 gallons |
| 4,000 gallons | 46 tons 14 cwt | 53 tons 3 cwt | 6 tons | 1,950 gallons |
| * This capacity was the official figure but presumably notional. | | | | |

'Castle' was by then working the 9.15am Plymouth-Penzance and the 1.25pm Penzance-Plymouth, or the 8.45pm Plymouth-Bristol, returning on the 2.50pm from Bristol. If the facilities were not yet operational, the eastward working would have been essential to refuel. By April No 5079 was a regular between Exeter and Bristol on the 10.40am Bradford express, returning on the 4.29pm from Bristol. Somewhat ironically, the Bradford service was soon cancelled in the interests of fuel economy, and this engine then reverted to Plymouth-Penzance work.

By the end of May 1947 ten more 'Halls' were at work (all with 4,000-gallon (water) tenders, unlike No 3950, which kept its small tender until early 1948). Known shed allocations were Old Oak Common (Nos 3903/3952-54), Bristol Bath Road (Nos 3900 and 3902), and Laira (Nos 3901, 3904 and 3955). In July No 3904 was noted at Swindon fitted with electric headlamps and cab lights, powered by a small electric generator bolted to the right-hand side of the smokebox. Old Oak Common also had 'Castles' Nos 100 A1 and 5039 and 2-8-0 No 4800. Following conversion, 'Halls' were used on the 6.25pm Paddington-Oxford via High Wycombe and the 10.30pm Oxford-West Ealing milk train. 'Mogul' No 6320 was allocated to Swindon and regularly appeared on the 4.38pm Didcot-Reading, returning at 7.00pm from Reading.

The summer of 1947 saw the oil-burners broadening their operations. In mid-July No 5083 was noted at Craven Arms hauling the combined Cardiff-Manchester and Plymouth-Liverpool trains in each direction, alternating with No 1008 *County of Cardigan*. Also the 3.30am Plymouth (Tavistock Junction)-Bristol and the

reverse working that left Bristol at 2.25pm had become regular goods duties for oil-burners. Engines noted were Nos 4804 (SPM), and 4807 and 4855 (LA). In February 1948 oil-burners (including Nos 100A1, 3902 and 3952) were making their first appearances at Wolverhampton on the 7.05am from Paddington, returning with the 1.40pm to Birmingham; details of the return working from there to London have not been traced. By June the 9.45am Paddington-Worcester (always heavily loaded as far as Birmingham) and 6.15pm return from Worcester were regular turns for oil-burning 'Castles'. On the other hand, No 5079 remained at work between Newton Abbot and Penzance.

If the government's plan had been fully enacted, it was estimated that 184 converted locomotives (25 'Castles', 73 2-8-0s and 86 mixed-traffic engines) would consume 125,000 gallons of oil per day, thereby reducing annual coal usage by 173,000 tons. Once all storage facilities were in service there would have been a total capacity of about 2 million gallons, or roughly 14 days' supply. However, in August 1948 came the announcement of a change in policy under which the oil-burning programme would cease, with all locomotives reverting to normal. It was expected that no oil-burners would remain in service after September 1948 and, as no further operating details have been found, it seems that they stopped work in accordance with this schedule, once remaining fuel stocks were exhausted. The process of re-conversion

to coal-firing took about 18 months to complete. All the 'Castles', five 'Halls' and five 2-8-0s had been treated by the end of 1948, but 12 months later three 'Halls' and one 2-8-0 were still at Swindon awaiting entry to the works. No 3903 (4907) *Broughton Hall* was the last to return to original condition, in April 1950.

The abrupt cancellation was a big disappointment following so soon upon inauguration of the Old Oak Common facility. Despite teething problems and the need for critical mass to maximise the benefits, it was evident that the oil-burners could deliver what was promised. However, by 1948 the mining crisis was easing and, while standards never returned to pre-war levels, coal was to remain the most feasible energy source for the time being.

The decisive factor was the country's economic condition, as expectations of a return to pre-war international trading standards were hopelessly optimistic. The war had effectively bankrupted Britain, assets had been mercilessly exploited, and money for renewal investment was in short supply. Economic recovery would be a long process, and an early step was Exchange Control to protect scarce foreign currency reserves. Restoration of pre-war parity at £1.00 = US $4.20 proved unsustainable, and devaluation to $2.80 resulted in an overnight 30% increase in imported oil cost. The scheme thus became fundamentally uneconomic, even if foreign currency could have been made available.

In earlier times, the considerable investment in infrastructure and locomotive conversions under governmental suasion would have created grounds for compensation claims. However, by the time the scheme was terminated this was no longer an issue, as the GWR had ceased to exist.

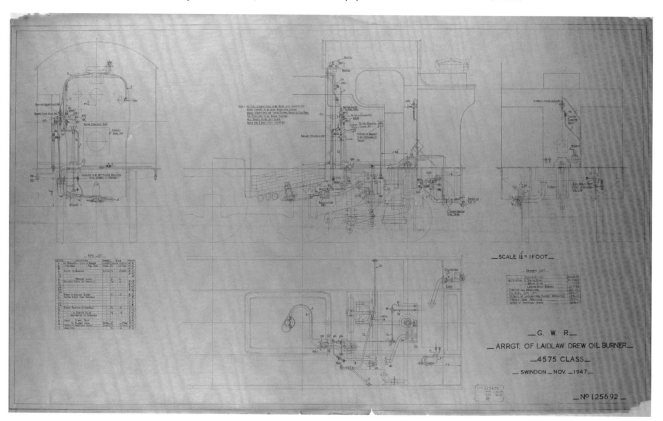

# CHAPTER 7
# POST-1940 STEAM CONSTRUCTION

Collett's reservations about the use of Swindon for munitions production were proved essentially correct by the scale of locomotive construction necessary from 1940 forward – although military hardware was also manufactured, mainly through adaptation of the Carriage Shop. So far as railway work was concerned, the emphasis rested on the locomotive and wagon fleets, with construction continuing unabated. Up until 1944 new building multiplied types introduced before the conflict, but plans under consideration showed Hawksworth's willingness to consider quite radical changes.

The breadth of ideas is apparent in surviving drawings that include a Class 42xx rebuilt as a 2-8-0 tender locomotive,, a lightweight 4-4-0 with a Standard No 10 boiler, a 2-6-0 pannier tank, and a lightweight 2-6-0 with a Standard No 2 boiler (as eventually appeared through the preservation movement). Other drawings evidence several iterations in respect of designs that finally became 0-6-0PT classes '94xx', '15xx' and '16xx'. Consideration was also given to the use of high tensile steel, and outside valve motion was seriously evaluated in more than one instance before eventually appearing with Class '15xx'.

With this radical thinking it was disappointing that circumstances beyond Hawksworth's control prevented more from being done. Of those engines that were built, shortages delayed deliveries, and some orders placed in the late 1940s were not fulfilled until 1956.

**ABOVE** The GWR had invested heavily pre-war in modernising its locomotives, albeit along traditional lines, but after the war reliance was still occasionally placed upon locomotives from an earlier era to undertake quite heavy duties. Ageing Dean Goods, carrying express passenger headlamps, were taking diverted trains over the Severn Bridge on Sundays, and 4-4-0s were called upon to haul loads that belied their size. Here 'Dukedog' 4-4-0 No 3015 (really a 'Bulldog' with a smaller, parallel boiler) has over 40 wagons in tow on a Class 'A' goods working at Iver in 1947. *Ian Allan Library*

Despite the problems, construction was prolific:

| | **1941-47** | **1948-56** |
|---|---|---|
| **Tender:** | | |
| '2884' 2-8-0 | 35 | - |
| 'Hall' 4-6-0 | 48 | - |
| 'Modified Hall' 4-6-0 | 22 | 49 |
| '2251' 0-6-0 | 38 | 2 |
| 'County' 4-6-0 | 30 | - |
| 'Castle' 4-6-0 | 10 | 30 |
| 'Manor' 4-6-0 | - | 10 |
| LMS-design 8F 2-8-0 | 80 | - |
| **Total** | **263** | **91** |
| | | |
| **Tank:** | | |
| '57xx' 0-6-0PT | 185 | 41 |
| '41xx' 2-6-2T | 20 | 20 |
| '94xx' 0-6-0PT | 10 | 200 |
| '74xx' 0-6-0PT | - | 20 |
| '15xx' 0-6-0PT | - | 10 |
| '16xx' 0-6-0PT | - | 70 |
| **Total** | **215** | **361** |

Wartime traffic needs centred on freight engines and shunters with the 2-8-0 type was preferred for long-distance work. Initially, Stanier's LMS 8F 2-8-0 was the Ministry of Supply standard, distributed around the UK and deployed in military service overseas. With large numbers required quickly, several builders were engaged and a batch of 80 was delivered by Swindon between 1943 and 1945 for use on the GWR. The Stanier 8F was later superseded by the War Department 'Austerity' 2-8-0, which could be completed faster and more cheaply by making extensive use of welded and fabricated components. Another wartime 2-8-0 type much in evidence was the United States Army Transportation Corps Class 'S160', built by Baldwin, Lima and the American Locomotive Co.

From 1942 the South Wales docks became important for disembarkation of personnel and equipment arriving from the United States, and 175 Class 'S160s' were lent to the GWR between January 1943 and February 1944 to help cope. They were allocated to the Wolverhampton and South Wales divisions, and all left for service overseas in September and October 1944. Because of the 8Fs and the 'S160s', the GWR had less need for 'WD' 2-8-0s, although there were short-term loans in 1944/45. This type returned in strength between 1946 and 1948 on permanent allocation, displacing the Swindon-built 8Fs, which moved to the LMS.

**RIGHT** Class 2884 No 3817 heads a down train of iron ore near Solihull on 20 August 1963. *M. Mensing*

For a locomotive works imbued with tradition, the construction and maintenance of these 'foreign' types was revelatory, exerting a profound impact on the insular Swindon culture. Hawksworth took heed by adopting new construction methods with the 'Modified Halls' and 'Counties' (as discussed in Chapter 4) and with the new post-war designs described below.

### The GWR eight-coupled fleet

Churchward's classic 2-8-0, first introduced in 1903, performed with consummate ease as the company's premier freight type, and by 1919 a total of 84 were in service. Construction then ceased with the availability of 'ROD' 2-8-0s of Great Central design origin, which had been built for war service and many of which had served in France. Continental European operators tried to purchase many of these engines after the war, but in its wisdom the British government insisted on their return to the UK. Disposal as war surplus material became a prolonged matter, with the asking price slashed in view of flagging buyer interest. Excluding 84 locomotives on short-term hire between 1919 and 1922 (some of which were later bought by the company), the GWR's purchase of 'RODs' fell into three categories:

**Nos 3000-19:** built in 1919 and acquired that year in virtually new condition

**Nos 3020-49:** built 1917 to 1919, fully reconditioned at Swindon in 1926-27

**Nos 3050-99:** built 1917 to 1919, deemed fit for limited service; given minor attention at Swindon in 1926-27; withdrawn by 1931

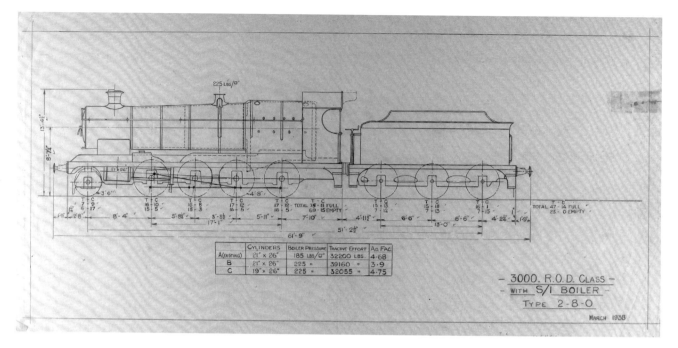

| | CYLINDERS | BOILER PRESSURE | TRACTIVE EFFORT | AD. FAC. |
|---|---|---|---|---|
| A (EXISTING) | 21" x 26" | 185 LBS/☐" | 32200 LBS. | 4·68 |
| B | 21" x 26" | 225 " | 39160 " | 3·9 |
| C | 19" x 26" | 225 " | 32055 " | 4·75 |

– 3000. R.O.D. CLASS –
– WITH S/1 BOILER –
TYPE 2-8-0

MARCH 1938

**ABOVE** A further manifestation of Collett's penchant for rebuilding was this proposal of early 1938 to rebuild Class '30xx' 'RODs' with the Standard No 1 boiler. *NRM*

In March 1938 it was proposed to rebuild the remaining 50 examples with Standard No 1 boilers as described in the accompanying drawing. Between 1944 and 1949 a similar scheme instigated by Thompson on the LNER covered 58 engines (new Class 'O1') from the fleet of ex-GCR/ex-ROD 2-8-0s that had become that railway's standard heavy freight type. Gresley had applied differing rebuilding treatments to some of these engines, but Thompson's work was the most radical, with new boilers and outside motion. The wisdom of reusing mainframes that were the 25-30 years old was questionable, and the same reservation applied to the GWR scheme.

A more sensible strategy commenced in the same month as the 'ROD'/No 1 boiler idea with the modernised version of Class '28xx', distinguished by the standard Collett side-window cab; 82 (Nos 2884-99 and 3800-66) appeared up to December 1942. The type's competence was recognised in a plan to build another 60 for military service overseas (where the loading gauge would not have been an issue), but this was rescinded following the fall of France. Post-1940 construction of Class '2884' comprised the residue of orders for GWR use:

| Lot No | Nos |
|---|---|
| 334 (part) | 3832-33 in 1941 |
| 341 | 3834 in 1941, 3835-43 in 1942 |
| 346 | 3844-66 in 1942 |

The remaining initiative with 2-8-0 tender locomotives derived from earlier tank engine designs and Swindon's focus on engineering at the expense of recognising market demand, specifically in the overproduction of Class '42xx' 2-8-0Ts. The timing of Lot No 233 (Nos 5245-74) of 1925-26 had been unfortunate, given the General Strike and decline in South Wales coal production, but nonetheless building resumed with Lot No 266, initially intended for 30 new

**BELOW** At Newport (Ebbw Junction) shed yard on 23 June 1963 are five Class '42xx' engines out of steam. Closest to the camera is No 5255, with Nos 5234, 4248, 5217, 5229 standing behind in that order. No 5255 was the first of the batch of ten built in 1940 and differs from the others in the raised footplate over the cylinders. *M. J. Stretton*

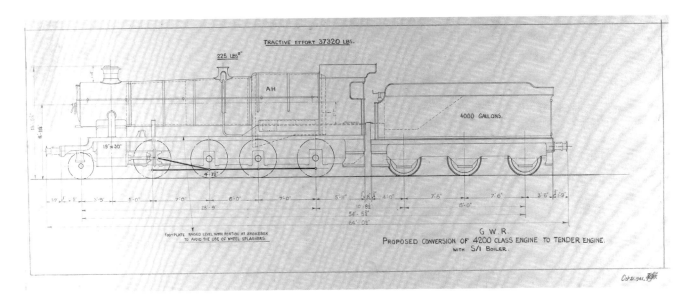

TRACTIVE EFFORT 37320 LBS.

225 LBS

AH

4000 GALLONS.

19"×30"

4'-7½"

FOOTPLATE RAISED LEVEL WITH PORTION AT SMOKEBOX
TO AVOID THE USE OF WHEEL SPLASHERS.

G.W.R.
PROPOSED CONVERSION OF 4200 CLASS ENGINE TO TENDER ENGINE.
WITH S/I BOILER.

**ABOVE** The proposal of October 1941 to rebuild Class '42xx' as a 2-8-0 with the Standard No 1 boiler. *NRM*

locomotives. Nos 5275-94 appeared in 1930, but the Lot was truncated by cancellation of Nos 5295-99 and 6200-04, while Lot No 270 (for Nos 6205-14) was cancelled completely in 1932. By then Nos 5265-94 were in store, some never having undertaken revenue-earning service.

Designed primarily for short-distance heavy mineral working in South Wales, restricted coal and water capacities limited their usefulness. Between 1934 and 1936, Nos 5255-94 were rebuilt as Class '72xx' 2-8-2Ts, then between 1937 and 1939 another 14 older examples were similarly treated. Their field of operations was thus expanded, but these impressive-looking machines could not be regarded as totally satisfactory. Axle loading excluded the use of the Standard No 1 boiler, fuel and water capacities were less than those of the Class '28xx', and their long overall wheelbase of 35ft 3in made them curve-shy on uneven track. These features reflected the design challenges endemic with large tank locomotives, where so much had to be crammed into the confined volume prescribed by a single carrying frame and the UK loading gauge.

Somewhat inconsistently, with Lot No 329 Collett resumed building Class '42xx' 2-8-0Ts in 1940 with (new) Nos 5255-64, but the remaining ten (Nos 5265-74) were cancelled in May 1941, shortly before his retirement. A basic change in direction during that period was evident in the proposal to rebuild members of Class '42xx' as 2-8-0s with Standard No 1 boilers. This intriguing design is so obvious a solution to a motive power need as to pose the question why it had not been considered earlier. Collett's treatment of Classes '42xx'/'72xx' had been characteristically minimalistic, resulting in the less-than-ideal 2-8-2T, whose abilities fell short of Class '28xx'. There were parallels in this cautious approach to the rebuilding of 'Saint' No 2925, which led to the

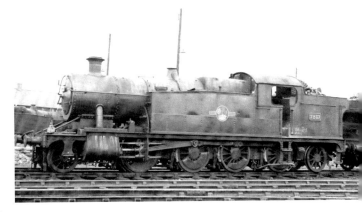

**ABOVE** Class '72xx' No 7237 stands at Newport (Ebbw Junction) shed on 19 November 1961. The first 20 of this class were rebuilds of Class '42xx' Nos 5245-74, which incorporated the raised footplate as with the second No 5255 depicted above. Later conversions, of which No 7237 was one, retained the straight footplate. This side view emphasises the considerable length of the rebuild.

'Halls', when more radical thinking could have yielded a still better engine, as finally emerged with the 'Granges'.

The drawing of October 1941 depicts a design suitable for the times with a higher pitched boiler and higher running plate to facilitate accessibility plus an austerity styled-windowless cab. These features were uncharacteristic of Swindon traditions and the proposal was contrary to Hawksworth's preference for new construction over rebuilding. Excluding completion of orders for Class '2884', this proposal was the final expression of GWR eight-coupled practice.

Leading dimensions of actual and proposed eight-coupled types are shown in Table 1.

| | | | | | | | |
|---|---|---|---|---|---|---|---|
| | | | | TABLE 1 | | | |
| Class/Type | Wheel arrangement | Cylinders | Max axle load | Coal | Water (gal) | Boiler pressure (lb/sq in) | TE (lb) |
| '28xx'/'2884' | 2-8-0 | 18.5in x 30in | 17 tons 5 cwt* | 6 tons | 3,500 | 225 | 35,380 |
| '28xx' with No 7 boiler | 2-8-0 | 18.5in x 30in | 18 tons 15 cwt | 6 tons | 3,500 | 225 | 35,380 |
| 4700 (prototype) | 2-8-0 | 19in x 30in | 17 tons 16 cwt | 6 tons | 3,500 | 225 | 30,460 |
| '47xx' | 2-8-0 | 19in x 30in | 19 tons 12 cwt | 6 tons | 4,000 | 225 | 30,460 |
| 'ROD' | 2-8-0 | 21in x 26in | 17 tons 7 cwt | 6 tons | 4,000 | 185 | 32,200 |
| 'ROD' with No 1 boiler | 2-8-0 | 21in x 26in | 17 tons 12 cwt | 6 tons | 4,000 | 225 | 39,160 |
| | | 19in x 26in | | | | 225 | 32,055 |
| '42xx'* | 2-8-0T | 19in x 30in | 18 tons 14 cwt | 4 tons 2 cwt | 1,800 | 225 | 33,170 |
| '72xx' | 2-8-2T | 19in x 30in | 18 tons 14 cwt | 6 tons | 2,500 | 225 | 33,170 |
| '42xx' rebuilt with tender | 2-8-0 | 19in x 30in | ** | 6 tons | 4,000 | 225 | 33,170 |

* Later examples
** Maximum axle loading is not stated but is unlikely to have been significantly different from Class '28xx'/'2884'

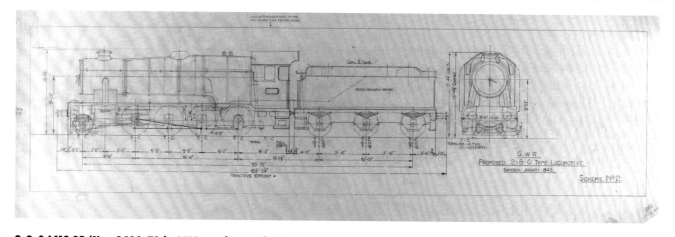

### 2-8-0 LMS 8F (Nos 8400-79 in LMS number series)

These were of standard design, built to orders of the Ministry of Supply and formally lent to the GWR until 1946/47. Workshop tools acquired for their construction were retained and used most notably in providing the 'Counties' with a shortened version of the 8F boiler. This episode would have reminded Hawksworth of earlier collaboration with Stanier, while giving the latter satisfaction in seeing his old employer build one of his fine designs.

On transfer to the LMS, they were replaced by War Department 2-8-0s that had been built after cessation of hostilities. In the 1950s, with the remaining Class 'ROD' 30xx 2-8-0s due for withdrawal, a number of Stanier 8Fs were transferred back to BR's Western Region, including some that had been built at Swindon. Of those that stayed on the London Midland Region, four (Nos 48400, 48410, 48423 and 48476) stayed in service until the end of British Railways steam in August 1968. The Swindon-built 8Fs were:

**ABOVE** A drawing of the proposed 2-8-0 with a Stanier 8F boiler, which is incomplete as estimated weights are not included. This seems to have been an exploration of what could be done with this boiler, although, judging by the date, the exercise was superfluous as 8F production was shortly to commence. The chassis is a modified version of that for Class '28xx' with a higher pitch for the boiler and a raised footplate to eliminate splashers. *NRM*

| Lot No | Nos |
|---|---|
| 348 | 8400-09 in 1943 |
| 349 | 8410-26 in 1943, 8427-29 in 1944 |
| 351 | 8430-39 in 1944 |
| 353 | 8440-62 in 1944, 8463-79 in 1945 |

ABOVE Three generations of 2-8-0 appear in this view taken at St Philip's Marsh, Bristol, on 16 June 1957. In the foreground is LMS-design 8F No 48410, built at Swindon in 1943. Behind the Stanier engine is a 'WD' 2-8-0, and behind that a GWR Class '2884'. In conjunction with the withdrawal of the remaining First World War vintage 'ROD' 2-8-0s of Class '30xx', a number of Stanier 8Fs were transferred to BR's Western Region in the 1950s. They were distinguishable by the modified ejector pipe on the left-hand side of the boiler. *R. K. Blencowe negative archive*

ABOVE Late in their careers a number of Stanier 8Fs acquired Fowler-type 3,500 tenders in an exchange with 'Jubilees'. No 48426 was at Carlisle, Kingmoor, on 11 July 1964 with a tender that looked as equally incongruous as it previously had with the 4-6-0s. *R. K. Blencowe collection*

## 0-6-0 Class '2251'

This class was introduced in 1930 as a replacement for the 0-6-0 Dean Goods, the earlier examples of which were by then well over 40 years old. Sixty had appeared by September 1939, and 20 more were built in 1940 in partial substitution for the 108 Dean Goods sold that year into military service. The shortfall was covered by 2F and 3F

ABOVE The final batch of Class '2251' engines (Nos 3200 to 3219) was built between February 1946 and January 1948. The time taken to complete delivery indicates the pressures on Swindon during this period and the low priority accorded expansion of this class. No 3200 is in tidy condition at Oswestry on 29 August 1954 with a considerably older tender. *John K. Morton*

0-6-0s on loan from the LMS, and Class 'J25' from the LNER. These locomotives were returned to their native systems from 1944 onwards.

The need for more small tender locomotives for secondary services was briefly considered in 1944 in the form of a lightweight outside-cylinder 4-4-0, largely to replace remaining outside-framed 4-4-0s. The accompanying drawing shows a combination of Standard No 10 boiler, modern cab, and outside Walschaerts valve gear, together with inclined cylinders (another departure from tradition). By comparison, the Class '2251' could be considered regressive, but the 4-4-0 was a specialised design with limited applicability. It was evidently concluded that more 0-6-0s were more appropriate, and construction restarted in October 1944.

BELOW This appears to have been an informal sketch rather than a properly sanctioned design exercise, as by the late 1940s there would have been little need for a modern replacement of the few remaining outside-framed 4-4-0s. Its principal value is in demonstrating how far modern thinking on cylinder and valve layout had permeated. *NRM*

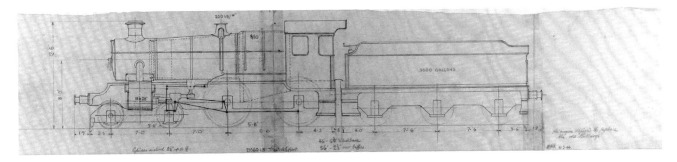

**ABOVE** No 3219, introduced in January 1948, had the distinction of being the second 0-6-0 built by BR and the last of this wheel arrangement built for service in England. *M. Edwards*

**ABOVE** Class '31xx' 2-6-2T No 3141, built in March 1906, was part of the first batch of 'Large Prairie' tanks introduced by Churchward. These engines went through changes such as lowering the cab roof, installation of outside steam pipes and adoption of curved front drop ends. No 3141 became No 5141 in January 1929 and survived until October 1952. *Ian Allan Library*

Although generally similar in size and power, the use of the heavier taper boiler placed them in the 'Yellow' route availability category, which meant that they could not entirely replace the uncoloured Dean Goods. Their duties typically comprised longer-distance branch services and pick-up freight trains. Their construction was accorded low priority:

| Lot No | Nos |
|--------|-----|
| 347 | 2231-40 in 1944, 2241-50 in 1945 |
| 360 | 3200-09 in 1946, 3210-17 in 1947, 3218-19 in 1948 |

## The tank classes

The tradition of tank engine orientation was never more apparent than in the 15 years up to 1956, when construction averaged almost 40 per annum. This was remarkable considering the industry-wide development of diesel shunters, and the impending expansion of the diesel multiple unit fleet. An indication of how out-of-step was this programme compared with contemporary trends was the GWR-designed diesel shunters Nos 15101-15106, delivered in 1948 and working until 1967. Two hundred Class '94xxs' built between 1949 and 1956 had all gone by the end of 1965.

## 2-6-2T Class '51xx'

The history of the 'Large Prairie' tanks was complex, starting with the prototype No 99 (later the first No 3100), which was built under Churchward's 1901 Scheme. When Hawksworth was appointed CME, the 'Large Prairie' fleet could be summarised as shown in Table 2.

At the end of 1930 this fleet had been at its most homogeneous, with Class '5100' and the new Class '5101' (then under construction) carrying Standard No 2 boilers, while Class '3150'

**BELOW** Class '81xx' 2-6-2T No 8109 stands at Swindon shed on 24 September 1956. There were ten members of this class, created by rebuilding withdrawn members of Class '51xx' – this particular engine had been No 5115. This programme, started by Collett in September 1938, was truncated by the Second World War, with No 8109 appearing as the last example in November 1939. Plans had covered 50 engines (Nos 5100 and 5111 to 5149, plus possibly Nos 5101 to 5110 that had been built as recently as 1929), but the scheme was not revived after the war. Class '81xx' had all the latest refinements applied to the 'Large Prairies', including new No 2 boilers with 225 lb per sq in pressure, more modern curved drop ends and the lower-profile cab roof. They were intended for suburban passenger services and closely resembled Class '61xx' except for having 5ft 6in driving wheels to aid acceleration. It is doubtful whether the cost of this deviation from the Churchward standard was justified. *G. Wheeler*

| | | | | | TABLE 2 | |
|---|---|---|---|---|---|---|
| Class | Running Nos | Introduced | Boiler | BP (lb/sq in) | Driving wheels | Comments |
| '51xx' | 5100/5111-49 | Sep 03 to Mar 06 | No 2 | 200 | 5ft 8in | Previously old Class '31xx' renumbered in same sequence 1928-30 (less ten later rebuilt as Class '81xx') |
| '5101' | 5101-10/5150-99/4100-39 | Nov 29 to Dec 39 | No 2 | 200 | 5ft 8in | Built as new engines |
| '61xx' | 6100-69 | Apr 31 to Nov 35 | No 2 | 225 | | Built as new engines |
| '81xx' | 8100-09 | Sep 38 to Nov 39 | No 2 | 225 | 5ft 6in | Rebuilds of Class '51xx' |
| '3150' | 3150-90 | Apr 11 to Jan 08 | No 4 | 200 | 5ft 8in | Less five rebuilt as new Class '3100' |
| '3100' | 3100-04 | Dec 38 to Oct 39 | No 4 | 225 | 5ft 3in | Rebuilds of Class '3150' |

**RIGHT** Class '5101' No 4177 was one of the last of the type, introduced by BR in November 1949. It is in early BR lined mixed-traffic livery at Penarth. *B. J. Miller*

used the Standard No 4 boiler. Although there were minor variations among the older locomotive as details were modernised, all major dimensions were in conformity. In 1931 the Class '61xx', with higher boiler pressure, was introduced for London area suburban services, where they were welcome replacements for the unpopular 4-4-2T 'County Tanks'.

The Class '61xx', with 5ft 8in driving wheels, wrought a considerable improvement, and in early 1932 No 6116 was rebuilt with 5ft 3in driving wheels to improve accelerative capacity further. This was part of a programme to test the concept of 'high acceleration locomotives' – see Chapter 8.

In 1938 Collett started two new classes ('81xx' and '31xx') by rebuilding first-generation small- and large-boilered 'Prairie' tanks, a programme that stopped with the war. Fifteen locomotives so rebuilt were created between September 1938 and November 1939, while in October to December 1939 another 18 new members of Class '5101' were introduced. Therefore, in the two calendar years 1938 and 1939, 33 'Large Prairies' were introduced, among which were two different boiler sizes, two different boiler pressures, and three different driving wheel diameters. The Class '81xx' engines (like the earlier '61xxs') were mainly confined to suburban passenger work, but the remainder seemed to have been used indiscriminately on a variety of duties.

Once again there had been concurrent introduction of different classes broadly intended for the same type of work. The cause would appear to have been Collett's passion for management accounting gymnastics, and if this was indeed the case he seems to have lost the plot in injecting complexity for little or no identifiable advantage. The traffic profile was essentially unchanged from the 1900s, and it is difficult to understand what he was intending. Above all, it was paradoxical that this arch-disciple of the Churchward model could reject well-founded proposals (e.g.

higher degree superheat), but then complicate the core vision of standardisation.

Hawksworth showed clarity of thought by simplifying this muddled situation. He abandoned plans for more of Classes '81xx' and '31xx' (new) through rebuilding, and reverted to 40 new examples of Class '5101' to replace life-expired members of Classes '51xx' and '3150'. Later replacements of the early 'Large Prairies' took the form of BR Standard 2-6-2Ts before the onset of dieselisation. The Hawksworth 'Prairies' were:

| Lot No | Nos |
|---|---|
| 335 | 4140-49 in 1946 |
| 361 | 4150-59 in 1947 |
| 369 | 4160-69 in 1948, 4170-79 in 1949 |

### 0-6-0 pannier tanks

Construction of the archetypal GWR tank locomotive continued unabated through the war, and extended beyond nationalisation, last examples appearing in 1956:

**ABOVE** William Dean's first six-coupled tank engine was No 1813, built in September 1882 as a side tank, converted to saddle in 1897, and to pannier in 1903. It was the direct ancestor of the Swindon larger pannier tank lineage – Dean's Classes '1854' and '2721' and Collett's Class '57xx', concluding with Hawksworth's '94xx'. While still a side tank, No 1813 was sold to the Pembroke & Tenby Railway, where it became No 7 and acquired the name *Holmwood*. It returned to the GWR in 1896 and retained its name through the tank changes until withdrawal in 1928. *Stephenson Locomotive Society*

| Class | Number built | Running Nos |
|-------|--------------|-------------|
| '57xx' | 226 | 3687-99/4600-99/6570-79/9600-82 |
| '74xx' | 20 | 7430-49 |
| '94xx' | 210 | 3400-09/8400-99/9400-99 |
| '15xx' | 10 | 1500-09 |
| '16xx' | 70 | 1600-69 |

### Classes '57xx' and '74xx'

These were continuations of pre-war types that do not warrant particular mention except to note that the smaller Class '74xx' was introduced for routes where Class '57xx' engines were prohibited. The need for this distinction was eliminated by reassessment of route availability of the larger type in 1950 ('Blue' to 'Yellow' category). Post-1940 construction:

**ABOVE** Crossing point: No 8749 on the 7.35am Llanelly-Llandillo train passes No 9621 on the 8.25am Llandovery-Llanelly at Derwydd Road on 25 July 1962. The engine on the left was the last of Class '57xx' to be built with the old-style cab (in 1931), while the other was built under Hawksworth in October 1945. *L. Sandler*

**ABOVE** The Class '74xx' 0-6-0PTs were introduced in 1932. No 7439 was one of ten ordered by Hawksworth and delivered in 1948 (ten more appeared in 1950). They were outwardly similar to Class '57xx' but had a smaller boiler (with a pressure of 165 lb per sq in), giving them 'Yellow' route availability. This distinction was eliminated in 1950 with re-categorisation of Class '57xx' to 'Yellow' (except for the condensing engines of series 9700 to 9710). *J. N. Westwood*

**LEFT** Class '57xx' No 9672 is at Swindon in April 1958. Only 30 more of this large class were completed after this engine appeared in June 1948. *R. K. Evans*

| Lot No | Nos |
|---|---|
| 330 (part) | 3687-99, 4600-04 in 1941, 4605-34 in 1942 |
| 336 | 4635-41 in 1942, 4642-60 in 1943 |
| 352 | 4661-67 in 1943, 4668-89 in 1944, 4690-99, 9600-21 in 1945 |
| 355 | 9622-32 in 1945, 9633-9641 in 1946 |
| 356 | 9642-51 in 1946 |
| 362 | 9652-61 in 1946, 6750-59 in 1947 |
| 370 | 9662-72 in 1948 |
| 371 | 7430-39 in 1948 |
| 374 | 6760-65 in 1948, 6766-69 in 1949 |
| 378 | 9673-82 in 1949 |
| 379 | 6770-79 in 1950 |
| 380 | 7440-49 in 1950 |

## Class '94xx'

Hawksworth apparently intended to add more of Class '57xx' beyond those delivered up to 1950. At the start of 1945 80 of Class '1854' (built 1890-95) and the entire 80-strong Class '2721' (1897-1901), together with even older examples of the genre, were due for replacement. As the largest remaining contingent of pre-Grouping GWR origin, this was a natural continuation of the modernisation programme. New construction would also eliminate the remaining engines absorbed from the Welsh companies. The Class '56xx' 0-6-2Ts had allowed removal of older, heterogeneous elements in the 1920s, and that wheel arrangement had been a deferral to local tradition. It was later recognised that 0-6-0PTs would have been adequate for working most coal traffic, i.e. loaded trains downhill from the valleys to the docks.

**BELOW** Only ten of Class '94xx' were built at Swindon, of which No 9409 was the last example; contractors constructed another 200 after nationalisation. The Swindon engines differed from the rest in having the space between the frames on the front running plate enclosed with a sloping panel. Internally, they were fitted with superheaters, an expensive luxury for engines expected to be engaged in short-distance work and shunting. *A. R. Carpenter*

**ABOVE** No 9410 displays the open space between the frames that was typical of the remainder of the class. All the contractor-built engines had saturated boilers. *Brian Morrison*

When approval for more of Class '57xx' was sought, Sir James Milne (apparently reflecting the wishes of the Board) asked for a modern appearance, apparently because the traditional pannier tank did not reflect a progressive image. Certainly, the domeless Class '94xx' was to be much in evidence on empty carriage work at Paddington, the location where the public was most likely to come into close contact with tank engines. Maybe a more forceful CME would have stood his ground, insisting that a variation on the 0-6-0PT theme was unreasonably expensive.

The easiest way of achieving the desired effect was to use the Standard No 10, which was the smallest domeless boiler. Originally designed for rebuilding locomotives from South Wales, it had been adopted for the Class '2251' 0-6-0s. The first scheme for the new class was prepared in 1945 with drawings (numbered 1 and 2, both dated June 1945), clearly depicting the Standard No 10 boiler. Drawing No 1 shows shallow, full-length 1,250-gallon pannier tanks, while drawing No 2 has tanks shortened so that the front face is just behind the chimney centre line, with capacity reduced to 1,210 gallons. This version states 'smokebox and cylinders as for 2251'. Drawing No 3, dated July 1945, shows 1,300-gallon tanks, with their front face in line with the chimney centre line.

The first ten of Class '94xx' appeared between February and May 1947 as a smaller-wheeled tank version of Class '2251'. This echoed the earlier practice of creating tank versions of tender engines and vice versa, reflecting the relationship between the Dean Goods and larger 0-6-0STs of the 19th century. However, just as Class '2251', by virtue of its heavier taper boiler, could not entirely replace the older 0-6-0, so Class '94xx' suffered a similar weight penalty in comparison with Class '57xx'.

In some areas weight was not a great drawback. Many Welsh Valleys routes were short but built to trunk-line standards. Class '56xx' engines had 'Red' route availability and, at the time of the arrival of Class '94xx', approximately 140 pre-Grouping Welsh engines remained

**ABOVE** An unidentified member of Class '94xx' at Bagnall's works on 10 September 1949. *Modern Transport*

in service that were similarly restricted. However, as traffic in that area declined together with contraction of secondary services elsewhere, an 0-6-0 tank engine with route availability equivalent to that of a 'Castle' became increasingly superfluous. Extended periods in store and short working lives were inevitable; the most extreme example was No 9499, built in May 1955 and withdrawn in September 1959.

Mechanically, the new engines were similar to earlier pannier tanks except that trailing axle coil springs were replaced with under-hung leaf springs. This yielded more space in the cab, but to the detriment of riding qualities. Externally, the width over the welded pannier tanks at 8ft 7in matched that of the cab and bunker. This allowed for 100 gallons more water and 4 cwt more coal but, as with the 'Counties', direct access from the cab to the front end was no longer possible; it was necessary to descend to ground level and use the footsteps mounted on the running plate valences, equidistant between the leading and centre axles. The capacity increases were of marginal benefit for engines habitually used on short-distance work, but the wider cab was a definite disadvantage; look-out was reduced through the spectacle plates, and the brake valve handle had to be extended as initially it could not be reached by the driver while leaning out of the cab, as was essential during shunting. Also, the wider cab reduced clearance in confined areas – goods sheds and near lineside structures, for example. These shortcomings suggest lack of awareness of everyday running conditions.

Construction seems to have been initiated in haste by diverting materials earmarked for new Class '2251' engines. If this was indeed the case, it would explain why the first ten engines had superheaters. It is doubtful whether the extra cost and greater weight of taper boilers yielded any worthwhile benefit for smaller locomotives on secondary work, but it had long been recognised that superheaters yielded a net deficit. For short journeys, or work involving coasting or long periods stationary, there was usually ample time for a boiler to recover from strenuous use, making a

superheater detrimental to fuel consumption. Nos 9400-09 were unique in being the only superheated pannier tanks. Nevertheless, a source who worked with the class has reported that they were masters of the work to which they were assigned, and the superheated examples were competent on reasonably loaded semi-fast duties, aided by their adequate boiler capacity.

The greatest measure of obloquy heaped upon this class, apparently arising latterly, relates to the prolonged construction period. Delivery of the later examples has been criticised in the context of dieselisation then in hand – a situation akin to that with later members of the BR Standard 2-10-0 9Fs. With hindsight it is easy to criticise on the grounds that too many were delivered too late. However, construction was a continuation of the well-established scrap-and-replace programme, and in 1947 it was not clear what would be the policy under new ownership. In these circumstances, the decision was reasonable, based on information available and on the need to displace ageing motive power.

**ABOVE** Class '94xx' No 9468 is seen in brand-new condition at Swindon, shortly after delivery from Robert Stephenson & Hawthorn Ltd. The coupling rods are still to be fitted. *R. H. G. Simpson*

**BELOW** Swindon was engaged in overhauling steam engines into the 1960s. No 8481 is at Swindon on 23 April 1964 following a General Repair. *G. H. Wheeler*

**RIGHT** A case of Class '94xx' engines in foreign parts was the loan of No 9401 to BR Eastern Region at Stratford in 1957, as shown here in company with ex-LNER Class '12/3' No 61573. The arrangement lasted only a few days as apparently the 0-6-0PT took offence at the sharp curves that abounded in the yards of east London, and presumably because the crews did not like an engine that was not one of 'their own'.

Whether so many were really needed forms part of broader questions concerning utilisation, as discussed in Chapter 2.

Construction of Nos 9410 to 9459 under Lot No 382 was intended to commence at Swindon in 1948, but continuing supply and capacity issues led to none appearing that year. All remaining examples were built by contractors, with deliveries starting in 1949. Lot 382 was actually built complete by Robert Stephenson & Hawthorn in 1950/51, while the remaining 150 contractor-built engines used boilers manufactured at Swindon.

The decision to outsource could not evade the issue of material shortages, particularly steel, which plagued all manufacturing industry, and GWR/BR Western Region management had little experience in negotiating for supply of locomotives from contractors. Significant numbers had been acquired in this manner before the war to meet different conditions, i.e. spare manufacturing capacity and relief of unemployment. The '94xx' contracts were somewhat loosely worded and, with little commercial experience upon which to draw, the parties in good faith strove to work out the situation in what was considered the best way possible. Unfortunately the industry was changing rapidly, making decisions taken in 1947 increasingly anachronistic by the early 1950s. There was tacit acceptance of a costly situation, when decisive action to cancel and to agree compensation would have been preferable.

In earlier times, with a completely in-house manufacturing programme, planned locomotives later considered surplus to requirements would have invoked cancellation and reallocation of surplus materials to other projects. The Class '94xx' story was a forerunner of the contractual structures now common for railway activities that rely heavily on outsourcing. The construction programme is shown in Table 3.

Delivery, by years, took place as shown in Table 4.

| TABLE 3 | | | |
|---|---|---|---|
| **Lot No** | **Builder** | **Nos** | **Builder's Nos** |
| 365 | GWR Swindon | 9400-09 in 1947 | - |
| 382 | Robert Stephenson & Hawthorn, Newcastle | 9410-33 in 1950, 9439-59 in 1951 | 7547-96 |
| 383 | Robert Stephenson & Hawthorn, Newcastle | 9460-62 in 1951, 9463-88 in 1952, 9489 in 1953 | 7611-40 |
| 384 | W. G. Bagnall | 8400-07 in 1949, 8408-24 in 1950, 8425-29 in 1951, 8430-39 in 1953, 8440-49 in 1954 | Between 2910 and 2959 |
| 385 | Yorkshire Engine Co | 8450-54 in 194, 8455-66 in 1950, 8467-75 in 1951, 8476-79 in 1952 | Between 2443 and 2472 |
| 386 | Robert Stephenson & Hawthorn, Darlington (as sub-contractor to Hudswell Clarke) | 8480-99 in 1952 | 7450-7469 |
| 387 | Yorkshire Engine Co (as sub-contractor to Hunslet Engine Co) | 9490-97 in 1954, 9489-99, 3400 in 1955, 2544-53, 2575, 3401-09 in 1956 | 2576-84 |

| TABLE 4 | | | | | | | | | | | |
|---|---|---|---|---|---|---|---|---|---|---|---|
| **Builder** | **1947** | **1948** | **1949** | **1950** | **1951** | **1952** | **1953** | **1954** | **1955** | **1956** | **Total** |
| GWR Swindon | 10 | | | | | | | | | | 10 |
| Robert Stephenson & Hawthorn, Newcastle | | | | 24 | 29 | 26 | 1 | | | | 80 |
| W. G. Bagnall | | | 8 | 17 | 5 | | 10 | 10 | | | 50 |
| Yorkshire Engine Co | | | 5 | 12 | 9 | 4 | | 8 | 3 | 9 | 50 |
| Robert Stephenson & Hawthorn, Darlington | | | | | | 20 | | | | | 20 |
| **Total** | **10** | **0** | **13** | **53** | **63** | **30** | **11** | **18** | **3** | **9** | **210** |

## Class '15xx'

Although the prototype of this class did not appear until mid-1949, it was apparent that the acceptance of outside valve motion for Swindon-designed locomotives occurred some years previously. The earliest drawing of what eventually appeared as Class '15xx' was dated 28 February 1944, thus substantiating the recurring speculation concerning the GWR's intentions.

Above footplate level, there was dimensional and physical resemblance to Class '94xx', but the chassis was quite different. Main-line British 0-6-0 tank locomotives with outside cylinders were usually restricted to smaller types, but the US Army Transportation Corps had favoured this layout for its shunting locomotives. Known as the 'USA' tanks, the Southern Railway purchased 14 from the War Department in 1947. Although conceptually similar, there is no evidence of that type directly influencing the Swindon design.

The inclined outside cylinders required the leading driving wheels to be sited further back, and to provide the requisite balance the trailing axle was placed further forward. This reduced the overall wheelbase to 12ft 10in (compared with 15ft 6in for Classes '57xx' and '94xx'), thus confining the type to slow-speed work. The shorter wheelbase allowed curves as tight as 3½ chains radius to be negotiated, although the engines were not heavily used in docks and yards where such features abounded; their weight would have limited their usefulness in such locations where uneven, poorly laid track was common.

Low maintenance was a key expectation and, being bereft of running plate and splashers, their appearance was suitably austere. They were distinctly un-GWR in using single slide-bars and in lacking a crosshead vacuum pump (there being no room to mount one). As with Class '94xx', welded construction of the superstructure was used wherever feasible.

**RIGHT** Several of the class were used on empty carriage workings into and out of Paddington, for which work they were painted in BR lined black mixed-traffic livery. No 1504 is at Old Oak Common on 17 November 1957. *C. P. Boocock*

**LEFT** The penultimate class designed under GWR auspices was the BR Class '15xx' 0-6-0PT, which appeared after nationalisation. Tanks, boiler, cab and bunker were in the style initiated with Class '94xx', but there were significant changes to the chassis. The outside cylinders and Walschaerts valve gear were departures from traditional practice, confirming Hawksworth's exploration of fresh (for the GWR) design principles. Outside cylinders dictated that the wheelbase had to be short while the thrust effect of outside motion induced instability at speed. These engines were therefore a specialised heavy shunter that provided an inkling of where GWR design practice might have gone next with a larger engine using a leading bogie or pony truck. No 1501 is at rest at Southall on 8 May 1960. *A. A. G. Delicata*

**BELOW** Class '15xx' engines were often used on shed pilot duties. No 1502 is on a locomotive coal train at the entrance to Oxford shed yard on 12 May 1953. *Dr G. D. Parkes*

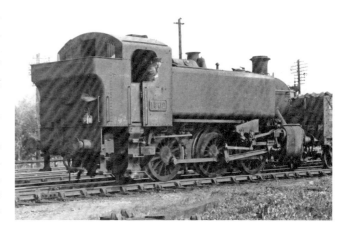

Despite the efforts towards simplicity and austerity, the Class '15xx' engines were the heaviest of all the panniers by virtue of the outside motion and the cross-bracing needed to support the cylinders. From inception the pannier concept had been a brilliant compromise between saddle and side tanks that neatly avoided the poor access implicit with the latter. While the 15xx layout improved access yet further, this advantage was offset by

ABOVE Class '15xx' also penetrated South Wales. No 1507 is at Newport. *Ian Allan Library*

the weight factor, which constrained their sphere of operations. They were mainly used on empty stock workings at Paddington and heavy shunting at Newport. They were constructed in a single Lot:

| Lot No | Nos |
|--------|-----|
| 373 | 1500-09 in 1949 |

Viewed in the round, neither Class '94xx' nor Class '15xx' yielded sufficient benefits to justify the presence of either. More Class '57xx' engines would have been cheaper and more sensible – regardless of that offending dome.

### Class '16xx'

If the taper-boilered types threatened a design revolution, the very last pannier tank class was a reassuring reversion to tradition. At nationalisation all but 20 of the 140-strong Class '2021', built

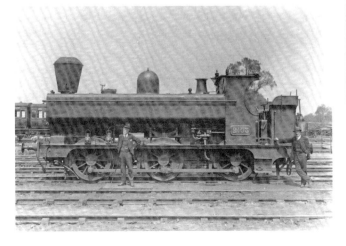

ABOVE There can be no stronger evidence of Swindon's commitment to its traditions than with the final class of pannier tanks. Class '16xx' No 1600 is at Swindon shed on 6 June 1959. The cab and bunker are of modern design but this engine is an obvious descendant of No 2103 in the photograph below left. Introduced after nationalisation, this class was pure Great Western in every respect. *P. H. Wells*

BELOW Class '16xx' No 1616 is seen at Gloucester, fitted with a spark arrester chimney. *P. J. Sharpe*

LEFT Small 0-6-0 tank engines were useful machines that reached all parts of the system on a variety of secondary duties. Class '2021' No 2103 was just such an example, built in 1902 as a saddle tank and equipped with pannier tanks in 1917. The date and location of this view are unknown, but the engine has a spark arrester chimney that was fitted late during the First World War for shunting at sensitive locations such as ammunition stores. *Ian Allan Library*

**ABOVE** Class '16xx' No 1622 at Cardiff Canton on 24 June 1956.
*R. J. Buckley*

between 1897 and 1905, remained in service, together with more than 40 of the similar but older Class '850'. These Wolverhampton-built engines were smaller than the main body of 0-6-0PTs, and their uncoloured route availability made them especially useful. At nationalisation they were the remaining significant element of the pre-Grouping fleet and their replacement was facilitated by 70 of Class '16xx', a design for which the earliest drawing is dated 2 May 1946.

Other than their welded assembly, they were entirely traditional with attractive lines. They were widely distributed over routes with tight curves and restricted clearances. Delayed introduction was again caused by supply problems, and their careers paralleled those of Class '94xx' in replacing older locomotives, before becoming swiftly obsolete through service contraction and dieselisation. No 1669 was delivered as late as May 1955, yet withdrawals started less than four years later. With hindsight it would have been more economic to eke out the lives of the ageing members of Classes '850' and '2021' that they replaced. The construction programme:

| Lot No | Nos |
|--------|-----|
| 381 | 1600-19 in 1949, 1620-29 in 1950 |
| 389 | 1630-49 in 1951 |
| 417 | 1650-54 in 1954, 1655-69 in 1955 |

## Proposed 2-6-0PT

The drawing for this type is among the most interesting of the surviving records of GWR designs proposed but not constructed, providing further evidence of Swindon's acceptance of outside valve motion. The drawing's date of April 1945 indicates an intention to expand upon the 0-6-0PT Class '15xx' layout that had already been agreed, but which would not appear until after nationalisation. The degree to which outside motion had permeated design thinking is also borne out by the previously featured drawing of a 4-4-0 as a suggested replacement for surviving 'Bulldogs'. This is a detailed sketch rather than a formally endorsed proposal, while the 2-6-0PT provided an altogether more realistic basis for further development.

The combination of existing dimensions and components would have created a versatile design with a superior operating range to Classes '94xx' and '15xx'. Also, it is readily apparent that removal of the pannier tanks and shortening of the frames at the rear would have resulted in an austerity-style tender 'Mogul' with 'Yellow' or even uncoloured route availability.

The Dean Goods boiler was to remain in production until 1950 and the plan anticipated the use of this type, with modified firebox and top feed (the latter feature had appeared on a few of Class '2301'). In the hope that the Board would not take umbrage at retention of the dome, this would have been an ideal arrangement. Conceptually such a locomotive would have been similar to the LMS Ivatt Class 2 2-6-0 – whose steaming was improved following comparative testing at Swindon against a Dean Goods in 1949-50.

The leading dimensions of the six pannier tank classes constructed/planned under Hawksworth's auspices are shown in Table 5.

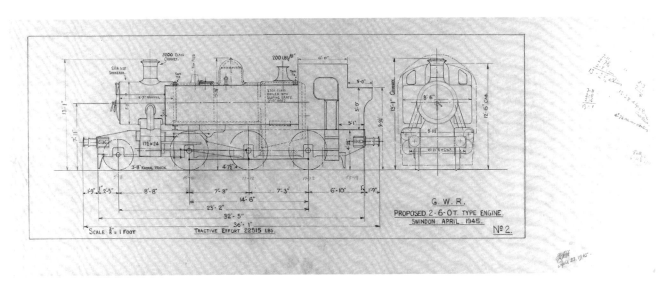

**ABOVE** The proposal for an 2-6-0PT with outside motion and inclined cylinders. *NRM*

| TABLE 5 | | | | | | |
|---|---|---|---|---|---|---|
| Class | '57xx' | '74xx' | '94xx' | '15xx' | '16xx' | 2-6-0PT (proposed) |
| Cylinders | 17.5in x 24in | 16.5in x 24in | 17.5in x 24in | 17.5in x 24in | 16.5in x 24in | 17.5in x 24in |
| Boiler | | | | | | |
| - barrel | 10ft 3in | 10ft 6in | 10ft 3in | 10ft 3in | 10ft 1in | 10ft 3in |
| - diameter | 4ft 5in | 4ft 3in | 4ft 5in-5ft 0in | 4ft 5in-5ft 0in | 3ft 10in | 4ft 5in |
| Firebox length | 5ft 3in | 5ft 6in | 6ft 0in | 6ft 0in | 5ft 0in | 4ft 8in |
| Heating surfaces (sq ft) | | | | | | |
| - tubes | 1,076 | 1,004 | 1,246* | 1,246 | 877 | 1,012 |
| - firebox | 102 | 82 | 102 | 102 | 80 | 102 |
| Grate (sq ft) | 15.3 | 16.8 | 17.4 | 17.4 | 14.9 | 15.3 |
| Boiler pressure (lb/sq in) | 200 | 165 | 200 | 200 | 165 | 200 |
| Wheel diameter | 4ft 7.5in | 4ft 7.5in | 4ft 7.5in | 4ft 7.5in | 4ft 1.5in | 4ft 7.5in |
| Wheelbase | 7ft 3in + 8ft 3in | 7ft 4in + 7ft 4in | 7ft 3in + 8ft 3in | 6in 4ft + 6ft 6in | 7ft 4in + 7ft 4in | 8ft 8in + 7ft 3in + 7ft 3in |
| Weight per axle | | | | | | |
| - pony truck | n/a | n/a | n/a | n/a | n/a | 5t 8c |
| - leading | 16t 15c | 14t 17c | 17t 2c | 19t 14c | 13t 16c | 15t 8c |
| - centre | 16t 15c | 15t 2c | 19t 0c | 19t 14c | 13t 18c | 17t 12c |
| - trailing | 14t 0c | 15t 13c | 19t 5c | 18t 16c | 13t 18c | 17t 12c |
| Total weight | 47t 10c | 45t 12c | 55t 7c | 58t 4c | 41t 12c | 55t 18c |
| Tractive effort (lb) | 22,515 | 16,510 | 22,515 | 22,515 | 18,515 | 22,515 |
| Tank capacity (gal) | 1,200 | 1,100 | 1,300 | 1,350 | c1,000 | 1,300** |
| Bunker capacity | 3t 6c | 3t 4c | 3t 10c | 3t 5c | 2t 10c | 3t 10c** |
| Route availability | Blue*** | Yellow | Red | Red | Uncoloured | Blue |

\* Nos 9400-9409: tubes, 1,069sq ft, superheater 74sq ft
\*\* Estimated
\*\*\* 'Yellow' after 1950, except Nos 9701-10

# CHAPTER 8
# FIXED-FORMATION TRAINS

Although the GWR had a penchant for random assembly of its coaching sets, combining different styles and vintages, there was a recurrent interest in forming trains on a fixed basis from the 1900s onwards. In a planning sense, the most advanced thinking about fixed-formation trains used diesel-electric power dating from early 1926, but this initiative lost momentum around 1931. The departure of Sir Felix Pole in 1929 and his subsequent pre-eminence in electrical manufacturing may not have been entirely coincidental in this regard. Fortunately, the principles of diesel power were not abandoned as single-unit mechanical-transmission vehicles made their appearance from 1933 forwards. The final examples (two powered DMU pairs) were precursors of the British Railways fleet, although it was not until the 1950s that BR adopted the basic DEMU principles that the GWR had started to consider in the 1920s.

## Steam railmotors and auto-trains

The GWR's experience with fixed-formation trains coincided with the span of Hawksworth's career. The first steps were a response to the competitive threat posed by the electric tramcar, which siphoned off commuter traffic that previously had been the sole

**ABOVE** Steam railmotor (SRM) No 30 was one of eight 59ft 6in branch-line units and the second of this type of vehicle to be built with panelling of similar style to contemporary 'Toplight' steam-hauled coaches; SRMs Nos 1 to 28 had been built with vertical matchboard sides. No 30 was built under Diagram H in January 1905 and was a late survivor, not being withdrawn until February 1935.

**RIGHT** SRM No 63, seen here in the lined all-brown livery and introduced in 1908, was a 70-foot vehicle for branch-line duties. Thirty-five SRMs were built to this format under Diagrams O and R, making them the most numerous type. Those numbered 61 to 72 of Diagram O were built by contractors, with the power units constructed by Kerr, Stuart and the bodies by Hurst, Nelson of Motherwell. They were identical with the Swindon-built variety except for the double doors to the passenger vestibule, whereas a single, wide door was more normal. Built in April 1906, No 63 survived in this form until September 1927, when it was converted to auto-trailer No 151 (Diagram A29). *Ian Allan Library*

preserve of the railways. Several companies experimented by combining a coach with a small steam power unit. Cab and controls in the coach end removed the need for a locomotive to run around the train at journey's end.

The GWR was the most prolific operator of the steam railmotor (SRM) in the pre-Grouping period. Ultimately the fleet comprised 99, introduced between October 1903 and February 1908. The range of operations was broadened, with later examples intended for branch-line services. In summary, the different types were:

| Coach number | Type | Body length | Number of seats |
|---|---|---|---|
| 1-2 | Suburban | 57ft | 52 |
| 3-8 | Suburban | 59ft 6in | 52 |
| 9-14 | Suburban | 59ft 6in | 54 |
| 17-28 | Branch | 59ft 6in | 51 |
| 29-36 | Branch | 59ft 6in | 49 |
| 37-40 | Branch | 70ft | 63 |
| 41-42 | Suburban | 59ft 6in | 50 |
| 43-52 | Suburban | 70ft | 64 |
| 53-58 | Branch | 70ft | 61 |
| 59-60 | Branch | 70ft | 63 |
| 61-72 | Branch | 70ft | 61 |
| 73-83 | Branch | 59'ft 6in | 45 |
| 84-99 | Branch | 70ft | 61 |

The engine units were 0-4-0VBTs with outside Walschaerts valve gear. Numbered in a separate series as 0801 to 0912, the 112 engine units were rotated on works visits so that each complete unit could be returned to work in the shortest possible time.

The SRM fleet was surprisingly large considering that the concept's disadvantages must have soon been apparent. In some areas they attracted new patronage, requiring attachment of trailer vehicles, and these had to be equipped with cabs and compatible controls for reverse running. Further, the power unit had to be small so as not to encroach unduly upon passenger space, and attachment of a single trailer vehicle was the normal maximum. A further restriction lay in the limited capacity of the boiler which could only be fired while stationary as firing on the move destroyed the draught.

**ABOVE** SRM No 74 was one of the last series of short, 59ft 6in SRMs (Nos 73 to 83 of Diagrams Q and Q1). The first eight were built by the Gloucester Railway Carriage &Wagon Co, and were distinguished by their double passenger doors. The three built at Swindon (Nos 81 to 83) had single doors and an 8-foot 'American' bogie under the passenger section. *Ian Allan Library*

**BELOW** Auto-trailer No 108 (Diagram A7) with vertical matchboard sides, a conversion of SRM No 10 built 1904, survived until September 1954. The locomotive is a push-pull-equipped Class '517' 0-4-2T, and the vehicle behind appears to be a purpose-designed 70-foot auto-trailer of Diagram U (built 1911/12), in early condition before the end windows in the luggage end were plated over. *Ian Allan Library*

Trailers were intended to cope with surges in demand, but fixed multiple units were first tried in 1905 when SRM Nos 59 and 60 entered service permanently coupled to trailers Nos 9 and 10 respectively. Driving cabs were installed in one end of the trailers with a rudimentary opening at the other to provide a connection with the coach section of the SRM. This was improved in 1911 with installation of conventional gangway connections. Despite having branch-type luggage accommodation, the pairs were built for commuter services between Plymouth North Road and Saltash in Cornwall. As the Royal Albert Bridge was the only fixed crossing

LEFT Although the 0-6-0STs of Class '1076' (the 'Buffaloes') were built for long-distance goods services, they were later popular on passenger work, and a number were auto-fitted in the 20th century. It is difficult to determine, but this locomotive might be either No 1235 (fitted in 1917) or 1265 (fitted in 1918) at the head of three auto-trailers coupled together. The control equipment was difficult to operate when linked through three coaches, and it was later preferred practice to sandwich the locomotive within the formation of three- or four-coach trains. *Stephenson Locomotive Society*

over the River Tamar in the area, the service provided an important passenger link. Saltash station's situation on a cramped site adjacent to the Cornish end of Brunel's great bridge meant that trains had to terminate and reverse on the main line, which favoured the use of SRMs. The two pairs worked in the area until 1913, and were withdrawn for rebuilding as conventional auto-trailers in 1917/18.

With a SRM, a crew of three was still necessary and a capacity seated payload of, say, 15-21 per head (roughly double with a trailer attached) was inefficient. By comparison, four-coupled tank engines often hauled quite lengthy rakes of four- or six-wheeled coaches, each of which could accommodate around 50 seated passengers, albeit without much comfort, yielding a payload of 50 to 100 passengers per crew member. Further, the tank engine enjoyed greater operational flexibility in being able to handle other duties.

There were other drawbacks. As the coach section could not be readily detached from the power unit, non-availability of the latter placed the entire assemblage out of commission. Routine maintenance for a locomotive takes longer than that for a coach, and this curtailed the availability of the revenue-earning passenger accommodation. Further, without purpose-designed facilities, the entire unit had to be serviced within the dirty confines of a locomotive shed, which compromised efforts to keep the passenger accommodation clean.

Dissatisfaction with SRMs was proven in their short working lives. Withdrawals commenced in 1915, and by the start of 1923 41 had disappeared. Eventually, three were sold as complete units, 12 were condemned and broken up, and the remainder converted to non-powered auto-trailers to operate in push-pull mode. By the start of

ABOVE This early post-nationalisation view shows a '14xx' 0-4-2T with two auto-trailers. The coach behind the engine (possibly No 1435) is purpose-built 70-foot No W62 (Diagram L), which lasted until 1956; the other vehicle is one of three purpose-built 70-foot trailers dating from late 1905 (Nos 11-13, Diagrams E and F), all of which survived until 1954/55. *Ian Allan Library*

RIGHT Auto-trailers were originally either conversions from steam railmotors or purpose-built. However, in 1936/37 two hauled non-corridor Brake 3rds and two Brake Composites were converted to driving trailers by the installation of cab and controls at the luggage end, followed by four purpose-built trailers in 1939 that were similar to the Brake 3rd conversions. Between 1953 and 1955 18 non-corridor All 3rds were adapted to work as intermediate trailers, and 12 Brake 3rds were converted in similar form to the 1936 version. Auto-trailer No W256W was converted in 1955 from Brake 3rd No 4345, built in 1935, and it is seen here in company with Class '14xx' No 1419 on a Lostwithiel-Golant-Fowey service on 16 April 1960. *D. Fereday Glenn*

**RIGHT** This undated view of a 'Hall' on what seems to be a secondary express comprising eight vehicles highlights the heterogeneous nature of some GWR train formations, and the inflexibility that could result from articulation. The first two coaches are an articulated pair – a Brake 1st and an All 1st – followed by a conventional Composite of Diagram E.127 (1st Class compartments leading) and a Brake 3rd. The fifth coach seems to be a 'Dreadnought' diner before modernisation, the sixth an All 3rd (possibly of the ubiquitous Diagram C.54), and the last appears to be a clerestory. The train thus has 11 compartments seating 66 1st Class passengers in the first three vehicles, as far as possible from the dining facilities.

1935 only ten (Nos 30, 37, 55, 65, 71, 88, 91, 92, 97 and 98) remained, and all had gone by the end of that year. These late survivors had been originally intended for branch services; No 30 was the last remaining 59ft 6in railcar, the remainder being 70 feet long.

Auto-trailers were originally used to work with SRMs, but it was soon recognised that, in partnership with small tank locomotives of greater tractive effort, operating flexibility improved. The availability of push-pull-equipped locomotives for other duties broadened their utilisation, and they were able to haul more passenger vehicles than a SRM power unit could manage. Virtually all the inherent disadvantages of SRMs were eliminated at a stroke.

A drawback that auto-trains (as they became known) shared with SRMs lay in the method of controlling the driving unit from the trailer cab. This equipment was mechanical, requiring regular lubrication and adjustment to keep it operable. There were early cases of a locomotive pushing three auto-coaches, but this was not really practicable. Two coupled together was the effective maximum, which limited auto-trains to four vehicles with the locomotive sandwiched in the centre of the consist, but even then the controls could be difficult. One-coach trains in later years almost invariably saw the engine coupled with its bunker adjacent to the trailer to minimise the distance between driving cab and footplate. There was occasional recourse to the totally irregular measure of propelling the trailer vehicle with the controls disconnected.

The most advanced example of auto-train operations was at Plymouth on services previously worked by SRM units Nos 59 and 60. For many years the preferred formation was two pairs of 70-foot auto-trailers with a tank locomotive (from the 1930s usually an 0-6-0PT Class '64xx') coupled in between. The ten auto-trailers of Diagrams Q and R were purpose-built in 1909 and 1913 for this work. The Diagram Q vehicles comprised driving cab and seating for 80 passengers in a single saloon, and were compatible with the Diagram R non-driving intermediate trailers, which sat 76 (later 84) passengers in a single saloon, and provided luggage space. A four-coach set thereby provided 328 seats as well as space for standing passengers, making this a high-capacity unit. The efficacy was reduced by there being only two means of access to each vehicle, but this was slightly mitigated by gangway connections. Some seem to have worked their entire careers of more than 45 years as fixed pairs.

## Articulation and designated sets

A more definite interpretation of the 'fixed' principle emerged with articulated carriages, an idea earlier championed by Gresley that significantly reduced the deadweight factor. By the mid-1920s the LNER had concluded that articulated sets lacked the flexibility needed for general service expresses, but they were retained for specialised trains and for commuter sets. Although the pros and cons were finely balanced, the GWR created nine articulated trains in 1925.

Initially, three non-corridor sets appeared comprising Brake 3rd + All 3rd + Composite + Composite + All 3rd + Brake 3rd. The body style was similar to ordinary suburban stock but reduced to a width of 8ft 6in and a length of 48 feet so that they could work over the City Widened lines. Shorter bodies carried on seven bogies reduced both deadweight and length by about 20% compared with a conventional six-vehicle set of 57-foot coaches. However, their accommodation was proportionately more efficient, with a 12% reduction in the number of passenger seats. The cramped compartments were unpopular but they remained on their intended duties until 1939, and were then moved to Bristol and South Wales from where they were withdrawn between 1957 and 1960.

The six main-line articulated trains achieved wider recognition but had shorter lives. The first train was exhibited at the Railway Centenary Exhibition of 1925, underlining the importance attached to the concept. The composition as introduced was: Brake 1st + All 1st (articulated pair)/Restaurant 1st + Kitchen car + Restaurant 3rd (articulated trio)/All 3rd + All 3rd + Brake 3rd (articulated trio). The generous provision of 1st Class accommodation emphasised the intended use on front-line services, but whether six trains could be fully employed was questionable. Discrimination between the two classes by the positioning of the kitchen car complicated the addition of 'filler' vehicles. The Restaurant 1st was soon found superfluous, and the three catering vehicles were replaced by one or two conventional restaurant cars. These sets served on front-line duties until about 1930 and were then cascaded to secondary expresses, ending up on Weymouth and Cheltenham trains. By 1936/37 they

ABOVE A down suburban service from Paddington is hauled by 2-4-0T 'Metro' No 458, and comprises six close-coupled coaches (Brake 3rd + All 3rd + two Composites + All 3rd + Brake 3rd). This configuration was known as a 'Local C Set' in the London Division, not to be confused with the same division's 'ordinary' C Set, which comprised five suburban coaches. Set designations varied between divisions and could be subject to change within divisions as traffic demands changed, making this a complex and sometimes contradictory subject. This view was very likely taken in the 1920s prior to the introduction of Class '61xx' 2-6-2Ts for use on Thames Valley suburban services. *Stephenson Locomotive Society*

RIGHT Here is another six-coach suburban set comprising vehicle types in the same order as in the previous photograph, but in this case they are articulated. The motive power is an unidentified 'Large Prairie', probably of Class '61xx'. Two corridor coaches are attached at the rear of the train. *Ian Allan Library*

BELOW A two-car close-coupled B-set in BR maroon livery is hauled by 0-4-2T No 5804 of the non-auto-fitted version of Class '48xx' ('14xx'). *Stephenson Locomotive Society*

were judged too inflexible for normal duties and rebuilding made most of them indistinguishable from ordinary stock. The All 1sts, which had housed five compartments within a 48-foot length, remained distinctive for their new, non-standard length of 55ft 5in with six compartments.

Fixed formations were also achieved by marshalling non-corridor coaching stock into designated 'sets' that were often close-coupled. The best-known were pairs of non-corridor Brake Composites, generically but sometimes misleadingly known as B-sets. The confusion arose because the Birmingham and Worcester divisions, at least in 1937/38, designated a B-set as four (specifically 57-foot) vehicles – Brake 3rd + two Composites + Brake 3rd – while elsewhere this combination was known as a D-set. Other designations varied between divisions, indicating compromise between the principles of fixed consists and the need for flexibility to meet local traffic demands.

The B-set as a pair of Composite Brakes appeared on longer rural services. Duplication of 1st Class, guard and luggage accommodation in such a short consist seemed unnecessary when corridors and toilet facilities would have been more useful. They were considered regressive, as travel in the saloon of a traditional auto-trailer with panoramic views was more pleasant. B-sets, perhaps more than any other hauled stock configuration, highlighted the drawbacks of trying to preordain traffic patterns.

## Diesel-electric multiple units and the High Acceleration Project

Later pursuit of fixed formations embraced the application of diesel power, a ground-breaking move that highlighted a dichotomy in motive power policy. The minimal progress in steam development was at odds with the adventurous modernity spearheaded by the DEMU evaluation project and the later diesel-mechanical railcar programme. Most of the team around Collett would have been intellectually resistant to the new order, while those (Stanier and Hawksworth) who showed by their later work to have recognised the potential, had learned since 1926 to keep their own counsel over iconoclastic initiatives. The impetus for the railcar programme has therefore remained something of a mystery, but the availability of apparently previously undisclosed information helps provide a possible explanation.

The earliest evidence is contained in a drawing prepared by William Beardmore & Co Ltd, 36 Victoria Street, Westminster SW, numbered 79975 and bearing a Swindon Drawing Office stamp dated February 1926. The four-car unit depicted comprised two articulated pairs: Driving Motor Brake Composite + Trailer Composite/Trailer 3rd + Driving Motor 3rd. Use of articulation conformed to contemporary thinking as discussed above with steam-hauled fixed sets, and was relevant in power-to-weight calculations. Each vehicle had a planned body of length of 49 feet and the total accommodation was 50 1st Class passengers in five compartments and 252 3rd Class passengers in 21 compartments, indicating non-corridor high-capacity accommodation. The practicality seems doubtful, as a steam-hauled articulated suburban All 3rd (Diagram C.53) housed 96 passengers in eight cramped compartments within a 48-foot length, while Beardmore hoped to squeeze 108 into nine compartments within 49 feet. (The post-war

steam-hauled 63ft 1in-long All 3rd suburbans of Diagram C.75 accommodated 100 passengers in ten compartments.)

Beardmore was a large, broadly based engineering and manufacturing organisation whose business was in gradual, inexorable decline in the 1920s. To arrest this trend, the group had entered the UK railway market (also as manufacturers of steam locomotives), and was aggressively promoting its wares. Information on the power unit is sparse, but two six-cylinder diesel engines were planned to drive electric generating plant weighing 10 tons 10 cwt (there are no details of power rating). Presumably the cooperation of a leading electrical manufacturer had been enlisted and the whole enterprise is likely to have appealed to Felix Pole's commercial instincts. A further element that might have been relevant was continuing uncertainty over UK coal supplies, which had been declining in quantity and quality for some years. The reasons were complex but sufficiently disquieting to lend urgency to evaluation of alternative energy sources – as underlined by the General Strike of that year, and by extremely distressed conditions in mining communities.

Further work was undertaken by Beardmore as evidenced in drawing No 83636A (Swindon Drawing Office stamp dated August 1927), which shows greater detail and a more realistic seating layout: Driving Motor Luggage Guard 3rd (40 seats) + Trailer Composite (24 1st Class/56 3rd Class) + Trailer Composite (24 1st Class/56 3rd Class) + Driving Trailer 3rd (80). As opposed to the earlier suburban intentions, this unit appears to have been for longer-distance or semi-fast work. The accommodation was improved with open saloons, but a notable omission was toilet accommodation.

There is no information about the power source other than an eight-cylinder diesel engine driving electric transmission, although the drawing indicates 'Approx Speed on Level (Loaded) 48 mph'. Drawing No 87480 (Swindon stamp November 1928) shows the empty/loaded train weights unchanged at 129 tons/150 tons, but

**BELOW** The draft proposal by William Beardmore & Co Ltd dated 2 February 1926 for a four-car DEMU (Swindon Drawing No 79975).

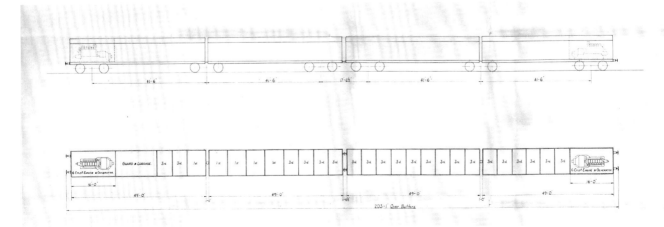

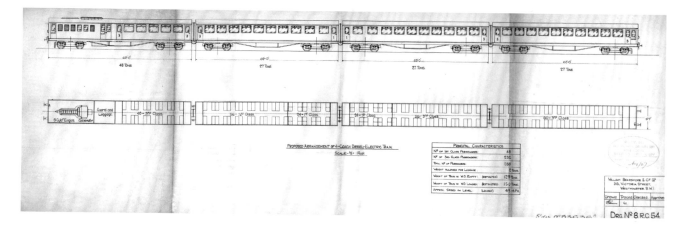

with the speed on the level (loaded) increased to 55mph. This later drawing has a pencil note appended to the engine compartment plan that reads '500 BHP'.

The information with these drawings allows comparison of passenger accommodation between a four-car DMU and a traditional four-car auto-train set comprising two Diagrams Q/R pairs (70-foot lengths) plus an 0-6-0PT as shown in Table 1.

The DEMU thus offered an approximate 8% increase in revenue-earning accommodation without allowing for an improved yield through reduction of the luggage space, e.g. if deployed exclusively on commuter duties. A factor against the DEMU was its dedication to a single purpose, while the pannier tank could work other duties – a repetition of the advantage of the auto-train over the steam railmotor.

A distinctive feature was the intention to use diesel-electric power, while the later railcars employed mechanical transmission. It seemed to become GWR policy to avoid diesel-electrics when considering alternative modes of traction, as the company only ever owned one example – a shunting locomotive – although more were under construction at nationalisation (see Chapter 9). This might in part have been due to experience with the four-car train depicted in drawing reference D1602A dated October 1927, prepared by Beardmore for the LMS Carriage & Wagon Dept, Derby. Apparently there was an open exchange of information as the drawing is of a promotional nature combining plans, side and end elevations with a photograph of the unit at work. This document bears the Swindon Drawing Office stamp dated 1928 (no month).

This stock had started life as an experimental third-rail electric set built by the Lancashire & Yorkshire Railway in 1916 for service between Bury and Holcombe Brook. In July 1927 the LMS agreed to Beardmore's proposal to convert this train using electrical equipment supplied by English Electric Co Ltd. The primary power source was a 500 horsepower, four-speed, eight-cylinder Beardmore diesel engine mounted above the generator, which was a 340kW 600-volt unit. Two 272bhp axle-mounted traction motors were fitted to the inner bogie of the motor unit. All vehicles were 60 feet long, and the configuration is shown in Table 2.

The train was used on passenger services daily (except Saturdays) between Blackpool Central and Preston via Lytham from July 1928 until April 1929. It was soon concluded that it was underpowered, with a power-to weight ratio of 3½hp per ton, which yielded poor acceleration. Weight distribution was also problematic, necessitating replacement of the outer non-powered bogie of the Driving Motor 3rd with a stronger version, and there was a three-month hiatus pending replacement of a broken crankshaft. The primary power source required frequent minor repairs, and the carriage heating system also proved unreliable.

While the unit was out of commission, a steam-powered push-pull service (presumably of similar carrying capacity) was substituted and detailed costings prepared. It was concluded that the all-in cost of the steam service equated to 5.8 pence per mile, while the diesel worked out at 7.9 pence per mile. When all related expenses (including interest, renewal and maintenance) were taken into account, it was calculated that there was a deficit of £877 per annum, which could only be eliminated by Beardmore reducing the capital cost of its equipment from £7,555 to £2,485, and hence the amortisation factor. It was noted that the train was out of service for repairs for 69% of its possible working days, and it was concluded that there was no demand for such a unit on LMS suburban lines. Following withdrawal in April 1929, the unit did no further work and was broken up in 1931.

The bases for the costings looked dubious. A one-off experimental prototype using fresh technology inevitably incurs more expense than production-series equipment that relies on time-honoured methods. There seems to have been no effort to try alternative or uprated power units. It is easy to see how conservative elements could seize

### TABLE 1

| | Crew | Seating capacity | Train length (ft) | Seats per foot |
|---|---|---|---|---|
| Four-car diesel-electric multiple unit | 2 | 280 | 248 | 1.13 |
| Four-coach auto-set Diagrams Q/R + Class '64xx' | 3 | 328 | 311 | 1.05 |

### TABLE 2

| Original L&YR No | LMS No | Category | Weight | Capacity (seats) |
|---|---|---|---|---|
| 3500 | 14570 | Driving Motor 3rd | 59 tons 7 cwt | 60 |
| 3601 | 14668 | Trailer 3rd | 26 tons 8 cwt | 85 |
| 3600 | 14669 | Trailer Composite | 26 tons 8 cwt | 32 1st, 45 3rd |
| 3501 | 14571 | Driving Trailer 3rd | 31 tons 17 cwt | 75 |

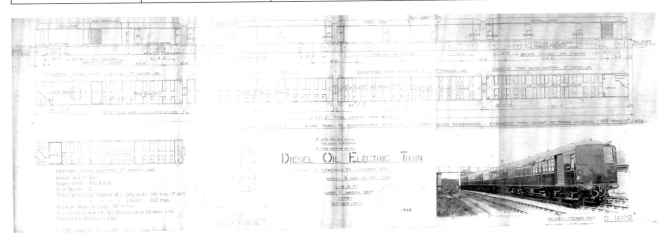

**ABOVE** A proposal by William Beardmore & Co Ltd dated 31 October 1927, and bearing the Swindon date stamp of 1928, for a four-car DEMU based on details submitted to the LMS in respect of the experimental train then on trial in the Blackpool/Preston area.

upon these conclusions, and upon the various causes of unreliability, to prove that this was not a viable replacement for steam power.

Cessation of the LMS Blackpool-Preston project and Pole's departure might have seen the end of DEMU initiatives, but correspondence indicates that the concept remained under active consideration. A fairly detailed tender dated 6 August 1931 was submitted by Sir W. G. Armstrong, Whitworth & Co (Engineers) Ltd for the supply of 'Standard Oil Electric Railcar Chassis'. Four different versions were proposed and each specification related only to the railcar chassis, bogies, control equipment and that portion of the body related to the cab and engine room. Engines were to be either six- or eight-cylinder airless injection Armstrong, Whitworth oil engines to generate power for electric motors axle-hung on the bogie below the engine. The power cars would incorporate passenger accommodation to be provided by another supplier, which would also provide the trailer vehicles. Estimated performance figures anticipated that the powered railcars would propel/haul one to four

trailers, depending upon the installed bhp. The maximum safe working speed was to be not less than 65mph in every version. The leading dimensions are shown in Table 3 (overleaf).

Payloads and power-to-weight ratios were a major consideration, especially in persuading steam-orientated operators seriously to consider diesel traction. Armstrong, Whitworth included appropriate estimates in the tender, as set out below. It should be noted that there was an element of supposition concerning the trailers, as different construction methods might have reduced overall weight and improved performance. (It was notable how weights increased with the GWR single-unit railcars discussed below – of the twin-engined vehicles, No 19 was 36% heavier than No 2.)

The power-to-weight calculations submitted by Armstrong, Whitworth were:

| **Engine bhp** | 250 | 350 | 450 | 600 |
|---|---|---|---|---|
| **Power-to-weight (bhp/ton):** | | | | |
| Single unit | 5.1 | 5 | n/a | n/a |
| + one trailer | 3.3 | 3.9 | 5 | n/a |
| + two trailers | n/a | 2.9 | 4.08 | 5 |
| + three trailers | n/a | n/a | 3 | 4 |
| + four trailers | n/a | n/a | n/a | 3 |

| TABLE 3 | | | | |
|---|---|---|---|---|
| Armstrong, Whitworth Drawing No | LD322 | LD270 | LD275 | LD268 |
| Drawing date | 17/04/31 | 03/02/31 | 11/08/31 | 30/01/31 |
| Engine bhp | 250 | 350 | 450 | 600 |
| Chassis weight (tons)* | 38.5 | 41.9 | 51 | 65.3 |
| Railcar weight, empty (tons) | 44.25 | 47.5 | 56 | 71.5 |
| Railcar weight, full passenger complement (tons) | 49 | 53.5 | 62.75 | 79 |
| Seating capacity | 60 | 55 | 50 | 71.5 |
| Max axle loading (tons) | 15.35 | 17.5 | 17.5 | 15 |
| Length over buffer beams (ft in) | 59 6 | 59 9 | 59 9 | 78 7 |
| Motor bogie wheelbase (ft in) | 8 0 | 8 0 | 8 9 | 8 0 |
| Trailer bogie wheelbase (ft in) | 8 0 | 8 0 | 8 0 | 8 0 |
| Bogie centre distance (ft in) | 42 0 | 42 0 | 42 0 | 21 3 + 40 7 |
| Price for single unit | £7,153 | £8,225 | £9,285 | £12,835 |
| Unit price for batch of 12 | £6,480 | £7,445 | £8,720 | £12,155 |
| Maximum number of trailers | 1 | 3 | 3 | 4 |

* Cab and engine carried on separate chassis articulated with passenger section.

| TABLE 4 | | | | | | |
|---|---|---|---|---|---|---|
| | Crew | Seating capacity | Length (ft) | Seats per foot | Tare (tons) | Seats (per ton) |
| Six-car diesel-electric multiple unit | 2 | 470 (unclassified) | 419 | 1.12 | 277 | 1.51 |
| Six-coach suburban set + 2-6-2T Class '61xx' | 3 | 64 1st, 400 3rd | 379 + 41 | 1.1 | 187 + 74 | 1.78 |

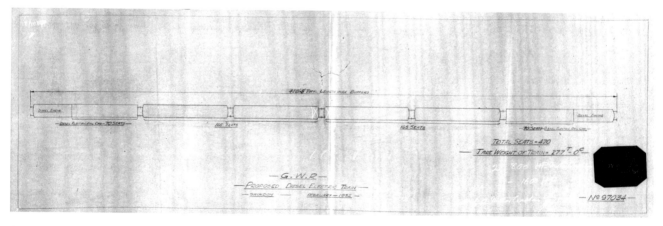

Consideration of the possibilities of DEMU operations culminated in two schematic drawings dated 17 February 1932, prepared by the Swindon Drawing Office rather than a commercial manufacturer. Drawing No 97034 describes a six-car 'Diesel Electric Train' with a Driving Motor vehicle at either end, each with accommodation for 70 passengers, together with four trailer vehicles with aggregate space for 330 passengers. In broad terms, the concept anticipated accommodation for 470 passengers within a train 418 feet long and weighing 277 tons.

**ABOVE** Schematic drawing No 97034 by the Swindon Drawing Office dated 17 February 1932 depicting a six-car DEMU.

No information is provided about the nature of the accommodation or the division between classes, but pencil notes appended indicate that each Driving Motor vehicle would have housed an 800bhp diesel-electric unit. If the Armstrong, Whitworth estimate that 600bhp would be adequate for a five-car set was accepted, then 800bhp for six cars would be logical. The use of

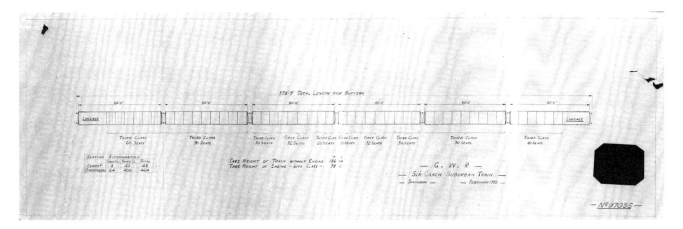

two engines yielding an installed power of 1,600bhp seems an excessive increase that might simply have been an error. The total cost would have been £25,000. (The similarity between the four-car plans of 1927/28, this configuration, and the BR Southern Region 'Hastings' units introduced in 1957 indicates that either the GWR investigations were indeed visionary or the post-war efforts were out-of-date.)

Schematic drawing No 97035, also dated 17 February 1932, was clearly prepared for direct comparison between steam and diesel motive power. The definition of the non-corridor accommodation is clearer: Brake 3rd + 3rd + Composite + Composite + 3rd + Brake 3rd (the Brake 3rd had 60 seats in six compartments, the 3rd 90 seats in nine, and the Composite 32 1st in four compartments and 50 3rd in five). The vehicles were all 60 feet long, yielding a train length, excluding locomotive, of 378ft 9in. The tare weight was 186 tons 14 cwt plus 78 tons for a 2-6-2T Class '61xx' (see Table 4).

While the capacity figures were broadly comparable, certain advantages lay with steam haulage. The seats-per-tare-ton factor was better, and it was probably well within the ability of a 'Large Prairie' to add one or two more coaches without adverse impact on schedules. Also, the locomotive could be used on other duties.

These comparisons were connected with what became known as the High Acceleration Project to improve the performance of steam locomotives on Paddington-based suburban services, and presumably those at other major population centres. Schematic drawings dated March 1932, evidently by A. W. J. Dymond, on file at York show that five possibilities were considered:

| Scheme No | Wheel arrangement | Driving wheels | Cylinders |
|---|---|---|---|
| 1 | 2-6-2T | 5ft 3in | (2) 19in x 30in |
| 1A | 2-6-2T | 5ft 3in | (2) 19in x 30in |
| 2 | 2-6-2T | 5ft 8in | (2) 19in x 30in |
| 3 | 4-6-2T | 5ft 8in | (4) 14.5in x 26in |
| 4 | 2-6-2T | 5ft 6in | (2) 19in x 30in |

These drawings were accompanied by relative adhesion factors and rather theoretical estimates of accelerative capacity. There were only minor differences between Schemes 1 and 1A, and this concept had already taken shape in the rebuilding of the Class '61xx' 2-6-2T No 6116 in January 1932; the larger-boilered version appeared in 1938 with the new Class '31xx'. Scheme 2 was simply the existing Class '5101' format, while Scheme 4 appeared in 1938 in Class '81xx'.

The most radical idea was Scheme 3, which married a 'Star'-type chassis with 5ft 8in driving wheels and a trailing axle. A new standard boiler as a derivative of the No 1 type was contemplated. It was convention for four-cylinder engines to use inside Walschaerts valve gear, but this arrangement lacked the 'punch' on starting imparted by the Stephenson link motion. A further complication was the question of adequate clearances with the 'Star' layout using driving wheels of the size proposed. It seems likely that this proposal would have been quite unsuitable for suburban work, making it hard to believe that Collett would have been interested. Nothing quite so exotic had been seen in the panoply of GWR tank locomotives since broad gauge days.

The rebuilding of No 6116 apparently marked closure of initiatives with diesel-electric traction for suburban work. This was a solution to a traffic need with which Collett in his customary caution would have felt comfortable. Had the timing been slightly different, it is possible that the company would have reverted to an all-steam motive power policy. However, the advantages of diesel power had been recognised by others, as by then the project to produce the first diesel-mechanical railcar was under way. This raises the question of who sponsored these developments.

Progress was only feasible with outside technical support, and Collett in his habitual antipathy towards commercial manufacturers is unlikely to have been directly involved. Auld was a dyed-in-the-wool steam man with plenty on his plate, while Hannington held the demanding Works Manager job. It seems probable that,

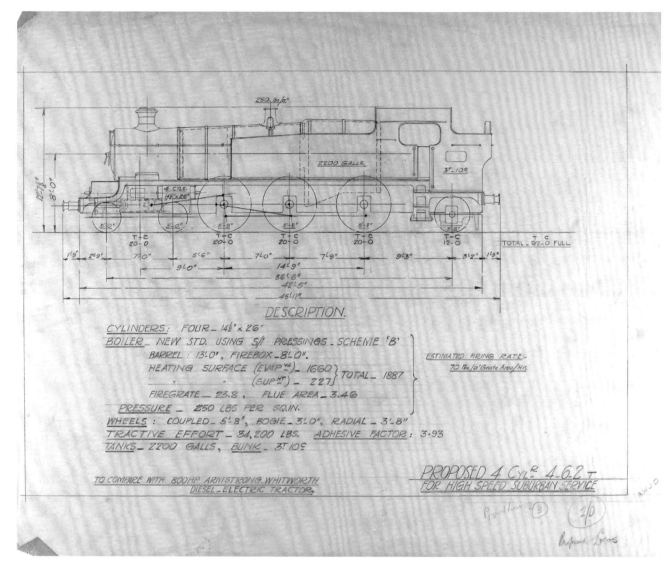

**ABOVE** The most radical alternative considered under the High Acceleration Project was Scheme 3. *NRM*

following Pole's resignation, Stanier had led the post-1929 DEMU investigative work and, following his move to the LMS, the diesel-mechanical railcar programme became Hawksworth's responsibility. This contention is borne out by his assiduity in completion of the final examples during the difficult wartime period. In this respect there is a circular nature to the saga, as the railcar pairs (Nos 35 to 38), augmented by intermediate trailer coaches, were conceptually similar to the Beardmore-sourced proposals of August 1927.

## The diesel railcar programme

The DEMU proposals submitted by Beardmore and later by Armstrong, Whitworth were more advanced than the GWR railcar fleet that actually appeared between 1934 and 1942. The styling of the latter vehicles was undoubtedly modernistic, but in mechanical terms they were essentially conservative. This might have been another expression of Collett's usual attitude, but the wisdom of this decision was supported by the reliability that the railcars were to enjoy.

However, another factor that might have influenced GWR policy comes from a brief addendum to the Armstrong, Whitworth tender documents that reviewed the relative merits of electric versus mechanical transmission, based on a survey of 332 'cars' at work in the USA (189 with mechanical drive and 133 with electric). It was noted that the number of diesel-electric units in service was increasing at a faster pace and that this configuration was preferred for power ratings of 150bhp or more, which would be understandable given typically greater train weights. The data presented definitely favoured the diesel-electric arrangement in terms of availability and estimated transmission working life:

|  | **Mechanical** | **Electric** |
|---|---|---|
| **Availability** | 82.6% | 91.6% |
| **Life expectancy (years):** | | |
| - car body | 20-30 | 20-30 |
| - power plant | 10-15 | 10-15 |
| - transmission | 5-10 | 10-25 |

It may not be coincidental that the GWR railcars reflected caution in using technically simpler mechanical transmissions driven by individual power units that did not exceed 121bhp.

Although much of the early work took place outside the Swindon Drawing Office, the results would have crossed Hawksworth's desk. Railcar No 1 was actually the second to be powered by internal combustion. The first was a four-wheeled petrol-electric vehicle (numbered 100 in the SRM series) built in 1911 by British Thomson-Houston, which also designed the power equipment. There were driving cabs at both ends with the power unit behind one of the cabs. The unit seated 44 passengers in a single saloon and the general style anticipated the four-wheeled British Railways diesel railbuses of the 1950s. No 100 was used on branch services and, while little is known of its performance, it apparently worked well enough before withdrawal and sale in 1919.

No 100's form was in the best tradition of 'early English perpendicular', but streamlined Railcar No 1 broke fresh ground in a startling statement of modernity through its Art Deco styling. It was the result of collaboration with Associated Equipment Co Ltd, which provided the diesel-mechanical power unit, and Park Royal Coachworks Ltd, a leading builder of omnibus bodies. The unit's thrusting snout, subtly curved body outline and full shrouding below solebar level implied speed and grace, achieved with the

help of a wind tunnel. *The Locomotive* of November 1933 was enthusiastic, describing the appearance as resembling a 'huge seaplane float', a view that accorded with contemporary images of progress.

This return to self-propelled passenger vehicles preceded withdrawal of the final SRMs, and the substitution of a diesel-powered unit promised several benefits. The fireman was no longer required; the chore of lighting up was eliminated; there was no need for servicing in the dirty environment of a steam shed; and overhaul of the power unit could be achieved more quickly. It was claimed that the body shape reduced wind resistance to one-fifth of that met with a conventional slab-ended vehicle. This seems hard to believe, but obviously aerodynamic efficiency was considered important in optimising power-to-weight and fuel consumption factors.

No 1 started work in December 1933, powered by a single 121bhp diesel engine with mechanical transmission to the axles of both bogies. The engine was similar to that being fitted to London buses and the overall weight was a mere 24 tons. Accommodation was simple: there was seating for 69 passengers in 2+3 format in two open saloons, with access through central double doors. A small compartment for guard and luggage was provided, and there were driving cabs at both ends. Intended for suburban duties, seating capacity exceeded that of a 57-foot corridor All 3rd coach. With No 1 and the next 16 railcars,

**BELOW** Petrol railcar No 100 (numbered in the SRM series). Cooling was a persistent problem with early internal combustion engines, and some railways ran railcars as driving motor pairs with the engine of the trailing vehicle shut down, which had an adverse impact on power-to-weight and performance factors. The solution applied with No 100 was to mount the radiator on the roof. *BR*

**ABOVE** This publicity photograph describes diesel railcar No 1 as 'G.W.R. Experimental Stream-Lined Heavy Oil Rail Car', and it is in apparently brand new condition at Southall.
*Stephenson Locomotive Society*

**RIGHT** Diesel railcar No 3 in new condition.
*Stephenson Locomotive Society*

**BELOW RIGHT** Diesel railcar No 13, with the skirting over one bogie removed. *Stephenson Locomotive Society*

concealed self-contained buffers and drawgear of a rudimentary nature were installed for haulage in case of breakdown.

Three more railcars appeared the following year as express units with a more complex internal layout. There were 1st and 3rd Class saloons, a small buffet, two lavatories, and space for guard and luggage. Seating capacity was reduced to 44. Two 121bhp engines were fitted, yielding a maximum speed of more than 75mph compared with No 1's 60mph. While No 1 had an obvious prototypical role as a test vehicle, the traffic objectives with Nos 2 to 4 were less clear. Their novelty stimulated new custom, leading to capacity constraints, and the economics were doubtful as, requiring a crew of three, the seat-to-crew ratio was 15 to 1.

Operational inflexibility was exposed when the buffet railcar services were relaunched with the October 1946 timetable. No 2 was allocated to Newport to work intensively on a 12-hour shuttle to

**ABOVE** The 17th railcar was designed for parcels traffic only in BR days. The skirting below the solebar impeded access to mechanical parts with Nos 1 to 17, and towards the end of their careers sections were removed, usually starting with those over the bogies.

Cardiff and Swansea. At first it ran Cardiff-Swansea non-stop, but loadings were very light so stops at Neath and Bridgend were added. No 3 was allocated to Landore to provide a Swansea-Cheltenham service, and No 4 soon moved to Landore to act as spare. Surges in passenger numbers necessitated the substitution of a three- or four-coach set (hauled by a 2-6-2T Class '31xx' from Severn Tunnel Junction) on the Newport-Swansea service, with timings below railcar standard as the steam engine had to take on water during the journey.

By 1948 the Monday service from Cheltenham had become so popular that Railcar No 4, by then the regular on this service, had to be replaced by a 'Hall' or 'Grange' and four coaches. Business passengers expecting a modern vehicle with on-board catering did not appreciate the substitution of a scratch coach set with no buffet. This showed the practical difficulties of coordinating railcars within conventional steam-hauled operations.

Railcars Nos 5-9 and 13-16 had seats for 70 in a similar format to that of No 1, whereas the capacity of Nos 10-12 was reduced to 63 to allow for a toilet. No 17 had the same outward profile but no windows or seating, being intended for parcels only. The bodies of Nos 5-17 were built by the Gloucester Railway Carriage & Wagon Co Ltd, with AEC power units. It was surprising that there were so many of this type, considering the operating limitations.

**LEFT** Railcar No 18 was the first equipped with buffers and drawgear to haul trailers. This publicity photograph shows the railcar in as-new condition with an auto-trailer in tow.

**BELOW** No 18 had a long association with the Lambourn branch, over which passenger traffic were usually modest. Here an increase in numbers was clearly anticipated on 30 July 1938 as the railcar was hauling an auto-trailer and a clerestory Brake 3rd, combining three generations of GWR passenger vehicles. *V. R. Webster*

Railcar No 18 of 1937 was an experimental, transitional vehicle intended for branch use that owed more to traditional railway practice than had the preceding vehicles. Art Deco styling remained, but without shrouding over the bogies, which were heavier, and normal drawgear permitted haulage of passenger trailers or goods vehicles. The power and transmission arrangements incorporated Bowden cable linkage and electrical

**BELOW** Diesel railcar No 34 was, like No 17, intended only for parcels traffic. In common with a number of other railcars, the drive shafts to the second axles have been removed. *Ian Allan Library*

**LEFT** Railcars Nos 19 to 33 were all of the same type, intended for branch-line duties. In BR days No W32W is seen at Mickleton on 9 May 1954, hauling a trailer. The latter was a unique and interesting vehicle, being a 70-foot parcels van with accommodation for guard, built as No 833 under Diagram M.13 in 1908. The body style was of 'Dreadnought' profile but with outside frames, as used with many 'Siphons'. *C. F. H. Oldham*

connections for control from the cab of a driving trailer. Seating capacity was reduced to 49 (to allow more spacious guard and luggage accommodation), and was therefore less of an operating constraint. No 18 proved successful and was mainly associated with the Lambourn branch, where it frequently hauled horseboxes.

Weight had progressively increased with the earlier series, Nos 10-12 being the heaviest at 29 tons 18 cwt. No 18 weighed in at 33 tons 12 cwt, while the next batch of passenger cars (Nos 19 to 33) were heavier still at 35 tons 13 cwt. AEC supplied the engines, but otherwise the railcars were Swindon products. External appearance was more restrained, with a razor-edge cab design, and operating objectives were less ambitious. They were geared down to a maximum speed of 40mph for branch and secondary duties; internal arrangements were generally similar to those of No 18, with seats for 48 plus guard and luggage accommodation. No 34 was outwardly similar to Nos 19-33 except that it was designed for parcels traffic, in the fashion of No 17.

**ABOVE** Diesel railcar pair Nos 36 and 35 sandwich a 70-foot All 3rd as intermediate trailer in June 1944 on what is believed to be a Bristol Temple Meads-Weymouth service. (All 3rd No 4509 of Diagram C.46 was noted with Nos 37 and 38 in May 1943.) *Swindon Drawing Office*

**RIGHT** Railcar pair Nos 38 and (rebuilt) 33, in standard BR DMU livery, back out of Evesham after arrival with the 6.15pm service from Worcester on 14 April 1962. *M. Mensing*

The Swindon-built railcars appeared between July 1940 and September 1941. The exigencies of the time prevented much in the way of fresh initiatives, but there remained one evolutionary stage, which in many respects was the most important. When passenger demand warranted, it was normal to couple two of the Nos 19-33 series together, but, as with the two-coach B-sets, this was an inefficient duplication of non-passenger accommodation resulting in a load capacity that fell short of what steam locomotives could handle. (A good example was No 29, which replaced 'Dukedog' No 3219 on the Ledbury branch in the autumn of 1941. The 4-4-0 then became Gloucester station pilot, but frequently worked goods duties to Kingham as well as local passenger services to Cheltenham that could comprise 13 or 14 bogies.)

The final four railcar vehicles introduced in 1941 were significant in reducing these limitations and in avoiding duplicated facilities. They were styled similarly to Nos 19 to 33, but each had a single driving cab with a gangway at the other end to operate in pairs. Nos 35 and 37 had seating accommodation for 60 passengers in two saloons plus a toilet; Nos 36 and 38 could seat 44 passengers in two saloons, plus a small buffet and guard's accommodation. Working as powered twins and geared up to 70mph, they were main-line units conceptually similar to express units Nos 2-4 but with a seat-to-crew ratio improved to almost 35:1. Initially used on Birmingham-Cardiff services, they also attracted custom in excess of their load capacity.

A steam-hauled All 3rd coach (usually No 1096 of Diagram C.77, built in 1938) was modified to work as an intermediate

**ABOVE** This unidentified railcar pair has a Collett Diagram E.148 Brake Composite as intermediate trailer. The train is approaching Bathampton as a Weymouth-Bath service in October 1949. *R. R. Bowler.*

trailer vehicle with one of the pairs. However, on 13 May 1943 Railcars Nos 37 and 38 worked with similarly adapted 70-foot All 3rd No 4509 (Diagram C.46, built in 1924) between Cheltenham (Malvern Road) and Stratford-upon-Avon at 3 minutes under the schedule, proving that there was no shortage of power. Traffic growth meant that this measure was soon inadequate and services reverted to steam haulage, with the DMUs moving to the less busy Bristol-Weymouth and Reading-Newbury routes.

The usefulness of Nos 35-38 was proven by the practice of substituting a double-ended unit if one of the single-enders was out of commission. In 1947 No 37 was the second railcar to cease work following fire damage (as had happened with No 9 in 1945). In August 1948 the combination of Nos 22 and 38 with No 1096 as intermediate trailer was covering the Yatton-Wells-Witham services. No 33 was rebuilt in 1954 with a single driving cab and gangway connection at the other end as a permanent replacement for No 37.

## The BUT trains

Although railcar construction ended in 1942, there was an indication of how the GWR might later have resumed the programme. Following his resignation from the GWR in November 1947 and his rejection of the chairmanship of the newly created Railway Executive, Dublin-born Sir James Milne, assisted by a team of senior British railway executives, was commissioned to review the parlous condition of Córas Iompair Eireann. Recommendations submitted in 1949 included a proposal that main-line diesel locomotives should be eschewed, based on concern about reliability of equipment that for financial and currency reasons could only be sourced in Britain. It was proposed that diesel multiple units should work between Dublin and Cork at an increased service frequency, replacing the variegated collection of 4-6-0s inherited from the Great Southern Railways. The dismissive attitude towards the 4-6-0s, some of which were good engines, was intriguing in view of the familiarity of Sir James and his ex-GWR colleagues in the team with this wheel arrangement. There was obviously substance to the belief in the advantages of diesel-mechanical power for main-line services.

The Milne Report affected the thinking of CIE, and by extension that of the Great Northern Railway (Ireland). Both organisations invested significantly in DMUs, and in 1957 the GNRI's last variant belatedly solved the recurring flexibility issue with its fleet of diesel-mechanical BUT trains (engines by British United Traction Company, then owners of AEC). To form these trains, there were eight powered cars (Nos 901-8) with a full-width cab at one end and a corridor connection at the other. There were also 16 powered cars (Nos 701-716), which had small driving cabs at both ends alongside the corridor connection, giving an appearance similar to the Southern Railway 4-COR 'Nelson' EMU sets. Each powered car had two diesel engines.

The BUT trains operated in four-, six- or eight-vehicle sets with a 'piped' non-driving trailer for each powered car, thus sustaining consistency in the power-to-weight relationship. A total of 27 trailer vehicles were used at differing times, being specially adapted steel-bodied steam-hauled stock, comprising a broad range of types: Buffet, Diner, Corridor 1st, Brake 1st Corridor, Corridor Composite, Brake 2nd Corridor, 2nd Open, and Brake 2nd Open. The trains could be assembled with differing combinations as traffic demanded, allowing considerable operational flexibility. They stayed at work until 1975 and, as the final evolution of plans that had commenced in the mid-1920s, gave an impression of how the GWR's post-war DMU programme might have developed.

**RIGHT** Construction of the BUT 700-series power cars was protracted. Rather than leave the fifth (No 705) standing idle awaiting completion of its companions, GNRB temporarily assigned it to a new high-speed service between Belfast and Enniskillen. This proved popular, quickly necessitating the addition of a non-driving trailer (GNRI Diagram D3 mahogany-panelled Brake 2nd No 396), increasing the total seating capacity to 96. No 705 (in GNRI blue and cream livery) therefore had to run round at journey's end, and also at Omagh, where the Enniskillen line trailed into the Belfast-Londonderry route. The efficiency of the concept thus generated fresh capacity problems. *Plus ça change…*
*Colin Hogg*

**ABOVE** A six-car BUT train arrives at Dublin Amiens Street on an up train with a 700-series power car leading. *Alan Wild*

**LEFT** The Great Northern Railway Board (which had taken over the independent GNRI in 1953) was divided between Córas Iompair Eireann and the Ulster Transport Authority in September 1958. This eight-car BUT train passed to CIE ownership and had acquired green livery with the 'flying snail' emblem when seen at Portadown North on the up (Dublin-bound) 'Enterprise' on 17 August 1959. This train was led by a 900-series power car, followed by four non-powered trailers, then two (700 series) double-ended power cars, and possibly another 900-series power car on the rear. *E. M. Patterson, courtesy Charles Friel Collection*

# CHAPTER 9

# ELECTRICITY AND INTERNAL COMBUSTION

Although always marginal, the GWR's experience with alternative traction was diverse: third-rail electric (through a joint venture); overhead electric (detailed investment evaluations); petrol (railcar and shunting tractors); diesel-mechanical (railcars and shunter); diesel-electric (shunter, together with consideration of multiple units and a main-line locomotive); and gas turbine-electric. The scope showed interest in technological progress that contrasted with the company's conservative image concerning steam power. There is no obvious explanation for this paradox, but the sequence of events suggests that Felix Pole generated the initial interest, and that senior elements were determined that the company should monitor those developments that would one day replace steam. It is uncertain who exercised direct executive responsibility but, as discussed in Chapter 8, it seems likely that Hawksworth was involved in the earlier non-steam initiatives. He was definitely engaged in the later stages of the railcar programme, with diesel shunters and, as discussed in the next chapter, gas turbines.

## Electrification

Physical participation in electric traction was confined to half-ownership of the Hammersmith & City Railway and its fleet of 40 motor coaches (built in 1902 with electrical equipment by Thomson-Houston), which appeared only as a book entry in the GWR's records. The company's partner was the Metropolitan Railway, which worked the system and numbered the stock as 2208-2247 in its series. The H&CR was absorbed into the London Passenger Transport Board in 1933 and the relevant stock was withdrawn in 1938.

Main-line electrification was formally considered on two occasions, but neither proposal proceeded beyond preliminary evaluation. The first was instigated in 1925 in respect of the Paddington-Bristol and Paddington-Birmingham routes, and Sir Philip Dawson, a leading electrical engineer, was retained to assess the potential. Dawson saw more opportunity in the Birmingham line, but anticipated complications with both routes in the need to run steam trains

**LEFT** Apart from railcar No 100, the GWR's experience with petrol-engined vehicles was limited to a fleet of Simplex yard shunters numbered 15, 23, 24, 26 and 27 in the steam locomotive series (together with some 2-foot-gauge shunters for use on temporary track). These vehicles barely registered as motive power in the accepted sense, being little more than shunting tractors, a form of traction common in some countries but quite rare in the UK. The first was No 15, seen here at Swindon Works yard in 1933 with steam railmotor No 86 in the background. *Stephenson Locomotive Society*

alongside electrified services. His study was therefore redirected to the Taunton-Penzance section, where conversion of all services could overcome mixed traction problems. Favourable factors were the severe gradients, seasonal traffic congestion, and the cost of supplying steam sheds remote from coal sources.

Minor routes, where conversion was unrealistic, were also included in the study (e.g. the 2 miles between Churston and Brixham). An alternative was briefly considered involving all routes west of Plympton, a strange option that removed any benefits from improved operations over the South Devon banks. It was estimated that 381 steam engines could be replaced by 233 electric locomotives: 56 express types of 1,400 to 1,600hp with a 2-4-2 or 4-4-2 wheel arrangement; 173 general-purpose engines (1,200 to 1,400hp Bo Bos); and four battery-electric engines. In addition, 32 steam heating vehicles would be needed to work with stock not solely dedicated to the electrified area. These vehicles would have added to the deadweight factor, while complicating shunting. Collett had already closely studied the North Eastern Railway's electrification schemes and was reportedly unenthusiastic.

The main advantages lay in the superior hill-climbing ability of electric locomotives. Dawson calculated that the new traction could sustain an average speed over the Taunton-Penzance route of 57mph hauling 518 tons, compared with 47mph and 257 tons for steam. The study, which was submitted in July 1927, went into considerable detail, including factors such as savings in personnel costs, but the estimated return on investment at about 7% per annum was insufficient to sway the Board. Their attention then moved to informal discussion of the potential with London suburban services.

Elements of this study had longer-term relevance. The operating department preferred services not due to call at Taunton to work through to their first scheduled stop in the electrified zone to change motive power – a condition that would have complicated traffic management and increased the requisite number of locomotives. This traditionalist mindset illustrated the need for a holistic approach to modernisation. It also foreshadowed problems with gas turbines and early dieselisation, where insufficient critical mass made integration into steam rosters obligatory, rendering poor utilisation. The report formed part of submissions made by the GWR in 1929 to the Ministry of Transport, which was investigating the potential for nationwide electrification.

Those studies were conducted by the Weir Committee and culminated in a report published in 1931. Of significance was continuing escalation in fuel prices, which was sharpened for the GWR by its reliance on Welsh steam coal, i.e. less scope for consumption of lower-grade cheaper coal from other fields. Reference was made in the report to the Dawson investigation, and to the conclusion that conversion of the Taunton-Penzance section was not viable. There was therefore some surprise when, in 1938, the company commissioned Messrs Merz & McLellan, electrical consultants, to re-evaluate the same route.

In the preceding 12 years or so, several factors favoured revisiting the subject, in addition to the trend in coal prices. The national electricity grid had been completed in 1933, greatly facilitating the steady supply of large amounts of energy. There had been progress in improving the performance and efficiency of electric motors. The challenges of remoteness from fuel sources, gradients and seasonal traffic congestion remained dominant issues in the South West.

On the negative side, 1,500-volt dc overhead electric power for mineral workings over the 18-mile Bishop Auckland-Shildon route of the LNER had been decommissioned in 1935 after little more than 20 years' service. The North Eastern Railway (with whom the GWR had maintained a close relationship) had been an enthusiastic pioneer in electrification. Ten electric locomotives had replaced a significant number of steam engines and each could competently handle loads up to 1,400 tons. Unfortunately, decline in local coal production and resultant changes in traffic patterns meant that the fleet was never fully used, providing a salutary warning of the risks with substantial capital investment.

The conclusions of the Merz & McLellan report (submitted in February 1939) were broadly similar to Dawson's earlier views, but with a lower estimated investment return. Conversion again anticipated inclusion of virtually all routes in the area, and it was considered that four classes comprising 164 locomotives would be adequate. The largest (eight locomotives) would have been slightly more powerful than the 'Kings', but with a lower axle loading allowing use in Cornwall. Two intermediate classes, roughly equivalent in power to the 'Castle' and '43xx' classes, would have comprised 40 and 55 locomotives respectively. The remainder would have covered all other duties.

Taunton presented seemingly insurmountable problems, as the convergence of trains from London and the North at Cogload Junction was the starting point of route utilisation difficulties. Four tracks extended from there to Norton Fitzwarren, which eased conflicting movements over the Minehead and Barnstaple branches, but thereafter all long-distance traffic used a two-track route. Motive power changeover would have created extra light engine movements, thus exacerbating congestion. To offset the impact, trains not scheduled to stop would have to be steam-worked, perhaps as far as Plymouth, thus removing some of the benefits. The situation at Taunton on summer Saturdays would

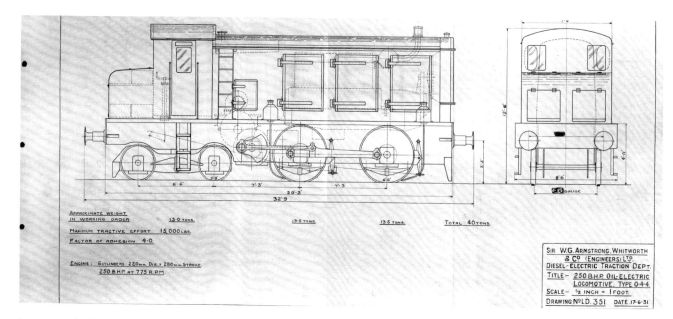

ABOVE A drawing of the 250hp diesel-electric locomotive described in the tender by Sir W. G. Armstrong, Whitworth & Co (Engineers) Ltd, dated 21 October 1931.

have resembled the break-of-gauge mayhem at Gloucester and elsewhere pre-1892.

Adoption of a 3,000-volt overhead supply was calculated to render the most favourable return. This system was permissible with Ministry of Transport sanction, the only other approved voltages following the Weir Report being 750 volts for third rail and 1,500 volts overhead. Even then the return was poor, without accounting for contingent matters such as temperature control in carriages equipped for steam heating. Interestingly, estimated reductions in journey times were modest, suggesting that superior hill-climbing might have been negated by the inadequacy of traditional vacuum brakes on downhill sections. In this regard, traffic levels outside the busy summer season were insufficient to justify regenerative braking.

The study was a useful survey of operating economics, equipment utilisation and the case for and against alternative motive power. It also provided a timely reminder that fresh technology did not necessarily offer a panacea, and this might have been relevant in considering options leading to the gas turbine project. In the longer term, history endorsed the conclusions as, until the opening of the Heathrow Express link in 1998, the former BR Western Region network remained unique in not having been subjected to any electrification.

It has been suggested that the main purpose of the Merz & McLellan study was to provide ammunition for negotiations with coal suppliers. The average price per ton had risen by about 34% between 1934 and 1937, and as the GWR purchased around 2 million tons annually, any measure that could help contain this trend was of interest. In this respect there was some success as prices eased, then held steady from early 1938 until the outbreak of war. Thereafter, the cost/quality scenario changed radically for the worse.

## Diesel-electric power

An omission in the alternative motive power suite beyond shunting engines was the diesel-electric combination, although reasons for the GWR's disinterest are not immediately obvious. As discussed in Chapter 8, the LMS experimental four-car DEMU tested between Blackpool and Preston in 1928/29 had not met expectations, but the relative technology continued to evolve overseas. In the 1920s and 1930s General Motors (Electro-Motive Corporation), Fairbanks-Morse, and the American Locomotive Company had commenced diesel-electric locomotive construction, and by 1939 even Baldwin had taken up the challenge. Concerns about reliability were certainly not supported by US railroad experience in working long distances and under varying climatic conditions. Any reservations based on prohibitive cost of modifications to suit the British loading gauge could be later largely discounted by the effectiveness of US-built diesel power in service with Allied forces in Europe and the Middle East. A more critical argument, although not recognised until 1947/48, rested on inadequate foreign currency reserves to pay for foreign-built locomotives.

Beyond the various proposals for DEMUs submitted between 1926 and 1931, the GWR remained a target customer for diesel-electric locomotives. In October 1931 Sir W. G. Armstrong, Whitworth & Co (Engineers) Ltd tendered to supply a '250 BHP Standard Oil Electric Freight and Passenger Locomotive' (that company's drawing reference LD 351/1). The wheel arrangement was described as 0-4-4 with outside connecting rods linked to a jack shaft drive. The leading dimensions quoted in the tender were:

| Bhp | 250 @ 775rpm |
| --- | --- |
| Cylinders | (6) 220mm x 280mm |
| Wheelbase: | |
| - coupled | 7ft 3in |
| - overall | 21ft 0in |
| Approximate working weight | 40 tons |
| Max axle loading | 13 tons 10 cwt |
| Tractive effort (starting) | 13,300lb |

The normal operating speed would be 45mph with a maximum of 55mph. The quoted price was £7,094 for a single locomotive (delivery within six months), reducing to £6,420 each in a batch order of 12.

## Petrol and diesel-mechanical power

Except for the diesel railcar project, incursion into internal combustion was limited to shunters, and there is no evidence of serious consideration of main-line locomotives, such as those being developed by the LMS and Southern railways. A few petrol-engined inspection trolleys were acquired during Collett's time, but these made no lasting impact. The first use of internal combustion locomotives in revenue-earning duties concerned five small petrol-engined 'Simplex' four-wheeled shunters built by Motor Rail & Tram Co Ltd of Bedford between 1923 and 1926. Numbered 15, 23, 24, 26 and 27 (in the steam locomotive series), by 1928 they were regarded as service vehicles working at locations such as Bridgwater Docks, Didcot Provender Yard, Reading Signal Works and the Engineer's Department at Taunton.

These units had four-cylinder engines developing 40bhp at 1,000rpm with two-speed gearboxes and chain drive to both axles. The equivalent tractive efforts and maximum speeds were low gear, 3,400lb and 3mph, and high gear, 1,540lb and 7.2mph. They were really shunting tractors, a motive power form quite common in some countries but never popular in Britain. No 15 was withdrawn in 1951 and the remainder in 1960. They appear latterly to have been classified as 'plant' rather than as locomotives.

There were two other Simplex shunters supplied in 1930 and built to the 2-foot gauge for use mainly on 'Jubilee' temporary track at construction sites. They weighed about 2.5 tons and developed 20bhp at 1,000rpm. Equivalent tractive efforts and maximum speeds were low gear, 1,250lb and 3.5mph, and high gear 956lb and 7mph. Unlike other machines of similar size and use that were classified as 'plant', they were numbered 22 and 25 in the steam locomotive series.

In 1933 more conventional power was introduced with the purchase of a coupled four-wheeled diesel-mechanical shunter built two years earlier by John Fowler & Co of Leeds as a demonstrator (Fowler Works No 19451). It was fitted with a six-cylinder diesel engine developing 70bhp, and equipped with a small auxiliary

**BELOW** One of the later Simplex yard shunters at Swindon.
*Stephenson Locomotive Society*

**ABOVE** The first diesel shunter purchased by the GWR seems to have been the opportunistic acquisition of a demonstrator unit built by John Fowler & Co (Leeds) Ltd. It was numbered '1' and confined to use in Swindon's yards. *Stephenson Locomotive Society*

petrol engine to aid starting. The four-speed gearbox yielded varying tractive efforts and speed maxima: 7000lb at 3mph, 3,500lb at 6mph, 2,060lb at 10.2mph, and 1,400lb at 15mph. Given the number '1' and handsomely finished in lined green express passenger livery, it was confined to shunting at Swindon Works. Placed on the spare machinery account in September 1939, it was sold early the following year. Details of its performance are not recorded, but it seems to have made no lasting impact on motive power policy.

No 2 was unique in being the only diesel-electric motive power unit owned by company, and was an altogether more substantial machine. It was a six-wheeled single-cab shunter, powered by a six-cylinder water-cooled diesel engine driving a 230kW generator that fed two motors hung on the outer axles. The centre axle was driven through coupling rods. The frames and mechanical equipment had been manufactured in 1935 by R. & W. Hawthorn, Leslie & Co, while the English Electric Company supplied the electrical equipment. It was purchased in April 1936, which suggests that it might also have had an earlier career as a demonstrator. In performance it was a considerable advance,

**ABOVE** Despite the investigative work into diesel-electric units in the 1920s, the only example of this power combination owned by the company was this shunter, purchased from the English Electric Co in 1936 and given the number 2. This was the only GWR locomotive to be renumbered at nationalisation, becoming No 15100, and it is seen here with coupling rods removed at Old Oak Common in March 1948. *R. S. Carpenter collection*

being capable of hauling 500 tons at speeds up to 19mph, or 1,000 tons at half that speed. Climbing a 1 in 100 gradient, the maximum load was 750 tons at a speed of 2.7mph. With a totally enclosed cab of generous proportions, it was broadly similar in appearance to Classes 08/09 of British Railways. During GWR days it was

**ABOVE** No 15105 near Cardiff East Dock on 3 September 1964. The cast number plates have been removed and painted numbers substituted, and there is the late-style BR emblem on the body side. *P. H. Groom*

continuously allocated to Acton except for a period during the war when it was used at the Swansea oil wharves.

In the renumbering scheme of 1946, No 2 was due to become No 500, but this never occurred; in 1948 it became No 15100, being the only GWR engine to be renumbered. Shortly before nationalisation, six machines with a similar technical specification were ordered, together with a seventh with a two-stroke engine. Delivered in BR days, Nos 15101-7 were an endorsement of general

satisfaction with No 2 (No 15100), but further development of the genre formed part of the BR diesel shunter programme associated with the Class 08 family.

These locomotives, like their later BR counterparts, were limited to shunting although their sphere of operations was more restricted by not having vacuum brakes. The nearest comparative and contemporary steam locomotives were the 0-6-0PTs of Classes '15xx', '16xx', '6750' and '94xx'. It was a sign of the rapidly changing motive power scene that GWR-design diesel shunters No 15100-15106 had longer working lives than their steam contemporaries (No 15107 was rather less successful).

The leading dimensions are shown in Table 1.

| TABLE 1 | | | | |
|---|---|---|---|---|
| **Nos** | **1** | **2 (later 15100)** | **15101-6** | **15107** |
| Introduced | 1933 | 1936 | 1948 | 1949 |
| Builder | John Fowler & Co | Hawthorn Leslie/English Electric | Swindon/English Electric | Swindon/Brush Electrical |
| Bhp | 70 | 350 | 350 | 360 |
| Traction motor hp | n/a | 2 x 170kw | 2 x 135kw | 2 x 116kw |
| Cylinders | (6) 120mm x 180mm | (6) 10in x 12in | (6) 10in x 12in | (4) 8.5in x 13in (two-stroke) |
| Main generator | n/a | 230kw | 190kw | 190kw |
| Auxiliary generator | n/a | 11kw | 4kw | 9kw |
| Wheels (ft in) | (4) 3 0 | (6) 4 0.5 | (6) 4 0.5 | (6) 4 0.5 |
| Wheelbase (ft in) | 5 6 | 5 3 + 5 3 | 5 3 + 5 3 | 5 3 + 5 3 |
| Tractive effort (lb) | See text | 30,240 | 38,500 | 35,000 |
| Weight | 18 tons 11 cwt | 51 tons 11 cwt | 46 tons 9 cwt | 46 tons 2 cwt |

# CHAPTER 10
# GAS TURBINES

Viewed from afar, the GWR's motive power policies in the inter-war years exposed intriguing contrasts. Collett, secure in his redoubt, exercised almost unchallenged authority to sponsor considerable progress in workshop and manufacturing techniques, while steadfastly refusing to countenance sensible design revisions. Concurrently, a separate tranche within the company hierarchy was exploring fresh technology options despite the CME's characteristic reticence and hostility to outside influences.

Hawksworth dispelled much of this potentially costly duality by embracing all options. Factors beyond his control limited these efforts, but his open-mindedness to new concepts, as exemplified with the 'Modified Halls', must have been a breath of fresh air after years of restraint. It was also to his credit that so much was achieved on a modest budget at a difficult time. This programme continued after his retirement, and the continued improvement of the 'Castles' at minimal expense reinforced the core excellence of Churchward's concept.

In general, the introduction of internal combustion engines was not markedly different from similar initiatives in these islands. The exception concerned plans for main-line motive power, where the GWR stepped well beyond accepted industry boundaries in a move

quite at odds with the company's conservative reputation. Records traced have failed to explain the rationale behind the decision to opt for gas turbine technology. Some commentators have written off the project as yet another effort by the company to be 'different', which is a flimsy proposition. Publicly owned companies led by responsible directors and managers might unwittingly harbour institutionalised inefficiencies (as discussed in Chapter 2), but they do not set about innovative investment programmes just for the novelty. Circumstantial evidence is set out below that might rationalise how the company came to take this revolutionary decision.

In the closing stages of the war the debate over non-steam motive power policy had considerable substance. The company, in the hope of continued independence, was on the cusp of crucial policy decisions with long-term consequences. The information garnered through the pre-war electrification evaluation was a valuable reminder of the risks and costs that new technology could encounter, especially where significant infrastructural investment was necessary.

The development of a pair of gas turbine locomotives for express duties, and their subsequent commissioning and operation under British Railways' auspices, has been comprehensively documented. An earlier work, *The Great Western Railway Gas Turbines – A Myth Exposed* by Kevin Robertson (Sutton Publishing 1989), provides extensive information on the trials and tribulations that befell these unusual machines. This diary documents an experimental project that commenced in 1946 through to its abandonment 13 years later, and elements of that work form the core of the technical description set out below.

However, an as yet unexplained aspect concerns the process by which the GWR Board chose to adopt an energy source that, in a railway context, had only once been tried before, in continental Europe. The company's diesel-mechanical railcars had shown considerable enterprise in exploiting road transport techniques, but the decision to pursue cutting-edge technology placed the gas turbine project in an altogether different league.

In 1946 Hawksworth advised that it had been decided not to proceed with main-line diesel-electric locomotives. This pronouncement's aleatoric essence was remarkable in its rejection of the latest American developments, and this conviction implies a crafted decision based on evaluation of alternatives that enjoyed Board support. Continuing problems with coal supplies and the residual, albeit reducing, hope that the company might retain its independence suggests that extensive discussions had taken place. As the price of fuel oil was then competitive with domestic coal, a strategy that included steam locomotives where conversion from coal to oil and vice-versa could be effected conveniently as market circumstances changed was attractive. This intent would have been compatible with expansion of the proven format of two- or three-car diesel railcar sets for longer-distant intermediate services. Thus adoption of a further technology in the form of gas turbines offered the company a range of energy sources that obviated the infrastructural investment needed with electrification.

Nevertheless, the decision to sidestep main-line diesels and make an unprecedented sally into the unknown suggests that something significant had occurred behind the scenes. Elements of the following explanation are based on deduction, and should be considered speculative in the absence of verifiable facts.

## Possible genesis

On several occasions the 'Big Four' considered exploitation of non-railway-sourced technology to improve locomotive performance and to redress the basic inefficiency of using reciprocation to make driving wheels revolve (e.g. cam-driven poppet valves). The Lentz, Caprotti and other valve systems yielded some theoretical gains, whereas turbine drive offered a process that relied solely on rotational movement, thereby improving mechanical performance.

BELOW Gas turbine No 18000 as built. *Ian Allan Library*

**ABOVE** Two views of No 18000 at Swindon on 20 April 1950.
*Both H. C. Casserley*

Steam turbines have been successful in electricity generation and in steam ships since the 1880s. Their effectiveness was greatly aided by double or triple compound expansion processes, and by absence of constraints on the volumes that boilers and turbines occupied. Thus a powerhouse or an engine room could be made as large as the estimated workload demanded, limited only by the maximum permissible size for manufacture and transportation of individual components. A further advantage with a powerhouse is that the turbine has a firm, stable base. Obviously this does not occur with a ship, although the turbine and attendant boilers are securely anchored to the hull/keel.

Turbines in a railway locomotive encounter challenges that do not exist elsewhere. Apart from the weight limitation, the base on which the turbine is mounted is inherently unstable through jolts and vibration imparted by the contact between metal wheel and rail. Further, design and layout must conform with the long narrow

volume dictated by the loading gauge. This latter constraint is a feature shared, for different reasons, with a turbine in an aircraft.

The first turbine drive steam locomotive owned by a British railway was the 'Turbomotive' introduced in 1935 by William Stanier on the LMS. This machine was inspired by successful Ljungstrom locomotives in Sweden and shared boiler, wheels, frames and many mechanical parts with the two conventional 'Princess Royal' 'Pacifics' (Nos 6200 and 6201) then in service. A large turbine mounted on the left-hand side of the boiler provided forward movement, while a smaller turbine on the right was for reverse running at reduced power and speed. The turbines were manufactured by Metropolitan-Vickers, and the engine cost roughly two and a half times that of a conventional 'Pacific'. Despite being an experimental one-off design, the 'Turbomotive' proved commercially effective and continued on main-line express duties until 1952. The smooth, even torque with absence of hammer blow allowed axle loadings up to 24 tons, a factor that underlined the potential for larger and more powerful machines.

Before the 'Turbomotive' entered service there was a development that had a far-reaching effect on LMS, and later GWR, steam practice. Stanier had joined the LMS fully imbued with the Churchward tradition of low superheat, but the turbine project stimulated a radical change of view. The locomotive's boiler differed from that used on the other two 'Pacifics' in one important respect. Condensation can cause serious damage to turbine blades, making dry steam obligatory and necessitating a superheater that raised the temperature to 650°F as compared with the 500°F originally applied to Nos 6200 and 6201. Pending completion of manufacture of the turbines, this boiler was spare and was experimentally fitted to No 6200. The resultant improvement in performance was a major influence on Stanier's thinking, forming the basis for his abortive attempt to persuade Collett to change GWR policy.

By the time of its appearance, the LMS restocking programme was progressing, but the 'Turbomotive' earned Stanier a personal profile in fields beyond the railway industry. This was demonstrated by leading American industrial designer Raymond Loewy, who was lavish in his praise of No 6202. Then in the late 1930s Stanier won governmental recognition through participation in two formal enquiries into matters concerning the state-owned Indian Railways. Sir Ralph Wedgwood, Chief General Manager of the LNER, led the first (October 1936 to March 1937) to investigate the cause of operating losses and to recommend remedial action. Stanier *inter alia* identified wastage through poor locomotive and stock utilisation, and in excessive numbers of engines awaiting repair (shades of the contemporary GWR). The second enquiry started in 1938 when he was part of a technical group convened to assess the poor riding qualities of 'Pacific' Classes 'XA', 'AB' and 'XC', one of which had crashed the previous year causing much loss of life. These two enquiries addressed contentious issues at a delicate time in the face of demands for Indian independence. They were a considerable drain on a busy man's time, but his successful participation was clearly appreciated.

In 1942 Stanier was seconded to the Ministry of Production as one of a team of three scientific advisors. Accounts of his work in this role seem to be slight, presumably falling under the 'hush-hush' colloquialism, so symbolic of innovation in those times. However, his work was sufficient to win both political and scientific recognition. He was knighted in early 1943, and a year later received the far more significant accolade of election as a Fellow of the Royal Society; the only other railway engineer so honoured had been Robert Stephenson.

The nature of some of his responsibilities might be divined by his appointment as Chairman of Power Jets Ltd, a company formed in January 1936 by (later Sir) Frank Whittle, inventor of the British jet aircraft engine. Power Jets initially operated in factory premises rented from British Thomson-Houston Ltd (a subsidiary of Metropolitan-Vickers) at Rugby, Warwickshire, with personnel seconded from BT-H and the Royal Air Force. The first turbojet engine was bench-tested in 1937, and in May 1941 the Gloster E.28/39 (popularly known as the 'Gloster Whittle') was the first British jet to fly. Whittle reluctantly agreed to the nationalisation of Power Jets in March 1944, and Stanier appears to have become chairman then. After the war the company was merged with the Turbine Division of the Royal Aircraft Establishment at Farnborough, to form the National Gas Turbine Establishment. Secrecy surrounding the technology was intense – for example, the Gloster Meteor, the first operational jet fighter to serve with the RAF (from 1944), was forbidden to fly over enemy territory lest one should fall into German hands.

Reviewing this chronology, there are several points of speculation:

1 Following Collett's rejection of the compound 'Castle' proposal in 1926, Stanier and Hawksworth might have jointly considered other ideas, although with rather more circumspection.

2 The pair were friends into retirement and their individual skills formed the basis for an ideal technical partnership. Stanier was a brilliant practical engineer with an interest in metallurgy (his father had established the laboratory at Swindon, and had worked with William Dean on a seminal paper on the use of metals in locomotive construction). Hawksworth's draughting skills and theoretical knowledge would have been invaluable in documenting new ideas.

3 Unlike the present day, where major corporate reorganisations are conducted by imported executive teams, Stanier went alone to the LMS, armed only with

**BELOW** Gas turbine No 18100 at Metropolitan-Vickers' Trafford Park Works, Manchester. *Metropolitan-Vickers*

many GWR locomotive drawings. He then drew upon the best talent that he could find within the ranks of his new employer. The drawings were taken with Collett's blessing, but any work related to investigations with Hawksworth might have been more sensitive, raising issues of ownership of Intellectual Property Rights.

4   Stanier's workload at the LMS was immense, yet it is intriguing that the 'Turbomotive' should have appeared so early in his tenure, being preceded only by the 'Princess Royal' 'Pacifics' and 5F 2-6-0s (1933), 4-6-0 'Jubilees'/Class 5s, and 4P 2-6-4Ts (1934). The decision to build this revolutionary machine followed a visit to Sweden in 1932, but there were significant delays in manufacture of the turbines. The timing suggests that design work might have started before he joined the LMS.

5   The introduction of the 'Turbomotive' broadly coincided with Whittle's early work on jet engines. Both he and Stanier collaborated with Metropolitan-Vickers and it seems probable that their mutual, non-competing interest in turbines meant that they were in contact from that time.

6   Robert Stephenson had became an FRS when steam was regarded as modern technology, a situation that definitely did not obtain in the 1940s. Stanier's only exposure to modern engineering issues that can be confirmed with certainty involved turbines. It would have been a natural thought process to recognise the potential for jet technology in powering railway locomotives, and to approach his old friend (Hawksworth) and his old employer with his ideas.

7   Although Stanier effectively gave up the position of CME in 1942, he did not officially relinquish the appointment until 1944. C. E. Fairburn acted in the role in the interim, and was then confirmed as successor. This was a slightly odd appointment for a concern that was mainly steam-powered, and likely to remain so for the foreseeable future, as Fairburn was predominantly an electrical engineer. Reputedly he had secured the promotion by outmanoeuvring other candidates with some questionable tactics, but his suitability became academic with his death at the age of 58 years in 1945. Stanier's last service to the LMS seems to have been to endorse H. G. Ivatt as Fairburn's successor. Nevertheless, the atmosphere might have been too reminiscent of the situation he encountered in 1932 for him to want any continuing involvement in LMS affairs.

8   Despite his work on the LMS, Stanier always knew where his core loyalties lay. In retirement he remarked to O. S. Nock, 'I've still got "GWR" embroidered on the seat of my trousers', and his re-engagement with his old employer, albeit it in an informal and discreet fashion,

would have been welcome. He knew how to keep his own counsel and was a skilled diplomat, as shown in his adjudication at the request of Edward Thompson in the torrid debate over the design practices of the late Sir Nigel Gresley. It would be entirely in character for him to lend his support in low-profile fashion.

9   Finally, in addition to the Hawksworth-Stanier collaboration on a technical plane, it is probable that Milne was fully informed of progress through his position as Stanier's brother-in-law.

It is reiterated that the evidence that Stanier acted behind the scenes as godfather to the gas turbine project is entirely circumstantial. However, there were too many coincidences for there not to be substance in the proposition.

## The gas turbine pair

The first written evidence of interest in gas turbine technology was a joint venture agreement signed with Metropolitan-Vickers in January 1946 to construct an express passenger locomotive that eventually became British Railways No 18100. Obviously the concept had been actively discussed at senior level during 1945, presumably following the end of the war in August, when freer access to fresh technology would have been permissible.

In early June 1946 Milne and Hawksworth attended the International Railway Congress in Switzerland and, during a two-week stay in that country, visited several engineering works to study construction methods. This displayed a spirit of enquiry reminiscent of Churchward's interest in foreign practice, and quite different from Collett's isolationism. Rolling stock construction that made use of alternative metals, particularly aluminium, was investigated in view of UK steel shortages. More specifically, the experience of Brown-Boveri in gas turbine power had direct relevance to the joint venture project by then under way with Metropolitan-Vickers.

On 27 June Hawksworth reported to the Locomotive Committee on the Brown-Boveri meetings. The following day the Board approved commencement of negotiations for acquisition of a gas turbine locomotive at an approximate cost of £100,000. It was anticipated that the contract would be formally confirmed by the end of September 1946 for delivery within 24 months. The haste displayed a sense of urgency, presumably in anticipation of time running out for the independent Great Western. Also, it seems probable that the Board had been fully briefed on intentions before the Swiss visit.

Although Metropolitan-Vickers had a head start, the Brown-Boveri machine was completed first, being numbered 18000 by British Railways. This was understandable, as the Swiss had already built a gas turbine locomotive, giving the advantage of practical experience. Swiss Federal Railways had ordered a 2,200hp gas turbine locomotive in 1939 for routes where traffic density did not justify electrification. The result was a locomotive with the unusual 1+A+Bo+A+1 wheel arrangement, and which had a tractive effort of 29,000lb delivered through four axle-mounted electric motors. It started working in 1941 and on test satisfied the manufacturer's expectations. It entered normal service in 1943 and Swiss Federal Railways assumed legal ownership in 1944. By August 1946 it had successfully covered 68,000 miles despite extended periods out of use due to fuel shortages, and on this basis there were optimistic hopes for No 18000.

Progress with No 18100 was slower. Metropolitan-Vickers had to cope with manpower and material shortages, and also the demands of post-war reconstruction – factors that had not affected Switzerland, as a neutral country. Also the ponderous nature of the joint venture proved an impediment, as even modest specification changes required both partners' approval. In contrast, Brown-Boveri, in following the terms of a construct and supply contract, were free to get on with the job.

Even so, Hawksworth was to be disappointed had he hoped to see No 18000 in service before retirement at the end of 1949. The locomotive was more or less complete by the beginning of that year, but there followed a number of delays for undisclosed reasons. Also, equipment for UK conditions had to be shipped for installation, e.g. buffers, couplings and ATC equipment, and a fitter/erector (S. C. Lewis) was seconded from Swindon for maintenance training and to report progress. Hawksworth visited Switzerland in May to witness successful bench-testing.

Lewis advised that completion was expected by the end of September 1949, but then had to modify this estimate to a month later. Hawksworth, accompanied by A. W. J. Dymond and W. A. L. Creighton (an electrical assistant), visited Switzerland in November to witness test running on freight and passenger trains, and performance was generally as promised. This visit was one of Hawksworth's last duties before retirement.

With further delays, No 18000 did not arrive at Harwich until 3 February 1950, reaching Swindon a few days later. It first moved under its own power on British metals in a return journey light engine to Stoke Gifford on 22 February. The leisurely pace at which the project had proceeded from the beginning of 1949 contrasted with the urgency in 1946. Relevant factors must have included diminishing enthusiasm with the GWR's impending demise, Hawksworth's waning interest with retirement approaching, and uncertainty over new corporate direction. However, the relaxed attitude of the manufacturers was possibly suspicious, suggesting that the test results might not have been as unequivocally positive as had been suggested.

With the Metropolitan-Vickers locomotive (BR No 18100), progress was further slowed by reservations expressed by the newly installed BR management. There were concerns about bogie design, which nevertheless proceeded against the preferences of R. A. Riddles, although his views were later justified by early frame cracking. Another point of contention was the selection and design of the train-heating boiler – an area of difficulty shared with No 18000, and with the early BR diesel locomotives.

No 18100's power unit was successfully bench-tested in November 1950 with hopes that the completed locomotive would be available for presentation at the Festival of Britain in March 1951. This proved unrealistic as the first movements under power were made at the Metropolitan-Vickers factory in November of that year. It was delivered to Swindon in December and made its first cautious test runs early in 1952, almost two years after the Swiss-built locomotive.

Both locomotives used jet engines of the 'ram air' type that had been invented by Sir Frank Whittle. As adapted for railway use, the essential elements are that large quantities of air are drawn into a compressor, then into a combustion chamber where fuel oil is burned. The resultant gases leave the combustion chamber at high speed, and that process in an aircraft engine generates the thrust that impels movement. In a locomotive, the high-speed gases turn a turbine connected directly to a shaft that drives an electric generator. The hot gases on emission from the turbine pass through a heat exchanger that preheats air passing from the compressor into the combustion chamber. Thereafter the gases are exhausted to the open air. The key stages in the cycle are shown in the accompanying diagram:

The layout of the components relevant to each other in the Brown-Boveri locomotive (No 18000) was made public in an official explanatory publication produced by the Railway Executive:

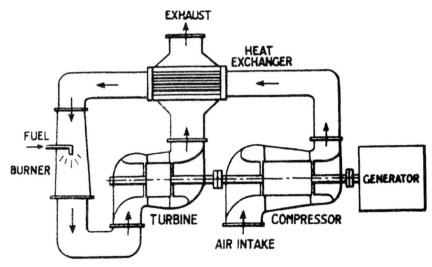

**ABOVE** A schematic drawing of a gas turbine engine with a single-stage compressor.

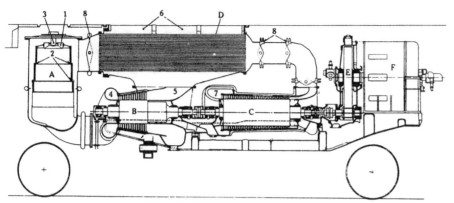

A. Combustion Chamber
B. Gas Turbine
C. Air Compressor
D. Heat Exchanger
E. Generator Reduction Gear
F. Generator

1 Combustion Air Swirl Vanes
2. Secondary Air Inlets
3. Burner Nozzle
4. Turbine Inlet
5. Turbine Exhaust
6. Exhaust louvres to atmosphere
7 Compressor air inlet
8. Expansion joints

**ABOVE** The Brown-Boveri power unit.

Both locomotives were rated as the equivalent of a 'King' for haulage and route availability purposes, but their leading dimensions show that they were potentially in quite different motive power categories:

| | 18000 | 18100 |
|---|---|---|
| Wheel arrangement | A1A+A1A | Co-Co |
| Weight | 115 tons 3 cwt | 129 tons 10 cwt |
| Continuous rating | 2,500hp | 3,000hp |
| Maximum tractive effort | 31,500lb | 60,000lb |
| Maximum speed | 90 mph | 90 mph |
| Fuel type | Heavy oil | Light oil |
| Auxiliary diesel | Yes | No |
| Height | 13ft 4in | 12ft 10in |
| Width | 9ft 2.5in | 9ft |
| Length | 63ft 0.5in | 66ft 9.25in |
| Wheel diameter: | | |
| - driving | 4ft 0.5in | 3ft 8in |
| - carrying | 3ft 2in | n/a |
| Bogie wheelbase | 11ft 9.75in | 15ft |

As neither the GWR nor Hawksworth played any role in their working careers, the operational history of both locomotives falls outside the scope of this work. However, to summarise, following extensive testing No 18000 entered normal service in May 1950, initially on London-Swindon duties, then London-Plymouth. As might be expected with a prototype using revolutionary technology, numerous teething problems and more serious failures were encountered. When working properly performance was

impressive, but a review of service between commissioning and October 1958 revealed that the locomotive had been out of service for 1,560 weekdays, which rendered an availability of less than 20%. Mileage covered in that period, at 319,000, was comparable with express steam engines but markedly below that typically delivered by BR diesels, even in their early days, when reliability was unimpressive. No 18000 stopped work in September 1959 and was officially withdrawn in December 1960.

No 18100 similarly underwent exhaustive testing before entering normal service in April 1952, likewise incurring numerous teething problems and failures. Towards the end of 1953 Swindon reported 25 major failures against a cumulative mileage of 75,000. Poor reliability must have been frustrating in view of the power potential, as demonstrated in load tests held in November 1952 when a 17-coach train (590 tons gross) was hauled unassisted from Plymouth to Newton Abbot. Continuing problems led to withdrawal in December 1953 for conversion by Metropolitan-Vickers to use heavy oil, as originally envisaged. This work encountered difficulties and by early 1956 had still not been completed. Abandonment of the project was then proposed, and the joint venture was finally wound up at the end of 1957. BR Western Region officially withdrew the locomotive in January 1958 although, like No 18000, it had a subsequent career as a test machine in other hands.

One contributory factor behind the operating problems echoed experiences of many years earlier with the servicing of steam railmotors at steam depots. The gas turbine machines also suffered under this system as, without special facilities, there was no easy means of keeping bogies and electric motors clean. The importance of these measures was not appreciated, and excessive accumulation of under-body dirt is believed to have caused several flashovers that damaged the electric motors. The worst occurred with No 18000 in 1956 when No 3 traction motor seized completely, leading to its removal and to the engine completing its working life with reduced haulage capacity.

These experiences fuelled Swindon's antipathy towards electric transmissions, providing evidence to help persuade higher authority that BR Western Region would be better served by diesel-hydraulic locomotives. The need for a purpose-designed maintenance infrastructure to support the gas turbines recalled conclusions drawn from the GWR's investigation of electrification. While new technology might provide advances at unit operating level, the

**ABOVE** No 18100 in ordinary service.

financial benefits were substantially less attractive when taking to account the infrastructural expense – an element that seems to have been underplayed in the promotion of steam replacement programmes. This is a complex topic but one that suggests that Riddles was making an effective point in sponsoring a fleet of modern, standardised steam locomotives during a period of scarce investment capital.

Hawksworth's involvement in the project was marginalised by the organisational structures needed to develop machines radically more complex than the traditional steam locomotive. The days when a railway company's works could produce all motive power needs inhouse were rapidly drawing to a close. In future, the role of the CME would require collaboration with a variety of knowledge sources and disciplines whose origins were far removed from the railway industry. In that respect, Hawksworth would have been conscious that much more was ending than just the independent GWR, and his own career.

# CHAPTER 11

# HAWKSWORTH-ERA ROLLING STOCK

Despite the reservations over diversion of Swindon's resources into war production, there was a revision of this attitude in late 1940 when an independent manufacturer that had been bombed out of its premises in Kent was relocated to the Carriage Shop. In normal times this facility could house around 250 coaches, but only a small section was retained for repair work and very limited new construction. The remaining floor space was adapted for the manufacture of munitions and aircraft parts.

The low priority accorded to new passenger stock meant that construction ceased in September 1941 following completion of orders placed pre-war. With the exception of Diagram Nos A.3/A.4 covering diesel railcars Nos 35-38 completed in February 1942, no new passenger vehicles were built in the years 1942-44. Construction resumed in 1945, but was limited to 20 Passenger Brake Vans to pre-war Diagram K.42 and a pair of special saloons for Royal Train service. Ambitious plans were prepared in 1944 for a new generation of main-line passenger

vehicles once peace was restored. This objective, a graphic demonstration of intent to achieve new standards for passenger accommodation on the modern railway, was delayed and largely frustrated by post-war shortages of materials and manpower.

A more generous body length of 64 feet was adopted to accommodate an unchanged seating capacity, and six new types were introduced and built between 1945 and 1951:

| Vehicle Type | Diagram Nos | Number built |
| --- | --- | --- |
| All 1st | A.23 | 29 |
| All 3rd | C.82/C.84 | 206 |
| All 3rd* | C.85 | 1 |
| Brake Composite | E.164 | 44 |
| Brake 3rd | D.131/D.133 | 157 |
| Composite | E.163/E.165 | 36 |
| Passenger Brake | K.45/K.46 | 45 |

* Experimental vehicle

**LEFT** All 3rd No W2113 (Diagram C.82), built in April 1949, forms part of a local service at Oxford in 1951. Despite the building date, the coach seems to be in chocolate and cream livery with the last form of GWR lining. *Patrick Kingston*

**RIGHT** Brand-new Hawksworth All 3rd coaches Nos 910, 911 and 912 (Diagram C.82) in 1948. These were from Lot No 1714 (Nos 855-924), built by the Gloucester Railway Carriage & Wagon Co. *Historical Model Railway Society*

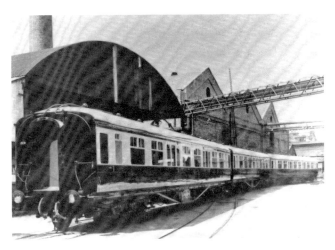

In the prevailing spirit of optimism, it was planned that the Works should build vehicles at the rate of five per week, with 260 intended in 1946, but this soon proved unrealistic. Eventually, only 518 new main-line carriages were delivered over seven years, with the help of contractors.

The new vehicles displayed clean crisp lines in keeping with modern trends, and were well received. Externally, the Hawksworth coaches introduced a new body profile with vertical slab sides, except for a slight inward taper just above solebar level. The roof ends were distinctive in sloping downwards in a fashion reminiscent of Gresley corridor panelled teak coaches. A further break with tradition was the mounting of destination boards immediately below the cantrail, rather than the previous position on the roof above the gutter.

The interior layout followed the format adopted with stock from 1938 onwards, but the extra body length allowed for more

**BELOW** All 3rd No W791W, built in 1948, is in BR 'blood and custard' at Marazion on 26 August 1958. *R. S. Carpenter collection*

commodious compartments and vestibules. A number of changes were made to interior panelling. Oak veneer was used initially, but with later vehicles enamelled hardboard was substituted, which proved very successful. Fluorescent lighting was tried, as pioneered by the London Passenger Transport Board on the District Line in 1944. Six 3rd Class coaches were so equipped but, with the technology in its infancy, the system was not completely satisfactory and further development was abandoned after nationalisation.

During their visit to Switzerland in 1946, Sir James Milne and Hawksworth paid particular attention to experiments being conducted by Brown-Boveri and Swiss Locomotive & Machine Works in the use of aluminium and light alloys in various locomotive components and in wagon construction. A key objective was a reduction of the unsprung weight of powered bogies. Very likely inspired by observations made during this visit, several of the new coaches embodied alternative techniques for body construction including the use of light alloys in sectionalised body panelling, body frames and ventilators. These features remained unique to these vehicles until British Railways revived the concept in the 1960s. All 3rd No 2239, completed in April 1950 under Diagram C.85, was especially interesting in having an aluminium chassis. Details of coaches with special features appear in Appendix G.

The new coaches were announced in mid-1945, but the slow construction rate meant that there were insufficient available when an exhibition train was displayed at Paddington in November 1946, together with oil-burner No 5091 *Cleeve Abbey*. Suitably restyled older vintage coaches were included to demonstrate the planned new interiors. The earliest report of ordinary service use that has been traced is dated September 1946, and states that All 3rd Nos 789, 791, 793 and 796 formed part of the 9.00am Paddington-Wolverhampton express. By November that year All 3rd Nos 785, 787, 790 and 792 were regularly rostered in the 'Cornish Riviera' sets. As more became available it was possible to make up complete

**LEFT** Experimental All 3rd No 2239 (Diagram C.85) had an aluminium frame.

**ABOVE** Hawksworth Composite No W7813W (Diagram E.165), built in November 1949, carries BR maroon livery at Barmouth on 13 September 1959. *Pamlin Prints*

train sets of Hawksworth coaches (excluding catering vehicles), particularly for the 'Cornish Riviera' and the 'Bristolian'.

Although catering vehicles were not included in the programme, details appeared in *The Locomotive* for November 1945 of plans to upgrade the interiors of Restaurant Cars using contemporary materials and styles, rather than to build new stock. This continued the custom whereby catering vehicles within otherwise matched train sets were readily identifiable by their differing body profiles. One idea promulgated with the 1945 plans was an 'Automat' Buffet Car. This idea envisaged the dispensing of food, drink and sundry non-edible items on a coin-in-the-slot basis from wall-mounted containers in the mode now associated with vending machines. This was probably incompatible with contemporary tastes and retailing habits, but at least demonstrated keenness to explore new ways of meeting passenger service expectations.

The provision of 29 All 1sts was notable as, although some new coaches in this category had appeared in the 1930s, the GWR usually preferred composite vehicles for the accommodation of 1st Class passengers. Brake Composites Nos 7372 and 7377 were retained for special duties in connection with special saloons Nos 9006 and 9007, which had been built for Royal Train duties under Diagrams G.64 and G.65 in 1945. The new-profile Hawksworth main-line stock was intended for general service use, but in addition there were four 1st Class Sleepers, Nos 9082-85 (Diagram J.18), fitted with six-wheeled bogies.

**RIGHT** Brake Composite (Diagram E.164) No W7377W is seen at Old Oak Common carriage sheds in the early 1950s. This was one of a pair set aside for Royal Train duties; its companion for this work (No W7372W) is standing behind. *Lens of Sutton*

After the war, some secondary services were still using ageing clerestory coaches supplemented by a sprinkling of four-wheelers in remote locations. These geriatrics would doubtless have disappeared but for the war, so plans were made for modernisation of vehicles used on suburban and branch duties. In terms of general styling, these new non-corridor coaches were similar to those built up to 1940, except with respect to body lengths. The pre-war series had varied: Brake Composites (Diagram E.161) and Brake 3rds (D.125) were 57 feet; Composites (E.156) were 59ft 3in; and All 3rds (C.75) were 55ft 3in. Similar categories were introduced after the war, but all shared the new standard length of 63ft 1in. Possibly the most interesting were the All 3rds, which accommodated 100 passengers in ten compartments, yielding a considerably better standard of comfort than BR's later application of the six-aside configuration for 3rd Class passengers.

The coaches introduced were:

| Vehicle type | Diagram Nos | Number built | Years |
|---|---|---|---|
| All 3rd | C.83 | 232 | 1948-51 |
| Brake Composite | E.167 | 32 | 1952-54 |
| Composite | E.166 | 36 | 1952-53 |
| Brake 3rd | D.132 | 141 | 1948-53 |

**BELOW** This Hawksworth Brake 3rd (Diagram D.131, number not discernible) is in BR 'blood and custard'. *S. V. Blencowe*

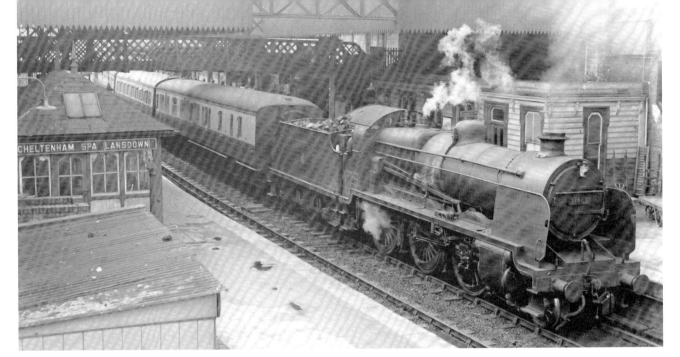

ABOVE LMS location, Southern locomotive, GWR coaches. Later in their careers Hawksworth stock was relegated to a variety of secondary duties. Here Southern Railway 2-6-0 Class 'U' No 31802 (rebuilt from a Class 'K' 'River' 2-6-4T in 1928) has arrived at Cheltenham Spa Lansdown station on a terminating service over the old Midland & South Western Junction Railway route from Andover. Cheltenham was the northern operating extremity of the MSWJR and this arrangement continued well into BR days. The first coach in the train is a Hawksworth Brake Composite.

ABOVE Hawksworth Passenger Brake Van No W319W (Diagram K.45) in BR maroon on 18 March 1966. The practice of assigning PBVs to specific routes persisted until quite late, as with this example, which is marked 'Paddington and Birkenhead' – on this occasion honoured in the breach as the location is Calstock, in Cornwall.

ABOVE Brake Composite No W7863W in BR maroon was photographed at Birmingham Snow Hill in about 1963. R. S. Carpenter collection

ABOVE Passenger Brake Van No W310W in tatty BR maroon.
R. K. Blencowe

ABOVE Twelve-wheeled 1st Class Sleeping Car No W9083W (Diagram J.18), built in February 1951, in BR maroon. There were four of these vehicles, the only carriages in the distinctive new styling that were not intended for general service. J. H. Aston

**ABOVE** 'Modified Hall' No 6993 *Arthog Hall* heads a secondary passenger train of five vehicles. The rear three coaches are corridor stock, but the first two are a Hawksworth Suburban Non-Corridor Brake 3rds (Diagram D.132), followed by a Suburban Non-Corridor All 3rd (Diagram C.83).

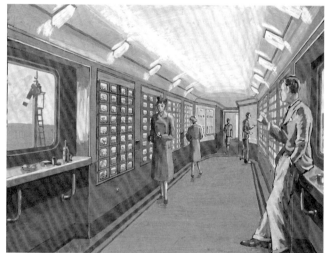

**RIGHT** An artist's impression of the interior of the proposed 'Automat' buffet car. *GWR*

**BELOW** Hawksworth Suburban Non-Corridor All 3rd (Diagram C.83) No 2002, seating 100 in ten compartments, is seen at Barmouth on 7 September 1959. *Pamlin Prints*

**ABOVE** Diagram A.39 auto-trailer No W220W at Bicester on 28 July 1961, with Class '54xx' 0-6-0PT No 5420. Rather oddly, this coach carried the name 'Wren' in sans-serif lettering midway along the side. Companion No W219W was named 'Thrush' in similar fashion, but no other auto-trailers were so blessed. *R. K. Blencowe collection*

**ABOVE** The typical auto-train in the final years was an 0-4-2T Class '14xx' with one or two of the post-nationalisation vehicles. No 1434 is seen with trailer No W226W at Tavistock with a service to Plymouth North Road on 5 June 1959. *J. H. Aston*

**BELOW** In 1958 three Hawksworth Brake Composites were rebuilt as slip coaches and repainted in BR chocolate and cream to harmonise with the sets of the 'Cornish Riviera'. One of these converted vehicles is seen on the last multiple slip working on 7 June 1960 approaching

Didcot West Curve Junction. The train was the 7.00am Weston-super-Mare to Paddington. (The very last single coach slip took place with the 5.10pm Paddington-Wolverhampton service at Bicester on 9 September 1960, with Hawksworth coach No 7374). *J. A. Coiley*

The build dates show that these 441 vehicles received lower priority than was given to main-line stock. They were of pure GWR design but were never operated by the company. They also had short lives, being rendered redundant with the arrival of diesel multiple units in the 1950s and 1960s. The last of pure GWR design were Diagram E.167 Brake Composites Nos 6276-85 (Lot No 1777 of 1954), which were used as two-coach B-sets.

There was one remaining coach type in the GWR style built at Swindon – a new generation of auto-trailers. By 1950 many of the steam railmotor conversions and older purpose-built auto-trailers were reaching the end of their working lives. Further, some were internally rather spartan and compared poorly with comfort standards of the post-war corridor and suburban coaches. The new auto-trailers used all-steel body construction with the new slab-sided profile and 'main-line' dimensions of 64 feet by 8ft 11in, but retained a family resemblance to the older auto-trailers. Internally they made use of modern materials, and back-to-back seating replaced most of the traditional longitudinal benches. Twenty-five were built and, because of variations in internal layout and decor, they were covered by four separate Diagrams. Technically these were not Hawksworth coaches, as they were designed after his retirement, but they reflected the standards of improved space and comfort that he had introduced. They were distributed widely through BR's Western Region and were common on the last auto services. They were pleasant vehicles in which to ride and preferable to contemporary BR non-corridor suburban stock.

Nos 235-244 of Lot No A.43 had the distinction of being the new last coaches built by BR to a non-standard design – not pure GWR, but not far from it. The auto-trailers were:

| Diagram Nos | Number built | Year |
| --- | --- | --- |
| A.38 | 13 | 1951 |
| A.39/A.40/A.43 | 12 | 1954 |

Details of the carriage fleet introduced under Hawksworth's auspices are set out in Appendix G.

### 'Siphons'

In contrast to the ambitious plans to build a new generation of coach stock, 'brown' vehicles introduced under Hawksworth and in the following period were modest in numbers and entirely traditional in concept. Around 1930 introduction of milk tank wagons suggested impending redundancy for the 'Siphon' fleet. Then, following reassessment of future needs, construction of 'Siphons G' was restarted for use on a wide variety of traffic. They continued to be known generically as 'milk vans' until the end of their days.

'Siphons G' built after 1941 were of the modern, inside-frame, gangway variety (50 feet long by 8ft 6in wide) with only minor

**RIGHT** A standard 'Mink A' to Diagram V.23, No 141812, is seen in BR days. More than 3,000 of this type were built between 1933 and 1941. *P. J. Sharpe*

**ABOVE** 'Siphon G' (Diagram O.62) No W1048 stands at Gloucester on 13 August 1980. *C. J. Tuffs*

differences from earlier Lots. Their final duties were mainly on newspaper services, for which their ventilation louvres were boarded over except for those between the outer side doors and the ends. A few were still to be seen at Paddington in the early 1980s, awaiting departure on evening newspaper trains. Despite their 'Rail Blue' livery, there was no doubt about their origins, providing a nostalgic reminder of times past. Their diagram details were:

| Diagram | Number built | Years |
| --- | --- | --- |
| O.33 | 30 | 1944-45 |
| O.62 | 60 | 1950-51 |
| O.62 | 20 | 1955 |

### Freight stock

Considerable numbers of wagons were built from 1941 onwards, often in continuation of programmes commenced before the war. There was little design change, but the demands of the times influenced the pattern of construction. There was a need for wagons designed to transport aeroplane propellers early in the war, but later demand grew for flat trucks to handle containers and palletised traffic. Few heavy-duty wagons (e.g. the 'Loriot'/'Macaw' families) appeared as, although there was vastly increased need to move loads for which such vehicles were intended, new construction went straight into military ownership.

**LEFT** 'CONFLAT' No W39155, Diagram H.6, stands at Maidenhead with a cement container on 21 July 1949. This wagon was part of a Lot built between 1933 and 1935, but basically similar vehicles were built from 1943 and on into BR days. *Topical Press Agency*

varnish. Redundant bogie coach chassis (designated 'Bocar A') were also modified, in this case with frames to support sheeted covers and sides for the transport of motor car bodies. As needs changed, some were converted to carry up to 9 tons of rails, for which they were designated 'Macaw Z' ('Borail A' after 1943), and were later converted back to 'Bocar A'. In addition, some four-wheel coach chassis were converted to become 'Bocar B'.

Appendix H summarises the wagon types built during Hawksworth's tenure, although several were continuations of construction programmes initiated years before.

The majority were vans ('Mink') and six-plank opens, continuing pre-war building programmes. There were minor variations but they basically followed the established style with the Morton brakes that had earlier displaced the Dean-Churchward type. A significant change occurred with later vans and 'Vanfits' (Diagrams V.37 to V.39 from 1947 onwards) in the use of plywood bodies to substitute for planked sides and ends, as suitable timber was in short supply.

Tradition remained strong as emphasised by shunter trucks ('gigs'), which were appropriately labelled and tailored individually for the locations where they were used. Those employed on carriage shunting were vacuum fitted with instanter couplings, whereas those that worked in goods yards were non-fitted. In 1940, with older trucks due for replacement, a building programme commenced under which new trucks even assumed the numbers of their predecessors.

Another long-standing tradition was the creation of 'Cordons' by mounting gas tanks on redundant coach and 'Siphon' chassis. This practice commenced in the late 19th century and conversions were effected as required through to BR days, normally but not exclusively involving nine gas cylinders mounted transversely on four-wheel (and sometimes six-wheel) chassis.

Variations on this theme occurred from 1938 onwards. Diagrams EE.1 and EE.2 were issued for 'Siphon' chassis that were modified to carry four tanks for the conveyance of paint and

**BELOW** Paint and varnish tank wagon No 39882 used the chassis from six-wheeled 'Siphon' No 1931. *Modern Transport*

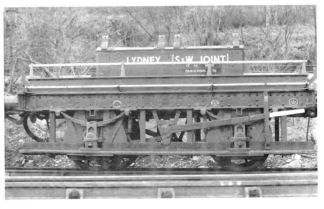

**RIGHT** The ubiquitous inhabitant of so many yards and stations – the shunters truck or 'gig'. Diagram M.5 No 41152 was built at Swindon in 1942 to replace an older truck carrying the same number and allocation details. It has heavy-duty buffing gear, vacuum pipes and instanter couplings, but retains spoked wheels.

# CHAPTER 12
# RETIREMENT AND REFLECTIONS

No records appear to have survived of Frederick Hawksworth's feelings at the end of his railway career, but his memories must have been flavoured with disappointment. He had witnessed the elegance of the Great Western in the late Victorian era, so closely associated with the great William Dean. He had played his part, albeit in a junior capacity, in the company's high summer under G. J. Churchward. He then achieved significant seniority shortly following endorsement of prevailing superiority of Swindon design practice in the 1925 Locomotive Exchanges.

After such a brilliant opening, the loss of momentum and the missed opportunities would have been frustrating. Equally, there could have been little satisfaction in knowing that his promotion upon Collett's retirement derived from the premature death of the preferred candidate, rather as the untimely passing of two senior colleagues had opened the way for his rapid elevation in the early 1920s. In his career advancement, he was thus both the beneficiary of circumstance and its victim.

With the Grouping, the Chief Mechanical Engineer became responsible for a larger workforce than any of his peers. The breadth and complexity of the position gave Collett cherished mental sanctuary. Someone less afflicted by loneliness might have welcomed retirement at age 65, and in Collett's case this would have roughly coincided with the company's Centenary celebrations. The closing years of his career were to prove expensive for the greater organisation in suppression of fresh thinking, and in manufacturing and resource management of questionable benefit.

None could have anticipated just how severe would be the circumstances that surrounded his eventual departure, nor the acute need for policy revisions that greatly added to the challenges facing his successor. These conditions notwithstanding, the inadequacy of Hawksworth's grooming and preparation for the role was an indictment of feeble strategic planning and limited foresight.

Viewed in this context, Hawksworth deserves more recognition and accolade than has so far been paid him. The role of chief executive officer is one where those close by, familiar with the scale of the issues, might empathise, and where those more distant, insulated by ignorance, might criticise, but only one man actually feels the burden. Whether or not Hawksworth was conscious of his shortcomings, the year 1941 was no time for introspection. Action was needed and he did not shirk the considerable load thrust upon his shoulders.

Excluding the LMS, where experience with CMEs was varied, there was similarity in the succession pattern of the 'Big Four'. Three individuals – Bulleid on the Southern in 1937, Thompson on the LNER in 1941, and Hawksworth – followed incumbents who had held their positions since pre-Grouping days. In each case they had grounds for disagreeing with elements of their predecessor's work, and each faced chronic difficulties in coping with vastly increased operational demands. A medium for judging Hawksworth as CME is to compare him against this peer group. Bulleid made little secret of his discontent over aspects of Maunsell's work, then set about creating a locomotive fleet whose technical complexity hardly accorded with contemporary needs. Thompson, acerbic in criticising practices of his deceased predecessor and in his treatment of subordinates, initiated a change of direction that yielded only mixed results.

Hawksworth had greater grounds for disquiet over what had gone before, yet kept his counsel. As circumstances allowed he introduced modest but effective improvements that paid generous dividends. Consideration of his contribution to the GWR 4-6-0 story typically focuses on the uncertainties of the 'Counties', while overlooking the simple yet profound changes that made very good engines of the 'Modified Halls' and the final 'Castle' sub-class. With regard to the latter, Hawksworth's improvements were finessed after his retirement with an idea he had pioneered with No 1000 – the double chimney. This exercise produced sparkling results at minimal extra cost, in stark contrast to the extravagance associated with the Southern's 'Pacific' hoard.

With secondary types, the saga of Class '94xx' disguised clarity of purpose that made a refreshing change from previous confusion. Perhaps the greatest source of frustration was that conditions prevented more change and rationalisation in the crowded nine years of his tenure. Delays in the gas turbine project must have added to regret over plans unfulfilled in the closing phase of his career.

Though he continued to live in his home town, Hawksworth showed little or no interest in the enthusiast community. Despite the presence of No 9400 in the Museum, he was seemingly devoid of the nostalgia that helped drive the preservation movement,

BELOW F. W. Hawksworth with his Principal Officers outside the CME's headquarters at his retirement in 1949.

ABOVE Old colleagues chat together in June 1959 after a Swindon Rotary dinner – K. J. Cook, Sir William Stanier, F. W. Hawksworth and A. W. J. Dymond.

apparently preferring social contact with professional engineers and former colleagues. Finding someone who had met him personally has proved hard, but late in this project contact was fortunately made with Mr Peter Lugg, who had commenced his career with the GWR as an engine cleaner at Old Oak Common before becoming a Locomotive Apprentice at Swindon. It is best to quote Mr Lugg's own words on his acquaintanceship and on Hawksworth's designs:

'Although I met him on a couple of occasions whilst I was involved with 18000, the Brown-Boveri gas turbine, I was then but a relatively junior Engineer and thus my relationship with him was rather more "master and worker" than colleague. I felt he was rather punctilious, even pedantic; but was courteous and very knowledgeable. His mind was open to relative observations, but one had the impression that "small talk" was not his forte! I recall that he questioned me on my footplate experiences with the "Counties" ("his" 10xx Class, not the 4-4-0s!), but appeared nonplussed when I commented upon the positioning of the fire hole! (As you will no doubt be aware, with the boiler being designed for an LMSR 8F, one is required to "lift" the shovel somewhat, to the fire hole – so different from a GWR-designed boiler where one shovels at footplate level)...

Insofar as the 10xx 4-6-0 "Counties" were concerned, my personal opinion of their performance was a little mixed. As originally constructed, with a 280psi boiler, they could be a little temperamental, and required careful enginemanship by the driver to avoid excessive slipping on starting; and with the cut-off well back the motion of the locomotive could be a little uncomfortable. Whilst still with 280psi boilers, the locomotives required great expertise on the fireman's part to maintain that boiler pressure when running. To a fireman brought up on the traditional design of tender, the Hawksworth pattern presented problems when "double-shovelling" – too much coal brought forward and it was not possible to get it out of the tender!

The 0-6-0 Pannier Tanks, the 94xx locomotives, were masters of the work to which they were assigned and, particularly when in superheated form, were competent performers on reasonably loaded semi-fast passenger work; and when properly fired, the boiler always had adequate steaming capacity. I do agree, however, that there was probably no need for the large numbers built.'

Except for the famous sally to destroy material relating to 'his "Pacific"', Hawksworth refrained from further involvement with 'inside' matters, unlike Churchward who, despite disenchantment

**ABOVE** On 11 December 1961 the traditional annual dinner of British Railways' (all regions) Chief Mechanical & Electrical Engineers (present and past) was held at the Charing Cross Hotel. Present (left to right) were K. J. Cook, C. T. Roberts, H. Ivatt, T. C. B. Miller, A. E. Robson, R. A. Smeddle, J. F. Harrison, W. J. A. Sykes, M. S. Hatchell and F. W. Hawksworth.

at the close of his career, found it hard to let go. Nevertheless, there is ample photographic evidence of his maintaining contact with old friends and colleagues at municipal events, Works Open Days and the like. A touching photograph records his presence among a small but distinguished group that met at Churchward's grave in St Mark's churchyard on 31 January 1957 to commemorate the centenary of the great man's birth.

It was a sad coincidence that those in charge at Swindon had little luck in achieving what might be considered a long and settled family life – a reminder of the herculean burden borne by those who occupied the position. Joseph Armstrong was patriarch of a large family, but a combination of professional commitments with numerous municipal and social responsibilities imposed a load regarded as the cause of his premature death. William Dean led the company through a period of extraordinary challenges and difficulties while building the foundations for the brilliant Edwardian phase, but at great personal cost. He was twice widowed, predeceased by two of his three children, and enjoyed only a short retirement before ill health took its toll.

G. J. Churchward maintained a range of outdoor pursuits that reflected his rural upbringing, while remaining a life-long bachelor. His demise has been attributed to his increasing deafness, and to his concern (practical railwayman to the last) to

inspect what he feared was a defective piece of track near Newburn House. This suggests failure mentally to adjust, with his continuing involvement reflecting loneliness. Collett left Swindon and saw out his years in Wimbledon. He maintained a reclusive existence until his death in 1952, apparently leavened only by obsession to redress his loss of almost 30 years earlier, through whatever means.

In contrast, Frederick Hawksworth lived on in the town of his birth, and continued to play his part in community affairs. For the historian, his retirement provided another lost opportunity as, irritated by being pestered over enquiries about the mythical 'Pacific', he showed no interest in discussing his career with

**BELOW** Mr & Mrs Hawksworth.

historians. A series of gentle, sympathetic interviews might have winkled out so much by way of recollections, memories and opinions that would have helped fill gaps about a truly memorable organisation of which so much has been recorded yet so much remains unexplained. Perhaps one day some notes might surface…

With the remaining pattern of his life apparently set, Hawksworth caused some surprise when he married his housekeeper of many years' standing about four years before his death in 1976. He lived until the age of 92 years, breaking the mould set by four of his predecessors in enjoying a long and companionable retirement.

For a true Swindonian, it was fitting that recognition of Frederick Hawksworth's achievements should have been essentially a local matter, in life and in death. The town and its largest employer had been the entire focus of his existence, and being granted the

**BELOW** The ceremony convened at St Mark's on 31 January 1957 to commemorate the centenary of the birth of G. J. Churchward. Present (left to right) were D. Murray John (Town Clerk), R. A. Smeddle, F. C. Hall, F. W. Hawksworth, C. T. Roberts, Canon Thomas, Mr Godsell, and Alderman N. Toze (Mayor).

**RIGHT** As a mark of respect, Swindon Borough Council named the extensive area of redundant land on the far side of the Gloucester line 'Hawksworth'. The site has developed into a successful industrial estate.

Freedom of the Borough in 1960 must have been a source of immense personal satisfaction. Equally, he would surely have been touched that, after his death, an industrial area immediately north of the junction with the Gloucester line was named 'Hawksworth'. It can be reached by means of Hawksworth Way.

And, finally, what of the findings of the Railway Research Service that so strongly pointed, in financial terms, to matters going badly wrong at Swindon in the late 1930s? Before these analyses could be digested, much less acted upon, the war turned a surplus of resources into an advantage, and although the implicit shortcomings remained then and in the aftermath, they were overridden by more immediate priorities. The survey was quietly forgotten, there being little motive to address its awkward conclusions. This was hardly in the best interests of the owner of the business – the shareholder and later the taxpayer. The beneficiary of this excess was he who reveres the Old Company and who is blessed that so many fine Swindon products remain extant.

# APPENDIX A

## Statistical comparison of the 'Big Four', 1923-37

The Railway Research Service of 4, Cowley Street, Westminster, London SW1 (an independent body) published a comprehensive survey on 1 June 1938, marked 'Private – For Official Use Only'. The survey's brief introduction was as follows:

'Inclusive of 1923, the results of fifteen years of working of the four main line railways of Great Britain are now available, and the period is of sufficient length to show up in true perspective the various trends exhibited by the figures contained in this study.

The present review follows the same general lines of the three earlier studies, on which the present one is based, published respectively in 1929 by the London and Cambridge Economic Service, in 1931 and again in 1934 by the Railway Research Service.

To include annual figures for the whole fifteen years would have made this review unwieldy and overweighted with statistical matter, whilst special features make several of the earlier years, such as 1926 and 1927, unreliable for comparative purposes. The year 1923 has been retained, however, for the reason that it was the first year of practically complete grouping, and 1929 has since come to be regarded, though not at the time in that light, as the year probably most approaching the normal, or perhaps, more accurately, the hoped-for normal.'

## Economic background

The survey commentary considered that the UK economy during the review period fell into three distinct periods:

**1924-30** – rising prosperity in general, though marred by the industrial troubles of 1926
**1931-33** – trade depression
**1934-37** – growing recovery.

This cycle was reflected in unemployment levels that had been 11.7% in 1923, peaking at 22.1% in 1932 and reducing progressively to 10.9% by 1937.

Deflation was dominant in the survey period, although by 1937 inflation had returned. Using 1924 as the base year, the cost of living index was measured: 1924 – 100; 1934 – 79; 1935 – 79; 1936 – 82; 1937 – 85

The railway companies' financial returns suffered depletion through deflationary forces over which they had no control. However, a greater source for concern was contraction in absolute numbers of passenger journeys and in freight tonnages:

|  | Passenger journeys* | Freight tonnage |
|---|---|---|
| **1923** | 1,319,000 | 419,500,000 |
| **1937** | 1,210,000 | 365,100,000 |

*Total includes season and workmen's tickets, so total number of passenger movements was considerably higher

Setting aside inflationary/deflationary distortions, the railway companies' businesses were contracting in real terms, but the decline was more extreme as the total transport market was expanding rapidly in real terms as evidenced by the population of road motor vehicles:

|  | Motor cycles* | Passenger vehicles | Goods vehicles |
|---|---|---|---|
| **1923** | 430,000 | 469,000 | 173,000 |
| **1937** | 488,000 | 1,884,000 | 478,000 |

*Numbers had peaked at 731,000 in 1929

## Railway industry trading performance

The survey summarised the decline of the railway companies' core business activities during the review period:

|  | 1923 | 1929 | 1930 | 1931 | 1932 | 1933 | 1934 | 1935 | 1936 | 1937 | % change, 1923-37 |
|---|---|---|---|---|---|---|---|---|---|---|---|
| **All companies: passenger traffic** | | | | | | | | | | | |
| Number of journeys (millions) | 1,319 | 1,187 | 1,161 | 1,097 | 1,069 | 1,084 | 1,119 | 1,149 | 1,173 | 1,210 | -8.3 |
| Receipts (£ million) | 70.3 | 61.7 | 58.6 | 54.1 | 50.9 | 51.1 | 52.5 | 54 | 56.2 | 59.5 | -15.4 |
| Average return per journey (pence) | 12.8 | 12.5 | 12.1 | 11.8 | 11.4 | 11.3 | 11.3 | 11.3 | 11.5 | 11.8 | -7.8 |
| **All companies: freight traffic** | | | | | | | | | | | |
| Tons conveyed (millions) | 420 | 403 | 374 | 332 | 309 | 310 | 332 | 333 | 346 | 365 | -13.0 |
| Receipts (£ million) | 107.4 | 103.5 | 96.5 | 87.8 | 78.9 | 78.5 | 83 | 83.8 | 87.7 | 92 | -14.3 |
| Receipts per ton-mile (pence) | 1.5 | 1.4 | 1.4 | 1.4 | 1.4 | 1.4 | 1.3 | 1.3 | 1.3 | 1.3 | -13.3 |

Total cash receipts fell at almost double the pace of passenger journey numbers. This meant that passengers were making increasing use of concessionary fares (excursions, weekend tickets, workmen's tickets and season tickets), or making shorter journeys. In 1923, by volume of ticket sales, more than 30% were on full-fare tariff (56% of passenger revenue) whereas by 1937 this had shrunk to less than 7% (less than 12% of revenue). The implication was that passengers with the discretion to choose were increasingly switching to alternative modes of transport (motor cycles, private cars, omnibuses, coaches and trams).

Fixed rates meant that there was less price/volume variance with freight revenue. Decline in tonnage, receipts and receipts per ton-mile therefore had a closer correlation and tended to move more in unison.

The inexorable decline in revenues had an impact on employee numbers, and on revenue earned per employee. By 1937 inter-company comparison reflected poorly upon the GWR's relative labour efficiency:

| EMPLOYEES (000s) | | | | | | | | | | | |
|---|---|---|---|---|---|---|---|---|---|---|---|
| | 1924 | 1930 | 1931 | 1932 | 1933 | 1934 | 1935 | 1936 | 1937 | 1937, total revenue (£000s) | 1937, revenue per employee (£) |
| GWR | 117 | 111 | 108 | 104 | 96 | 97 | 96 | 98 | 101 | 28,100 | 278 |
| LMS | 275 | 251 | 232 | 225 | 216 | 220 | 222 | 223 | 230 | 67,200 | 292 |
| LNER | 208 | 195 | 180 | 174 | 167 | 170 | 171 | 172 | 176 | 49,100 | 279 |
| SR | 70 | 71 | 68 | 68 | 61 | 63 | 65 | 66 | 68 | 22,100 | 325 |
| Total | 670 | 628 | 588 | 571 | 540 | 550 | 554 | 559 | 575 | 166,500 | |

## Trading performance by company

It was evident that three companies suffered proportionately generally similar declines in passenger revenue. The exception was the Southern Railway, whose catchment area was less affected by the economic depression.

| PASSENGER RECEIPTS (£ MILLIONS) | | | | | | | | | | |
|---|---|---|---|---|---|---|---|---|---|---|
| | 1923 | 1929 | 1930 | 1931 | 1932 | 1933 | 1934 | 1935 | 1936 | 1937 | % change, 1923-37 |
| GWR | 10.6 | 9.5 | 9 | 8.2 | 7.6 | 7.5 | 7.6 | 7.8 | 8.1 | 8.5 | -19.8 |
| LMS | 26 | 21.8 | 20.4 | 18.8 | 17.8 | 17.8 | 18.3 | 18.7 | 19.4 | 20.4 | -21.5 |
| LNER | 17.5 | 14.2 | 13.5 | 12.2 | 11.5 | 11.5 | 11.8 | 12.1 | 12.6 | 13.1 | -25.1 |
| SR | 14.8 | 14.5 | 14.1 | 13.2 | 12.3 | 12.6 | 12.9 | 13.4 | 13.9 | 14.7 | -0.7 |

Conversely, the Southern suffered the greatest proportionate decline in freight tonnage and revenue but, as this was from a much smaller base, there was less impact on the company's aggregate results. The business decline was generally consistent among the other three.

| FREIGHT RECEIPTS (£ MILLIONS) | | | | | | | | | | |
|---|---|---|---|---|---|---|---|---|---|---|
| | 1923 | 1929 | 1930 | 1931 | 1932 | 1933 | 1934 | 1935 | 1936 | 1937 | % change, 1923-37 |
| GWR | 18.3 | 18 | 17 | 15.3 | 13.8 | 13.9 | 14.5 | 14.8 | 15.4 | 16.4 | -10.4 |
| LMS | 47 | 43.8 | 40.4 | 37.2 | 33.7 | 33.3 | 35.2 | 35.9 | 37.9 | 39.6 | -15.7 |
| LNER | 36 | 36 | 33.5 | 29.9 | 26.5 | 26.5 | 28.4 | 28.3 | 29.5 | 31.1 | -13.6 |
| SR | 6.1 | 5.7 | 5.6 | 5.4 | 4.9 | 4.8 | 4.9 | 4.9 | 4.8 | 4.9 | -19.7 |

## Motive power utilisation per company

The survey compared efficiency in management of locomotive fleets. In 1923 all companies confronted maintenance backlogs, an excess of over-age or redundant units, and the need to modernise. Creation of the 'Big Four' also demanded workshop rationalisation, elimination of duplicated facilities, design standardisation and the adoption of the best practices from among the constituent companies. The differences between 1923 and 1929 largely reflect progress during the reorganisational phase. The figures thereafter show how well each company did in refining its mechanical engineering activities and in maximising efficient use of expensive capital assets.

| LOCOMOTIVE FLEETS | | | | | | | | | | | |
|---|---|---|---|---|---|---|---|---|---|---|---|
| | 1923 | 1929 | 1930 | 1931 | 1932 | 1933 | 1934 | 1935 | 1936 | 1937 | % reduction, 1923-37 |
| GWR | 3,944 | 3,871 | 3,861 | 3,857 | 3,745 | 3,754 | 3,608 | 3,593 | 3,587 | 3,632 | 7.9 |
| LMS | 10,289 | 9,797 | 9,319 | 9,032 | 8,450 | 8,225 | 7,996 | 7,885 | 7,660 | 7,657 | 25.6 |
| LNER | 7,388 | 7,378 | 7,316 | 7,194 | 7,092 | 6,901 | 6,846 | 6,787 | 6,718 | 6,576 | 11.0 |
| SR | 2,258 | 2,044 | 2,023 | 2,016 | 1,999 | 1,927 | 1,919 | 1,900 | 1,852 | 1,814 | 19.7 |

| LOCOMOTIVES UNDER OR AWAITING REPAIR | | | | | | | | | | |
|---|---|---|---|---|---|---|---|---|---|---|
| | 1923 | 1929 | 1930 | 1931 | 1932 | 1933 | 1934 | 1935 | 1936 | 1937 |
| GWR | 774 | 445 | 339 | 332 | 426 | 451 | 363 | 334 | 303 | 344 |
| LMS | 1,958 | 554 | 377 | 383 | 440 | 593 | 512 | 664 | 437 | 362 |
| LNER | 896 | 564 | 536 | 498 | 509 | 475 | 465 | 396 | 415 | 337 |
| SR | 266 | 153 | 151 | 137 | 136 | 157 | 144 | 137 | 149 | 156 |

| LOCOMOTIVES UNDER OR AWAITING REPAIR AS A PERCENTAGE OF THE FLEET TOTAL | | | | | | | | | | |
|---|---|---|---|---|---|---|---|---|---|---|
| | 1923 | 1929 | 1930 | 1931 | 1932 | 1933 | 1934 | 1935 | 1936 | 1937 |
| GWR | 19.6 | 11.5 | 8.8 | 8.6 | 11.4 | 12.0 | 10.1 | 9.3 | 8.4 | 9.5 |
| LMS | 19.0 | 5.7 | 4.0 | 4.2 | 5.2 | 7.2 | 6.4 | 8.4 | 5.7 | 4.7 |
| LNER | 12.1 | 7.6 | 7.3 | 6.9 | 7.2 | 6.9 | 6.8 | 5.8 | 6.2 | 5.1 |
| SR | 11.8 | 4.0 | 7.5 | 6.8 | 6.8 | 8.1 | 7.5 | 7.2 | 8.0 | 8.6 |

The achievements of the LMS were remarkable while, for a company lacking the financial resilience to implement intensive scrap-and-replace policies, the LNER's reduction of its heterogeneous fleet was impressive. The GWR undertook comprehensive modernisation during the period but the modest numerical reduction suggests little appreciation of how the new locomotives were to be best deployed, and indeed whether all were really needed.

It is particularly notable that by 1937, as a proportion of the fleet total, the GWR had approximately double the number of locomotives standing idle awaiting or under repair as did the LMS. In absolute terms, this equated to about 200 locomotives that were surplus to needs had LMS fleet management standards applied.

## Rolling stock utilisation by company

The decline in passenger numbers and in trading receipts stimulated reduction in unit numbers. Concurrently, the number of available seats actually increased (except for the LNER). This resulted from replacement of four-wheel, six-wheel and older, shorter bogie coaches with modern higher-capacity stock yielding an increase in the average number of seats per carriage.

### Carriage fleets

| CARRIAGE NUMBERS | | | | | | | | | | |
|---|---|---|---|---|---|---|---|---|---|---|
| | 1923 | 1929 | 1930 | 1931 | 1932 | 1933 | 1934 | 1935 | 1936 | 1937 | % reduction, 1923-37 |
| GWR | 6,768 | 6,820 | 6,768 | 6,576 | 6,343 | 6,185 | 6,167 | 6,143 | 6,128 | 6,248 | 7.7 |
| LMS | 19,663 | 19,771 | 19,536 | 19,059 | 18,679 | 18,171 | 17,911 | 17,546 | 17,522 | 17,409 | 11.5 |
| LNER | 14,314 | 13,748 | 13,620 | 13,409 | 12,965 | 12,730 | 12,611 | 12,613 | 12,538 | 12,430 | 13.2 |
| SR | 7,469 | 7,035 | 7,089 | 6,911 | 7,068 | 6,963 | 6,757 | 6,695 | 6,464 | 6,682 | 10.5 |

| SEAT NUMBERS (000s) | | | | | | | | | | |
|---|---|---|---|---|---|---|---|---|---|---|
| | 1923 | 1929 | 1930 | 1931 | 1932 | 1933 | 1934 | 1935 | 1936 | 1937 | % change, 1923-37 |
| GWR | 350 | 370 | 371 | 366 | 357 | 351 | 351 | 353 | 354 | 362 | 3.4 |
| LMS | 1,018 | 1,117 | 1,121 | 1,109 | 1,106 | 1,091 | 1,073 | 1,055 | 1,056 | 1,057 | 3.8 |
| LNER | 721 | 736 | 732 | 724 | 702 | 691 | 684 | 689 | 685 | 681 | -5.5 |
| SR | 401 | 408 | 411 | 402 | 412 | 406 | 398 | 398 | 390 | 404 | 0.7 |

| SEATS PER CARRIAGE (AVERAGE) | | | | | | | | | | |
|---|---|---|---|---|---|---|---|---|---|---|
| | 1923 | 1929 | 1930 | 1931 | 1932 | 1933 | 1934 | 1935 | 1936 | 1937 | % change, 1923-37 |
| GWR | 52 | 54 | 55 | 56 | 56 | 57 | 57 | 57 | 58 | 58 | 12.0 |
| LMS | 52 | 56 | 57 | 58 | 59 | 60 | 60 | 60 | 60 | 61 | 17.3 |
| LNER | 50 | 54 | 54 | 54 | 54 | 54 | 54 | 55 | 55 | 55 | 8.8 |
| SR | 54 | 58 | 58 | 58 | 58 | 58 | 59 | 59 | 60 | 60 | 12.6 |

### Wagon fleets

Nationwide freight operations suffered from the embedded inefficiency of private owner wagons, whose numbers exceeded the combined fleets of the 'Big Four'. Over the review period the average freight train size remained virtually static at 35 wagons in 1923 and 34 in 1937. Slightly more variance occurred in the composition of trains, where empty wagon numbers fluctuated between 31% and 36% of the total. Non-revenue empty wagon movements imposed a heavy direct and indirect cost upon the system, over which the railway companies could exercise little control. Thus it was important to maximise efficiency of those wagons whose deployment, subject to the rules of the Railway Clearing House, could be controlled.

| WAGON NUMBERS (000s) | | | | | | | | | | |
|---|---|---|---|---|---|---|---|---|---|---|
| | 1923 | 1929 | 1930 | 1931 | 1932 | 1933 | 1934 | 1935 | 1936 | 1937 | % reduction, 1923-37 |
| GWR | 83.9 | 83.4 | 83.3 | 83.0 | 81.3 | 79.1 | 78.1 | 78.2 | 78.0 | 81.4 | 3.0 |
| LMS | 297.2 | 292.5 | 286.9 | 283.3 | 277.0 | 267.2 | 264.8 | 265.7 | 268.1 | 276.3 | 7.0 |
| LNER | 277.2 | 268.5 | 268.4 | 264.4 | 258.8 | 250.4 | 243.5 | 240.4 | 239.8 | 249.2 | 10.1 |
| SR | 34.7 | 33.5 | 33.3 | 33.8 | 33.8 | 33.1 | 32.6 | 32.7 | 33.0 | 33.0 | 4.9 |

| AVERAGE CAPACITY PER WAGON (TONS) | | | | | | | | | | |
|---|---|---|---|---|---|---|---|---|---|---|
| | **1923** | **1929** | **1930** | **1931** | **1932** | **1933** | **1934** | **1935** | **1936** | **1937** | **% change, 1923-37** |
| **GWR** | 10.44 | 10.87 | 10.93 | 10.99 | 11.04 | 11.08 | 11.12 | 11.19 | 11.27 | 11.34 | 8.6 |
| **LMS** | 9.82 | 10.82 | 10.8 | 10.95 | 11.01 | 11.13 | 11.26 | 11.38 | 11.59 | 11.65 | 18.6 |
| **LNER** | 11.23 | 11.91 | 12.02 | 12.06 | 12.12 | 12.2 | 12.29 | 12.26 | 12.44 | 12.6 | 12.2 |
| **SR** | 9.97 | 10.44 | 10.55 | 10.64 | 10.68 | 10.76 | 10.96 | 11.12 | 11.17 | 11.22 | 12.5 |

Not only was the GWR the poorest performer in reducing its wagon fleet size (and thus commensurately in improving utilisation), but also its progress in increasing average carrying capacity was below par. This is surprising in view of the impression imparted of efforts to foster greater use of higher-capacity vehicles, as exemplified by the 20-ton Pole coal wagon.

## Docks and harbours

Following the Grouping, the GWR was regarded as the world's largest dock-owner through its inheritance from the Welsh companies (although the LNER actually commanded more wharf space). Investment did take place to improve efficiency in cargo handling but little could be done to arrest the decline in volumes resulting from the Great Depression. Some facilities were rationalised but only on a marginal scale, meaning that their size, and hence the attendant capital maintenance costs, remained essentially static:

| WHARFAGE (000FT) | | | | | |
|---|---|---|---|---|---|
| | **1923** | **1929** | **1932** | **1936** | **1937** |
| **GWR** | 172 | 173 | 165 | 164 | 164 |
| **LMS** | 96 | 96 | 97 | 92 | 92 |
| **LNER** | 201 | 210 | 204 | 209 | 198 |
| **SR** | 43 | 42 | 42 | 50 | 50 |

Against the fixed cost of managing the dock assets, income levels were fickle, being entirely driven by fluctuating levels of sea trade over which the company had no control. The Southern did well with its cross-Channel passenger traffic, while services across the Irish Sea were a major contributor to earnings for the LMS.

| NET RECEIPTS (£000) | | | | | |
|---|---|---|---|---|---|
| | **1923** | **1929** | **1932** | **1936** | **1937** | **% difference, 1923-37** |
| **GWR** | 718 | 560 | 145 | 120 | 342 | -52.3 |
| **LMS** | 18 | 88 | -85 | 13 | 35 | 94.5 |
| **LNER** | 403 | 198 | 63 | 184 | 248 | -38.5 |
| **SR** | 120 | 318 | 262 | 358 | 379 | 216.4 |

The decline in utilisation and hence revenue-earning capacity is illustrated by the following trends.

| NET RECEIPTS PER 1,000 FEET (£) | | | | | |
|---|---|---|---|---|---|
| | **1923** | **1929** | **1932** | **1936** | **1937** | **% difference, 1923-37** |
| **GWR** | 4,180 | 3,233 | 880 | 730 | 2,088 | -50.1 |
| **LMS** | 190 | 916 | -880 | 139 | 384 | 102.5 |
| **LNER** | 2,006 | 945 | 311 | 878 | 1,253 | -37.5 |
| **SR** | 2,801 | 7,495 | 6,263 | 7,168 | 7,603 | 171.4 |

### 'Big Four': dividend record

As reported in the LMS *Handbook of Statistics and Company Annual Reports*:

| PERCENTAGE DIVIDEND | | | | | | | | | | |
|---|---|---|---|---|---|---|---|---|---|---|
| | 1930 | 1931 | 1932 | 1933 | 1934 | 1935 | 1936 | 1937 | 1938 | 1939 |
| **GWR – Ordinary stock*** | 5.5 | 3 | 3 | 3 | 3 | 3 | 3 | 4 | 0.5 | 3.5 |
| **LMS – Ordinary stock** | 2 | 0.25 | nil | nil | nil | nil | 1.25 | 1.5 | nil | 3.5 |
| **LNER – Preferred ordinary stock** | 0.25 | nil | nil | nil | nil | nil | 0.5 | 1.75 | nil | nil |
| **LNER – Deferred ordinary stock** | nil | nil | nil | nil | nil | nil | nil | nil | nil | nil |
| **SR – Preferred ordinary stock** | 5 | 4 | 1 | 3 | 4 | 5 | 5 | 5 | 5 | 5 |
| **SR – Deferred ordinary stock** | 1.25 | nil | nil | nil | nil | nil | 0.5 | 1.5 | nil | 1.25 |

* The dividend record was a matter of prestige for the GWR, but this came at a cost. Between 1930 and 1935 it was sustained by drawing more than £4 million from revenue reserves, i.e. it was uncovered by distributable profits. The 1938 dividend has been linked with promotion of the 'Square Deal' campaign, high coal prices, and re-evaluation of plans to electrify lines in the South West.

# APPENDIX B

## R.A.G. Hannington

Robert Arthur George Hannington was born at Sandgate, Kent, in July 1883, and educated at Monkton Combe College, Somerset. He was connected by family with Hanningtons Department Store (the 'Harrods of Brighton'), which closed in 2001 after nearly 200 years. In 1912 he married Ithiel LeFeuvre at Bitterne, Hampshire.

He joined the Great Western in July 1903 as a pupil under Churchward, and his training period included spells in the Testing House, Laboratory and Drawing Office before being appointed a draughtsman in December 1906. In April 1909 he was appointed as Assistant Divisional Locomotive Superintendent under Stanier in the Swindon Division, and in September 1916 he became Assistant Divisional Locomotive Superintendent at Paddington.

From December 1916 until February 1919 he served as a Captain in the Railway Operating Division, Royal Engineers. While on leave from France Hannington called on Churchward at Swindon, who said that he wanted to send him to Worcester as Divisional Locomotive, Carriage & Wagon Superintendent, and enquired when he would be demobilised. Hannington promised to take the matter up the following day at the War Office. He went round numerous departments but every officer with whom he spoke rejected his request. In a last desperate effort, he knocked at a door and, on entering, a corporal sprang to attention and asked what he could do for him. Explaining that he wished to be demobilised, the corporal replied, 'Yes, Sir,' and in 10 minutes the process was completed.

Hannington stayed in the Worcester Division until April 1921 when he returned to Swindon as Manager of the Carriage & Wagon works. Following Stanier's appointment as Principal Assistant to the CME, he took over as Works Manager in July 1922, and K. J. Cook was appointed his assistant the following month.

During a visit to his daughter at her school in Ledbury, Herefordshire, on 26 June 1937 he dived into a swimming pool. He was an expert swimmer, but on this occasion he dived with his hands at his side. Although the water was 5 feet deep, he hit the bottom with such force that he was killed instantly.

(With acknowledgement to the archives of Mr Gerald Beesley.)

# APPENDIX C

## 'County' Class – early allocations and history

### Individual locomotive allocations

| No | New | 31/12/47 | 31/12/50 | No | New | 31/12/47 | 31/12/50 |
|------|------|----------|----------|------|------|----------|----------|
| 1000 | PDN | PDN | LA | 1022 | LA | LA | LA |
| 1001 | NA | NEY | NEY | 1023 | LA | TR | PZ |
| 1002 | BRD | BRD | BRD | 1024 | SRD | SRD | SRD |
| 1003 | PDN | PDN | LA | 1025 | SRD | SRD | SALOP |
| 1004 | LA | LA | LA | 1026 | PDN | PDN | PDN |
| 1005 | BRD | BRD | BRD | 1027 | WES | WES | NEY |
| 1006 | LA | LA | LA | 1028 | BRD | BRD | BRD |
| 1007 | BRD | BRD | BRD | 1029 | SRD | SRD | SRD |
| 1008 | PDN | PDN | PDN | | | | |
| 1009 | LA | NEY | NEY | | | | |
| 1010 | PDN | PDN | LA | | | | |
| 1011 | BRD | BRD | BRD | | | | |
| 1012 | PDN | PDN | LA | | | | |
| 1013 | BRD | LA | TR | | | | |
| 1014 | BRD | BRD | BRD | | | | |
| 1015 | PDN | PDN | LA | | | | |
| 1016 | SRD | SRD | SRD | | | | |
| 1017 | SRD | SRD | SRD | | | | |
| 1018 | NA | NA | PZ | | | | |
| 1019 | NA | PZ | PZ | | | | |
| 1020 | LA | EXE | NEY | | | | |
| 1021 | PDN | PDN | LA | | | | |

### Number allocated by shed

| Running shed | New | 31/12/47 | 31/12/50 |
|--------------|-----|----------|----------|
| Bristol Bath Road (BRD) | 7 | 6 | 6 |
| Exeter (EXE) | - | 1 | - |
| Laira (LA) | 6 | 4 | 9 |
| Newton Abbot (NA) | 3 | 1 | - |
| Neyland (NEY) | - | 2 | 4 |
| Old Oak Common (PDN) | 8 | 8 | 2 |
| Penzance (PZ) | - | 1 | 3 |
| Shrewsbury (SALOP) | - | - | 1 |
| Stafford Road (SRD) | 5 | 5 | 4 |
| Truro (TR) | - | 1 | 1 |
| Westbury (WES) | 1 | 1 | - |

RCTS (Part 12 Pages M26/ M28) is unequivocal that both Bristol Bath Road and Bristol St Philips Marsh shared the shedcode BL. Also, RCTS states that WSR became SRD as one of the later (very few) changes in shed code. The implication is that both BRD and SPM were unofficial classifications although Behrend in Gone With Regret uses them. In this book we have been consistent in referring to the late GWR/BR allocations, which although may be unofficial, are recognised by everyone:

Bristol Bath Road – BRD; Bristol St Philips Marsh – SPM; Wolverhampton Stafford Road – SRD

| No | County of... | Built | Named | Double chimney | Withdrawn | Mileage |
|---|---|---|---|---|---|---|
| 1000[a] | Middlesex | Aug 45 | Mar 46 | Mar 58[a] | Jul 64 | 733,933[b] |
| 1001 | Bucks | Sep 45 | Dec 47 | Dec 57 | May 63 | 664,361 |
| 1002 | Berks | Sep 45 | May 47 | Jun 58 | Sep 63 | 766,263 |
| 1003 | Wilts | Oct 45 | Aug 47 | Nov 57 | Oct 62 | 655,000 |
| 1004 | Somerset | Oct 45 | Aug 46 | Apr 57 | Sep 62 | 657,523 |
| 1005 | Devon | Nov 45 | Jul 46 | Dec 58 | Jun 63 | 710,034 |
| 1006 | Cornwall | Nov 45 | Apr 48 | Dec 58 | Sep 63 | 687,685 |
| 1007 | Brecknock | Dec 45 | Jan 48 | May 57 | Oct 62 | 658,967 |
| 1008 | Cardigan | Dec 45 | Jun 47 | May 58 | Oct 63 | 726,835 |
| 1009 | Carmarthen | Dec 45 | Feb 48 | Sep 56 | Feb 63 | 702,148 |
| 1010 | Carnarvon[c] | Jan 46 | Jan 46 | Jan 57 | Jul 64 | 779,055 |
| 1011 | Chester[d] | Jan 46 | Nov 47 | Nov 58 | Nov 64 | 728,610[b] |
| 1012 | Denbigh | Feb 46 | Jul 46 | Sep 57 | Apr 64 | 794,555[b] |
| 1013 | Dorset | Feb 46 | Jan 47 | Feb 58 | Jul 64 | 630,737[b] |
| 1014 | Glamorgan | Feb 46 | Mar 48 | May 58 | Apr 64 | 756,762[b] |
| 1015 | Gloucester | Mar 46 | Apr 47 | Nov 58 | Nov 62 | 724,192 |
| 1016 | Hants | Mar 46 | Sep 46 | Mar 57 | Sep 63 | 662,078 |
| 1017 | Hereford | Mar 46 | Mar 46 | Mar 59 | Dec 62 | 601,066 |
| 1018 | Leicester | Mar 46 | Apr 46 | Jan 59 | Sep 62 | 680,979 |
| 1019 | Merioneth | Apr 46 | Apr 46 | Mar 59 | Feb 63 | 662,550 |
| 1020 | Monmouth | Dec 46 | As built | Nov 58 | Feb 64 | 599,291[b] |
| 1021 | Montgomery | Dec 46 | As built | Oct 59 | Nov 63 | 747,718 |
| 1022 | Northampton | Dec 46 | As built | May 56 | Oct 62 | 590,659 |
| 1023 | Oxford | Jan 47 | As built | May 57 | Mar 63 | 592,957 |
| 1024 | Pembroke | Jan 47 | As built | Jul 58 | Apr 64 | 643,975[b] |
| 1025 | Radnor | Jan 47 | As built | Aug 59 | Feb 63 | 601,069 |
| 1026 | Salop | Jan 47 | As built | Oct 58 | Sep 62 | 621,007 |
| 1027 | Stafford | Mar 47 | As built | Sep 56 | Oct 63 | 650,666 |
| 1028 | Warwick | Mar 47 | As built | Aug 58 | Dec 63 | 723,639 |
| 1029 | Worcester | Apr 47 | As built | May 59 | Dec 62 | 555,216 |

[a] No 1000 carried a unique double chimney from new, and was converted to the standard type on the date shown.
[b] Official mileage to 28 December 1963 after which maintenance of records was abandoned
[c] Name amended to 'Caernarvon' in November 1951
[d] Original allocated name was the tautological *County of Cheshire*, but this was corrected before the name was placed on the engine. 4-4-0 'County' Class No 3814 had been similarly misnamed *County of Cheshire* from November 1906 until corrected in May 1907.

**LEFT** No 1011 *County of Chester* outlived the remainder of the class by several months and was eventually withdrawn in November 1964. On the 3rd of that month it is seen at Swindon MPD with nameplates removed and apparently out of steam, suggesting that withdrawal had taken place. In the preceding months No 1011 had been in demand for rail tours and its outward condition was not too bad by the standards of the time. The GWR number block has been restored to the front buffer beam, while both the smokebox number plate and the supporting lugs are no longer in evidence. The shedplate has also gone, but the legend on the footplate valence immediately behind the buffer beam advises in time-honoured fashion that No 1011 is a TYSeley engine. Some efforts were initiated to save No 1011, but a two-cylinder Collett 4-6-0 was considered a higher priority by the then small preservation community. Thus the 'Counties' departed the GWR scene – for the time being. *F. W. Sherlock*

# APPENDIX D

## 'Castle' Class – superheaters and double chimneys

As would be expected with a numerically large class built over 27 years, there were variations among the 'Castles' from new and those rebuilt from 'Stars', together with No 111. Notionally, the class consisted of:

**4073 sub-class:** Nos 4073 to 5012
**5013 sub-class:** Nos 5013 to 5082 and 5093 to 5097
**5098 sub-class:** Nos 5098, 5099 and 7000 to 7037

These were augmented by the 15 engines rebuilt from 'Stars' together with No 111, nominally rebuilt from *The Great Bear*.

Nos 111, 4000, 4009 (later 100A1), 4016, 4032 and 4037 were considered to be part of the 4073 sub-class. The ten 'Stars' (the former Nos 4063 to 4072), effectively rebuilt as Nos 5083 to 5092 between 1937 and 1940, were officially regarded as new engines and part of the 5013 sub-class, but differed in retaining the 'Star'/ early 4073 series-type 'joggled frames' (Nos 4073-4092 only). All engines up to No 5097 were built or rebuilt with the Churchward two-row superheater.

### 5098 sub-class

The first 'Castle' (No 5098) built under Hawksworth's regime introduced the three-row superheater, and all 40 of that series were so equipped. Further development led to the four-row superheater, and 27 locomotives later received this equipment. After experiments in 1956, a programme of fitting double chimneys commenced; the four-row superheater was almost exclusively associated with double chimneys. The fitting dates were as follows:

| No | Built | Four-row superheater | Double chimney | Withdrawn |
|---|---|---|---|---|
| 5098 | Apr 46 | Jan 59 | Jan 59 | Jun 64 |
| 5099 | May 46 | | | Feb 63 |
| 7000 | May 46 | | | Dec 63 |
| 7001 | May 46 | Sep 60 | Sep 60 | Sep 63 |
| 7002 | Jun 46 | Jul 61 | Jul 61 | Mar 64 |
| 7003 | Jun 46 | Jun 60 | Jun 60 | Aug 64 |
| 7004 | Jun 46 | Jun 56 | Feb 58 | Jan 64 |
| 7005 | Jun 46 | Nov 58 | | Sep 64 |
| 7006 | Jun 46 | Mar 60 | Mar 60 | Dec 63 |
| 7007 | Jul 46 | Jun 61 | Jun 61 | Feb 63 |
| 7008 | May 48 | Jun 59 | Jun 59 | Sep 64 |
| 7009 | May 48 | | | Mar 63 |
| 7010 | Jun 48 | Oct 60 | Oct 60 | Mar 64 |
| 7011 | Jun 48 | | | Feb 65 |
| 7012 | Jun 48 | | | Nov 64 |
| 7013ᵃ | Jul 48 | | May 58 | Sep 64 |
| 7014 | Jul 48 | May 57 | Feb 59 | Feb 65 |
| 7015 | Jul 48 | May 59 | May 59 | Apr 63 |
| 7016 | Aug 48 | | | Nov 62 |
| 7017 | Aug 48 | | | Feb 63 |
| 7018 | May 49 | Apr 58 | May 56/Apr 58ᵇ | Sep 63 |
| 7019 | May 49 | Jan 53 | Sep 58 | Feb 65 |
| 7020 | May 49 | Feb 61 | Feb 61 | Sep 64 |
| 7021 | Jun 49 | Nov 61 | Nov 61 | Sep 63 |
| 7022 | Jun 49 | Jan 53 | Jan 58 | Jun 65 |
| 7023 | Jun 49 | Oct 56 | May 58 | Feb 65 |
| 7024 | Jun 49 | Feb 56 | Mar 59 | Feb 65 |

| No | Built | Four-row superheater | Double chimney | Withdrawn |
|---|---|---|---|---|
| 7025 | Aug 49 | | | Sep 64 |
| 7026 | Aug 49 | | | Oct 64 |
| 7027 | Aug 49 | | | Dec 63 |
| 7028 | May 50 | Oct 61 | Oct 61 | Dec 63 |
| 7029 | May 50 | Jan 56 | Oct 59 | Dec 65 |
| 7030 | Jun 50 | Feb 56 | Jul 59 | Feb 63 |
| 7031 | Jun 50 | | | Jul 63 |
| 7032 | Jun 50 | Sep 60 | Sep 60 | Sep 64 |
| 7033 | Jul 50 | Jul 59 | Jul 59 | Jan 63 |
| 7034 | Aug 50 | Feb 56 | Dec 59 | Jun 65 |
| 7035 | Aug 50 | Jan 60 | Jan 60 | Jun 64 |
| 7036 | Aug 50 | Nov 57 | Aug 59 | Sep 63 |
| 7037 | Aug 50 | | | Mar 63 |

[a] 7013 was numbered 4082 wef February 1952, and received a double chimney while retaining the three-row superheater.
[b] 7018 had the three-row superheater until April 1958, but an experimental double chimney was fitted in May 1956.

The success of higher superheat led to replacement by the four-row type, the earliest being fitted to Nos 7019 and 7022 in January 1953, and surplus three-row superheater boilers were then cascaded to old class members.

## 4073 sub-class

On grounds of age, it was anticipated that withdrawals would commence with this sub-class, so comparatively fewer were uprated, although the second 'Castle' (No 4074) was found to be sufficiently sound for this treatment. While six of this series remained in service until the second half of 1964, No 5008 received the four-row superheater and double chimney in March 1961, but only remained in service for another 18 months.

| No | Three-row superheater | Four-row superheater | Double chimney | Withdrawn |
|---|---|---|---|---|
| 4074 | | Apr 57 | Apr 59 | Oct 63 |
| 4078 | Dec 57 | | | Jul 62 |
| 4080 | | Aug 58 | Aug 58 | Aug 64 |
| 4082[a] | | Nov 56 | | Sep 64 |
| 4087 | | Jul 56 | Feb 58 | Oct 63 |
| 4088 | | Nov 57 | May 58 | May 64 |
| 4089 | Feb 58 | | | Sep 64 |
| 4090 | | Apr 57 | Apr 57 | Jun 63 |
| 4093 | | Dec 57 | Dec 57 | Sep 64 |
| 4094 | Mar 60 | | | Mar 62 |
| 4097 | | Apr 55 | Jun 58 | May 60 |
| 5000 | Jun 57 | | | Oct 64 |
| 5001 | Jan 60 | Jul 61 | Jul 61 | Feb 63 |
| 5002 | Feb 60 | | | Sep 64 |
| 5007 | Aug 60 | | | Sep 62 |
| 5008 | | Mar 61 | Mar 61 | Sep 62 |

[a] 4082 was numbered 7013 wef from February 1952.

## 5013 sub-class

| No | Three-row superheater | Four-row superheater | Double chimney | Withdrawn |
|---|---|---|---|---|
| 5015 | Jul 61 | | | Apr 63 |
| 5016 | | Feb 61 | Feb 61 | Sep 62 |
| 5018 | May 57 | | | Mar 64 |
| 5019 | | Mar 61 | Mar 61 | Sep 62 |
| 5020 | Apr 60 | | | Nov 62 |
| 5021 | Sep 61 | | | Sep 62 |
| 5022 | | Feb 59 | Feb 59 | Jun 63 |
| 5023 | Apr 57 | | | Feb 63 |
| 5025 | May 57 | | | Nov 63 |
| 5026 | | Apr 55 | Oct 59 | Nov 64 |
| 5027 | | Apr 61 | Apr 61 | Nov 62 |
| 5031 | | Jun 59 | Jun 59 | Oct 63 |
| 5032 | Jul 57 | May 59 | May 59 | Sep 62 |
| 5033 | | Aug 55 | Oct 60 | Sep 62 |
| 5034 | Feb 57 | Feb 61 | Feb 61 | Sep 62 |
| 5036 | | Mar 55 | Dec 60 | Sep 62 |
| 5037 | | May 60 | | Mar 64 |
| 5038 | Jan 62 | | | Sep 63 |
| 5041 | May 61 | | | Dec 63 |
| 5042 | Feb 57 | | | Jun 65 |
| 5043 | | Dec 52 | May 58 | Dec 63 |
| 5044 | May 61 | | | Apr 62 |
| 5048 | Nov 60 | | | Aug 62 |
| 5049 | | Sep 47/Dec 53 | Sep 59[b] | Mar 63 |
| 5050 | Aug 57[a] | Aug 55 | | Sep 63 |
| 5055 | Feb 62 | | | Sep 64 |
| 5056 | | Nov 60 | Nov 60 | Nov 64 |
| 5057 | | Jun 54 | Jul 58 | Mar 64 |
| 5059 | Apr 61 | | | Jun 62 |
| 5060 | | Aug 61 | Aug 61 | Jun 62 |
| 5061 | | Jun 54 | Sep 58 | Sep 62 |
| 5063 | Apr 58[a] | Jun 54 | | Feb 65 |
| 5064 | | Dec 52 | Sep 58 | Sep 62 |
| 5066 | | Apr 59 | Apr 59 | Sep 62 |
| 5068 | | Mar 61 | Mar 61[c] | Sep 62 |
| 5069 | | Mar 57 | Nov 58 | Feb 62 |
| 5071 | Aug 50 | Mar 56 | Jun 59 | Oct 63 |
| 5072 | Jul 50 | | | Oct 62 |
| 5073 | | Sep 57 | Jul 59 | Feb 64 |
| 5074 | Jan 51 | Sep 61 | Sep 61 | May 64 |
| 5075 | Nov 50 | | | Sep 62 |

**ABOVE** Eighteen months after the appearance of No 2601, a second engine of the type was completed as a 2-6-0, and a further eight in 'Mogul' form were built in 1903. Quite why so many of an experimental unsatisfactory type were built has never been adequately explained, as all had gone by the beginning of 1907. It is thought that chassis and other parts were recycled for use with the successful 'Aberdare' 2-6-0s then being built; the boilers were adapted for stationary use. No 2610, the last to be built, displays a rather tidier appearance than the prototype.

| No | Three-row superheater | Four-row superheater | Double chimney | Withdrawn |
|---|---|---|---|---|
| 5077 | Sep 50 | | | Jul 62 |
| 5078 | May 60 | Dec 61 | Dec 61 | Nov 62 |
| 5079 | Jun 50 | | | May 60 |
| 5081 | May 50 | | | Oct 63 |
| 5082 | Oct 55 | | | Jul 62 |
| 5093 | Dec 50 | | | Sep 63 |
| 5094 | | Nov 52 | Jun 60 | Sep 62 |
| 5095 | | Mar 55 | Nov 58 | Aug 62 |
| 5096 | Nov 50 | | | Jun 64 |
| 5097 | Jun 50 | Jul 61 | Jul 61 | Mar 63 |

[a] Nos 5050 and 5063 unusually were four-row-equipped first, and later reverted to three-row
[b] No 5049 was the first 'Castle' to be fitted with a four-row superheater.
[c] No 5068 was equipped with an extended smokebox when the double chimney was fitted.

## Rebuilt 'Stars'

| No | Three-row superheater | Four-row superheater | Double chimney | Withdrawn |
|---|---|---|---|---|
| 5083 | May 57 | | | Jan 59 |
| 5084 | | Oct 56 | Oct 58 | Jul 63 |
| 5087 | May 60 | | | Aug 63 |
| 5088 | | Jun 58 | Jun 58 | Sep 62 |
| 5091 | Jan 60 | | | Oct 64 |
| 5092 | Nov 57 | Oct 61 | Oct 61 | Jul 63 |

# APPENDIX E

## Steam construction from 1 January 1941

F. W. Hawksworth took control at Swindon in July 1941, but for sake of clarity all locomotives introduced that year are included in the table below. In the period to 31 December 1947, the following numbers were built:

| | Type | 1941 | 1942 | 1943 | 1944 | 1945 | 1946 | 1947 | Total |
|---|---|---|---|---|---|---|---|---|---|
| **Tender classes** | | | | | | | | | |
| '2884' | 2-8-0 | 3 | 32 | | | | | | 35 |
| 'Hall' | 4-6-0 | 25 | 15 | 8 | | | | | 48 |
| 'Modified Hall' | 4-6-0 | | | | 12 | | | 10 | 22 |
| '2251' | 0-6-0 | | | | 10 | 10 | 10 | 8 | 38 |
| 'County' | 4-6-0 | | | | | 10 | 13 | 7 | 30 |
| 'Castle' | 4-6-0 | | | | | | 10 | | 10 |
| LMS-design 8F° | 2-8-0 | | | 26 | 36 | 17 | | | 80 |
| **Tank classes** | | | | | | | | | |
| '57xx' | 0-6-0PT | 18 | 37 | 26 | 22 | 43 | 29 | 10 | 185 |
| '41xx' | 2-6-2T | | | | | | 10 | 10 | 20 |
| '94xx' | 0-6-0PT | | | | | | | 10 | 10 |
| **Total** | | **46** | **84** | **60** | **80** | **80** | **72** | **55** | **478** |
| ° LMS Stanier design numbered 8400-8479 in that company's series | | | | | | | | | |

The post-1 January 1948 construction programme was:

| | Type | 1948 | 1949 | 1950 | 1951 | 1952 | 1953 | 1954 | 1955 | 1956 | Total |
|---|---|---|---|---|---|---|---|---|---|---|---|
| **Tender classes** | | | | | | | | | | | |
| 'Modified Hall' | 4-6-0 | 15 | 11 | 23 | | | | | | | 49 |
| '2251' | 0-6-0 | 2 | | | | | | | | | 2 |
| 'Castle' | 4-6-0 | 10 | 10 | 10 | | | | | | | 30 |
| 'Manor' | 4-6-0 | | | 10 | | | | | | | 10 |
| **Tank classes** | | | | | | | | | | | |
| '57xx' | 0-6-0PT | 17 | 14 | 10 | | | | | | | 41 |
| '41xx' | 2-6-2T | 10 | 10 | | | | | | | | 20 |
| '74xx' | 0-6-0PT | 10 | | 10 | | | | | | | 20 |
| '15xx' | 0-6-0PT | | 10 | | | | | | | | 10 |
| '16xx' | 0-6-0PT | | 20 | 10 | 20 | | | 5 | 15 | | 70 |
| '94xx' | 0-6-0PT | | 13 | 53 | 63 | 30 | 11 | 18 | 3 | 9 | 200 |
| **Total** | | **64** | **87** | **126** | **83** | **30** | **11** | **33** | **18** | **9** | **452** |

Summarised by Lots:

| Lot Nos | Year | Type | Nos |
|---|---|---|---|
| 330 | 1940 | 0-6-0PT | 3685 & 3866 |
| | 1941 | | 3687-3699 |
| | | | 4600-4604 |
| | 1942 | | 4605-4634 |
| 334 | 1940 | 2-8-0 | 3824-3831 |
| | 1941 | | 3832 & 3833 |
| 335 | 1946 | 2-6-2T | 4140-4149 |
| 336 | 1942 | 0-6-0PT | 4635-4641 |
| | 1943 | | 4642-4660 |
| 338 | 1940 | 4-6-0 | 6906-6910 |
| | 1941 | | 6911-6915 |
| 340 | 1941 | 4-6-0 | 6916-6935 |
| | 1942 | | 6936-6950 |
| | 1943 | | 6951-6958 |
| 341 | 1941 | 2-8-0 | 3834 |
| | 1942 | | 3835-3843 |
| 346 | 1942 | 2-8-0 | 3844-3866 |
| 347 | 1944 | 0-6-0 | 2231-2240 |
| | 1945 | | 2241-2250 |
| 348[a] | 1943 | 2-8-0[a] | 8401-8409 |
| 349[a] | 1943 | 2-8-0[a] | 8410-8426 |
| | 1944 | | 8427-8429 |
| 350 | 1944 | 4-6-0 | 6959-6970 |
| 351[a] | 1944 | 2-8-0[a] | 8430-8439 |
| 352 | 1943 | 0-6-0PT | 4661-4667 |
| | 1944 | | 4668- 4689 |
| | 1945 | | 4690-4699 |
| | 1945 | | 9600-9621 |
| 353[a] | 1944 | 2-8-0[a] | 8440-8462 |
| | 1945 | | 8463-8479 |
| 354 | 1945 | 4-6-0 | 1000-1009 |
| | 1946 | | 1010-1019 |
| 355 | 1945 | 0-6-0PT | 9622-9632 |
| | 1946 | | 9633-9641 |
| 356 | 1946 | 0-6-0PT | 9642-9651 |
| 357 | 1946 | 4-6-0 | 5098 & 5099 |
| | 1946 | | 7000-7007 |
| 358 | 1946 | 4-6-0 | 1020-1022 |
| | 1947 | | 1023-1029 |

| Lot Nos | Year | Type | Nos |
|---|---|---|---|
| 360 | 1946 | 0-6-0 | 3200-3209 |
| | 1947 | | 3210-3217 |
| | 1948 | | 3218 & 3219 |
| 361 | 1947 | 2-6-2T | 4150-4159 |
| 362 | 1946 | 0-6-0PT | 9652-9661 |
| | 1947 | | 6750-6759 |
| 365 | 1947 | 0-6-0PT | 9400-9409 |
| 366 | 1947 | 4-6-0 | 6971-6980 |
| | 1948 | | 6981-6990 |
| 367 | 1948 | 4-6-0 | 7008-7017 |
| | 1949 | | 7018-7027 |
| 368 | 1948 | 4-6-0 | 6991-6995 |
| | 1949 | | 6996-6999 |
| | 1949 | | 7900-7906 |
| | 1950 | | 7907-7919 |
| 369 | 1948 | 2-6-2T | 4160-4169 |
| | 1949 | | 4170-4179 |
| 370 | 1948 | 0-6-0PT | 9662-9672 |
| 371 | 1948 | 0-6-0PT | 7430-7439 |
| 373 | 1949 | 0-6-0PT | 1500-1509 |
| 374 | 1948 | 0-6-0PT | 6760-6765 |
| | 1949 | | 6766-6769 |
| 375 | 1950 | 4-6-0 | 7028-7037 |
| 376 | 1950 | 4-6-0 | 7920-7929 |
| 377 | 1950 | 4-6-0 | 7820-7829 |
| 378 | 1949 | 0-6-0PT | 9673-9682 |
| 379 | 1950 | 0-6-0PT | 6770-6779 |
| 380 | 1950 | 0-6-0PT | 7440-7449 |
| 381 | 1949 | 0-6-0PT | 1600-1619 |
| | 1950 | | 1620-6129 |
| 389 | 1951 | 0-6-0PT | 1630-1649 |
| 417 | 1954 | 0-6-0PT | 1650-1654 |
| | 1955 | | 1655-1669 |

[a] Lot Nos 348, 349, 351 and 353 were LMS Stanier 8F 2-8-0s built to the order of the War Department.

# APPENDIX F

## Oil-burning conversion programme

Between December 1945 and September 1947, 37 locomotives were converted before cancellation of the scheme in August 1948. Restoration to coal-burning condition commenced in September 1948 and was completed in April 1950 with 'Hall' No 3903 (4907). The locomotives and tenders in the programme were:

| Class | Number | Re numbered | Converted | Restored |
|---|---|---|---|---|
| 'Hall' | 4907 | 3903 | May 47 | Apr 50 |
| | 4948 | 3902 | May 47 | Sep 48 |
| | 4968 | 3900 | Apr 47 | Mar 49 |
| | 4971 | 3901 | Apr 47 | Apr 49 |
| | 4972 | 3904 | May 47 | Oct 48 |
| | 5955° | 3950 | Jun 46 | Oct 48 |
| | 5976 | 3951 | Apr 47 | Nov 48 |
| | 5986 | 3954 | May 47 | Feb 50 |
| | 6949 | 3955 | Apr 47 | Apr 49 |
| | 6953 | 3953 | Apr 47 | Sep 48 |
| | 6957 | 3952 | Apr 47 | Mar 50 |
| 'Castle' | 100A1 | n/a | Jan 47 | Sep 48 |
| | 5039° | n/a | Dec 46 | Sep 48 |
| | 5079 | n/a | Jan 47 | Oct 48 |
| | 5083 | n/a | Dec 46 | Nov 48 |
| | 5091° | n/a | Oct 46 | Nov 48 |
| '43xx' | 6320 | n/a | Mar 47 | Aug 49 |
| '28xx' & '2884' | 2832 | 4806 | May 46 | Apr 49 |
| | 2834 | 4808 | Jul 47 | Jan 50 |
| | 2839 | 4804 | May 46 | Oct 48 |
| | 2845 | 4809 | Aug 47 | Dec 49 |
| | 2847 | 4811 | Sep 47 | Jun 49 |
| | 2848 | 4807 | Jun 47 | Jul 49 |
| | 2849 | 4803 | May 46 | Apr 49 |
| | 2853 | 4810 | Aug 47 | Jun 49 |
| | 2854 | 4801 | Nov 45 | Feb 49 |
| | 2862 | 4802 | Feb 46 | Sep 48 |
| | 2863 | 4805 | May 46 | May 49 |
| | 2872 | 4800 | Oct 45 | Sep 48 |
| | 2888 | 4850 | Nov 45 | Sep 48 |
| | 3813 | 4855 | Jul 47 | Jun 49 |
| | 3818 | 4852 | Jan 46 | Sep 48 |
| | 3820 | 4856 | Jul 47 | Jun 49 |
| | 3831 | 4857 | Aug 47 | May 49 |
| | 3837 | 4854 | Jun 47 | Aug 49 |
| | 3839 | 4853 | May 47 | Nov 49 |
| | 3865 | 4851 | Dec 45 | Apr 49 |

° 3,500-gallon tenders were attached to Nos 5955 (3950) from June 1946 to early 1948 (tender identity not known), 5039 from December 1946 (tender No 2141), and 5091 from October 1946 to February 1947 (tender No 2014)

Thirty-nine tenders were fitted with oil tanks, indicating that further locomotive conversions were in hand when the scheme was stopped:

**ABOVE** A rear three-quarter view of No 4857. *P. Ransome-Wallis*

**3,500-gallon**

| No | Built | No | Built |
|------|--------|------|--------|
| 1640 | May 05 | 2061 | Aug 19 |
| 1652 | Apr 06 | 2141 | Apr 21 |
| 1657 | Jul 06 | 2146 | Apr 21 |
| 1739 | Oct 07 | 2174 | Dec 22 |
| 1852 | Nov 12 | 2236 | Mar 23 |
| 1863 | Nov 13 | 2315 | Jan 22 |
| 1883 | Apr 14 | 2317 | Jan 22 |
| 1936 | Jun 14 | 2318 | Jan 22 |
| 1990 | Dec 16 | 2331 | Jan 22 |
| 2014 | Nov 17 | 2359 | Apr 22 |
| 2034 | Jun 18 | 2372 | Sep 23 |

**4,000-gallon**

| No | Built | No | Built |
|------|--------|------|--------|
| 2721 | Jun 37 | 2877 | Oct 42 |
| 2764 | Jan 39 | 2883 | Oct 42 |
| 2767 | Jan 39 | 2884 | Oct 42 |
| 2782 | Sep 39 | 2886 | Oct 42 |
| 2792 | Oct 39 | 2892 | Jul 42 |
| 2809 | Apr 40 | 2908 | Jan 43 |
| 2814 | Apr 40 | 2918 | Apr 43 |
| 2827 | Jul 40 | 2933 | Sep 44 |
| 2840 | May 41 | | |

# APPENDIX G

## Hawksworth carriage stock

Initial orders were placed in 1944, but only a few had appeared by the end of 1945, with volume production increasing gradually the following year. With such a slow rate of production, considerable delay between first delivery and completion of certain Lots was inevitable.

| Lot No | Completed | Vehicle type | Diagram | Dimensions | Gangway/non-corridor | Running Nos |
|--------|-----------|--------------|---------|-----------|---------------------|-------------|
| 1685 | Apr 50 | All 3rd | C.85 | 64ft 0in x 88ft 11in | Gangway | 2239 |
| 1688 | Nov 49 | All 1st | A.23 | 64ft 0in x 88ft 11in | Gangway | 8001-8003 |
| 1689 | Oct 48 | Composite | E.163 | 64ft 0in x 88ft 11in | Gangway | 7252-7262 |
| 1690 | Dec 48 | Brake Composite | E.164 | 64ft 0in x 88ft 11in | Gangway | 7372-7285 |
| 1691 | Jun 48 | All 3rd | C.82 | 64ft 0in x 88ft 11in | Gangway | 781-832 |
| 1692 | Dec 47 | Brake 3rd | D.131 | 64ft 0in x 88ft 11in | Gangway | 833-854 |
| 1693 | Nov 48 | All 3rd | C.83 | 63ft 1in x 88ft 11in | Non-corridor | 374-413 |
| 1694 | Oct 48 | Brake 3rd | D.132 | 63ft 1in x 88ft 11in | Non-corridor | 414-438 |
| 1702 | Feb 51 | Sleeper 1st | J.18 | 64ft 0in x 88ft 11in | Gangway | 9082-9085 |
| 1703 | Jan 51 | All 1st | A.23 | 64ft 0in x 88ft 11in | Gangway | 8053-8064 |
| 1704 | Nov 49 | Composite | E.165 | 64ft 0in x 88ft 11in | Gangway | 7798-7816 |
| 1705 | Jul 48 | Brake Composite | E.164 | 64ft 0in x 88ft 11in | Gangway | 7838-7847 |
| 1706 | Apr 49 | All 3rd | C.84 | 64ft 0in x 88ft 11in | Gangway | 1713-1737 |
| 1707 | Jul 49 | Brake 3rd | D.133 | 64ft 0in x 88ft 11in | Gangway | 1772-1786 |
| 1712 | Aug 49 | All 3rd | C.83 | 63ft 1in x 88ft 11in | Non-corridor | 2002-2016 |
| 1713 | Apr 50 | Brake 3rd | D.132 | 63ft 1in x 88ft 11in | Non-corridor | 2087-2106 |
| 1714 | Nov 48 | All 3rd | C.82 | 64ft 0in x 88ft 11in | Gangway | 855-924 |
| 1719 | Jan 47 | PO Sorting Van | L.25 | 63ft 1in x 88ft 11in | Gangway | 843-847 |
| 1720 | Apr 49 | All 3rd | C.82 | 64ft 0in x 88ft 11in | Gangway | 2107-2136 |
| 1722 | Dec 49 | Passenger Brake | K.45 | 64ft 0in x 88ft 11in | Gangway | 290-299 |
| 1726 | Sep 50 | All 3rd | C.83 | 63ft 1in x 88ft 11in | Non-corridor | 1840-1859 |
| 1732 | Nov 50 | Brake 3rd | D.133 | 64ft 0in x 88ft 11in | Gangway | 2137-2185, 2187-2223, 2225, 2238 |
| 1734 | Jul 50 | All 1st | A.23 | 64ft 0in x 88ft 11in | Gangway | 8112-8125 |
| 1735 | Apr 50 | All 3rd | C.84 | 64ft 0in x 88ft 11in | Gangway | 2264-2292 |
| 1736 | Aug 51 | Auto Trailer | A.38 | 64ft 0in x 88ft 11in | Non-corridor | 222-234 |
|  |  |  | A.39 | 64ft 0in x 88ft 11in | Non-corridor | 220 |
|  |  |  | A.40 | 64ft 0in x 88ft 11in | Non-corridor | 221 |
| 1737 | Sep 50 | Composite | E.165 | 64ft 0in x 88ft 11in | Gangway | 7817-7822 |
| 1738 | Dec 50 | Brake Composite | E.164 | 64ft 0in x 88ft 11in | Gangway | 7848-7867 |
| 1739 | Aug 50 | All 3rd | C.83 | 63ft 1in x 88ft 11in | Non-corridor | 2017-2026 |
| 1740 | Nov 50 | Passenger Brake | K.45 | 64ft 0in x 88ft 11in | Gangway | 300-324 |
| 1744 | Jan 51 | Brake 3rd | D.133 | 64ft 0in x 88ft 11in | Gangway | 2240-2259 |
| 1745 | Jun 51 | All 3rd | C.83 | 63ft 1in x 88ft 11in | Non-corridor | 2601-2690, 2700-2720 |
| 1746 | Jul 52 | Brake 3rd | D.132 | 63ft 1in x 88ft 11in | Non-corridor | 2721-2765, 2776-2790 |
| 1748 | Nov 51 | All 3rd | C.83 | 63ft 1in x 88ft 11in | Non-corridor | 2797-2832 |
| 1750 | Oct 52 | Brake Composite | E.167 | 63ft 1in x 88ft 11in | Non-corridor | 7081-7090 |
| 1752 | Jul 51 | Passenger Brake | K.46 | 64ft 0in x 88ft 11in | Gangway | 325-334 |
| 1762 | Apr 52 | Composite | E.166 | 63ft 1in x 88ft 11in | Non-corridor | 7173-7208 |
| 1764 | 1953 | Brake 3rd | D.132 | 63ft 1in x 88ft 11in | Non-corridor | 4126-4131, 4133, 4134, 4136, 4137, 4139-4142, 4152 |
| 1766 | Sep 54 | Auto Trailer | A.43 | 64ft 0in x 88ft 11in | Non-corridor | 235-244 |
| 1767 | Aug 53 | Composite | E.166 | 63ft 1in x 88ft 11in | Non-corridor | 7183-7208 |
| 1775 | 1953 | Brake Composite | E.167 | 63ft 1in x 88ft 11in | Non-corridor | 7386-7397 |
| 1777 | Sep 54 | Brake Composite | E.167 | 63ft 1in x 88ft 11in | Non-corridor | 6276-6285 |

Special features associated with Hawksworth coaches (all gangwayed stock):

| Lot No | Vehicle type | Diagram | Running Nos | Features |
|---|---|---|---|---|
| 1685 | All 3rd | C.85 | 2239 | Aluminium frame prototype; also fitted with laminated plastic panelling |
| 1690 | Brake Composite | E.164 | 7374-7376 | Converted to double-ended Slip Composite in 1958 |
| 1691 | All 3rd | C.82 | 784 | Prototype fitted with laminated plastic panelling |
| " | " | " | 790 | Fluorescent lighting prototype; also with Empire veneer panelling |
| " | " | " | 796 | Withdrawn in 1961 and converted to Dynamometer Car No DW 150192 |
| " | " | " | 797 | Laminated plastic panelling, fluorescent lighting |
| " | " | " | 804 | Decolite flooring |
| " | " | " | 813 | Aluminium body panelling and window ventilators |
| 1702 | Sleeper 1st | J.18 | 9082-9085 | Fitted with Stone's pressure ventilation |
| 1714 | All 3rd | C.82 | 855-924 | Built by Gloucester Railway Carriage & Wagon Co |
| 1720 | " | " | 2107-2136 | Built by Gloucester Railway Carriage & Wagon Co |
| 1735 | All 3rd | C.84 | 2264-2288 | Aluminium body panelling |
| 1744 | Brake 3rd | D.133 | 2240-2259 | Built by Metro-Cammell |

## 'Brown' vehicles

### 'Siphon G" (50 feet by 8ft 6in), also known as 'Milk Vans':

| Lot No | Completed | Diagram | Running Nos |
|---|---|---|---|
| 1664 | 1945 | O.33 | 2937-2946, 2975-2994 |
| 1721 | 1950 | O.62 | 1310-1339 |
| 1751 | 1951 | O.62 | 1001-1030 |
| 1768 | 1955 | O.62 | 1031-1050 |

BELOW 'Siphon G' (Diagram O.62) No W1024, seen at Reading on 27 April 1982, was one of the last six of this Diagram in service, all of which were withdrawn in January 1983. The very last 'Siphon G' in normal service appears to have been No W2938 (Diagram O.33, built in September 1944), withdrawn in January 1985. *C. J. Tuffs*

# APPENDIX H
## Hawksworth era wagons

| Diagram | Built | Description | Load (tons) | Telegraph code | Number | Notes |
|---|---|---|---|---|---|---|
| B10 | 1942 | Roll | 15 | - | 2 | Converted from 'Beaver E' |
| C29 | 1945 | Trolley | 35 | CROCODILE E | 2 | Converted from Diagram C29 |
| E4 | 1938-41 | Aeroplane Propeller | 12 | AERO | 175 | |
| G34-6 | 1934, 1946 | Motor Car Bodies | 5 | BOCAR B | 26 | |
| G40 | 1940-44 | Well | 20 | LORIOT N | 15 | |
| G41 | 1943-48 | Trolley for Excavators | 2 | LORIOT W | 2 | |
| G42 | 1943-45 | Well | 25 | LORIOT P | 35 | |
| G43 | 1946-47 | Motor Car Van | 12 | MOGO | 100 | |
| G44-5 | 1946 | Motor Car Bodies | 5 | BOCAR A | 22 | |
| H9 | 1943-44 | Flat (Containers) | 12 | CONFLAT | 200 | |
| H10 | 1944-48 | Flat (Containers) | 12 | CONFLAT | 357 | |
| H11 | 1945-BR | Flat (Containers) | 12 | CONFLAT | 243 | |
| J24 | 1943 | Bogie Flat | 30 | MACAW E | 10 | Rebuilt from 'Bocar' G28/29 |
| J28 | 1939-46 | Bogie Bolster | 30 | MACAW B | 250 | |
| J29 | 1940-49 | Bogie Rail Wagon | 40 | GANE A | 63 | Engineering Dept |
| J30 | 1940-41 | Bogie Bolster | 25 | MACAW H | 20 | |
| J31 | 1947 | Bogie Bolster | 38 | BOBOL A8 | | |
| M5 | 1940-BR | Shunters' Truck | - | - | 48 | |
| N34 | 1944-BR | Loco Coal | 21 | - | 300 | |
| O37 | 1939-45 | Open | 13 | OPEN | 2751 | |
| O38 | 1944-47 | Open | 13 | HYFIT | 849 | Six-plank |
| O39 | 1945-47 | Open | 13 | HIGH | 500 | Six-plank |
| O40 | 1945-47 | Open | 13 | HYFIT | 100 | Six-plank |
| O41 | 1945-47 | Tube | 21 | TUBE | 100 | Four-plank |
| O42 | 1945-48 | Open | 13 | HYFIT | 250 | Six-plank |
| P18 | 1939-41 | Ballast/Sand | 10 | - | 201 | |
| P19 | 1941 | Ballast | 14 | - | 100 | |
| P20 | 1942 | Ballast | 10 | - | 150 | |
| P21 | 1942-48 | Ballast | 14 | - | 200 | |
| P22 | 1945-49 | Hopper Ballast | 20 | - | 250 | |
| P23 | 1945-48 | Ballast | 20 | - | 100 | |
| S13 | 1948 | Fish (Refrigerated) | 8 | INSIXFISH | 50 | |
| T13 | 1942-44 | Chaired Sleepers | 18 | - | 6 | |
| V23 | 1933-41 | Goods Van | 12 | MINK A | 3097 | |
| V24 | 1933-43 | Goods Van | 12 | MINK A | 2389 | |
| V34 | 1941-45 | Goods Van | 12 | VAN | 1200 | |
| V35 | 1942-43 | Goods Van | 12 | VAN | 650 | Built by Southern Railway |
| V36 | 1944-47 | Goods Van | 12 | VANFIT | 700 | Plywood panels |
| V37 | 1947-BR | Goods Van | 12 | VAN | 114 | Plywood panels (all by BR) |
| V38 | 1947-BR | Goods Van | 12 | VAN | 230 | Plywood panels (all by BR) |
| V39 | 1947-BR | Goods Van | 12 | VANFIT | 100 | Plywood panels (all by BR) |
| AA23 | 1942-49 | Goods Brake | - | TOAD | 326 | |
| DD4 | 1897-BR | Gas Tanks | - | CORDON | 77 | |
| DD6 | 1946 | Drinking Water Tanks | - | - | 6 | |
| EE1 | 1938-47 | Container Tank | 12 | - | 13 | 3,000-gallon, glass-lined |
| EE2 | 1947-BR | Container Tank | 12 | - | 2 | |
| FF1 | 1942 | Trestle Plate | 9 | - | 10 | |

# APPENDIX I

## GWR ships in the Second World War

All parts of the GWR were engaged in the war effort, but there are few reference to the fortunes of the GWR shipping fleet, briefly summarised as follows:

SS *St Andrew* Present at the Dunkirk evacuation. Participated in the Salerno landings in Italy in September 1943, serving as a hospital ship. While supporting the Anzio landings in early 1944, she helped pick up survivors from the SS *St David*. Later that year struck a mine off Taranto and was severely damaged, but managed to limp back to England for heavy repairs.

SS *St David* Present at the Dunkirk evacuation. Later served as hospital ship in Italian theatre and was sunk at Anzio Bay on 24 January 1944.

SS *St Helier* Transferred to Fishguard service early in war. Then taken over by Government to carry troops, mail and cargo from Southampton to Cherbourg and Le Havre. In May/June 1940 made one crossing to Calais and seven to Dunkirk, evacuating 10,200 troops and 1,500 civilians. Involved in two collisions with other ships while manoeuvring. Participated in D-Day landings. She had regularly worked on the Weymouth-Channel Islands service and fittingly was present at the liberation of those islands in May 1945.

SS *St Julien* Taken over as troopship in 1939. Present at Dunkirk evacuation, working as hospital ship; despite markings, was bombed by enemy aircraft but escaped. While serving in Italian theatre, evacuated more than 9,000 injured troops from Anzio beachhead. Present at D-Day landings; struck a mine but managed to return to Britain for repairs.

SS *St Patrick* Requisitioned as troop transport in October 1939. Later returned to GWR service between Fishguard and Rosslare. Bombed and sunk off Fishguard in June 1941.

SS *Roebuck* This small cargo ship was at Dunkirk and evacuated more than 1,000 troops despite being ill-equipped to recover men from water or small boats. Then moved down Channel to help in evacuation from Brittany. At St Valéry came under enemy gunfire with loss of life to crew. Participated in D-Day landings.

SS *Sambur* Another small cargo ship, she joined *Roebuck* at St Valéry and was similarly attacked. Participated in D-Day landings.

SS *Great Western* Stayed in company service but was under enemy air attack on several occasions.

Plymouth tenders *Sir Francis Drake*, *Sir Walter Raleigh* and *Sir Richard Grenville* were called up in August 1939 and served as Admiralty examination craft. *Sir John Hawkins* stayed in company service until severely damaged in an air raid in January 1941. She was repaired, then taken into naval service.

The GWR vessel possibly best known to passengers was *The Mew*, which operated the Kingswear-Dartmouth river ferry. With the Dunkirk evacuation well under way, she left Kingswear with her decks heavily laden with coal and steamed up the Channel at full speed, but on arrival at Dover she was too late to play any active role. She returned safely to the River Dart and saw out the war on the duties for which she had been built.

# REFERENCES

**Chapter 1**

[1] *The Armstrongs of the Great Western* by H. Holcroft, pages 89-92 (Railway World Ltd, 1953)

**Chapter 4**

[2] *The Churchward 2-6-0s* by David Andrews, pages 60-62 (Line One Publishing, 1985)
[3] *The GWR Mixed Traffic 4-6-0 Classes* by O. S. Nock, page 40 (Ian Allan Ltd, 1978)
[4] *'Halls', 'Granges' & 'Manors' At Work* by Michael Rutherford, pages 36-37 (Ian Allan Ltd, 1985)

**Chapter 6**

[5] 'Swindon's Acquaintance with Rotary Cam Valve Gears' by L. A. Summers, pages 347-351/437-442, *Backtrack*, June/July 2012

# BIBLIOGRAPHY

Allen, Cecil J., *The Locomotive Exchanges*, Ian Allan Ltd, Undated

Atkins, D. G., Beard W. and Tourret R,. *GWR Goods Wagons*, Oxford Publishing Co, 2013

Chacksfield, J. E., *Sir William Stanier – A New Biography*, The Oakwood Press, 2001

Chacksfield, J. E., *CB Collett – A Competent Successor*, The Oakwood Press, 2002

Clements, Jeremy and McMahon, Michael, *Locomotives of the GSR*, Colourpoint Books, 2008

Cook, A. F., *LMS Locomotive Design and Construction*, RCTS, 1990

Haresnape, Brian, *Ivatt & Riddles Locomotives*, Ian Allan Ltd, 1977

Harris, Michael, *Great Western Coaches from 1890*, David & Charles, 1985

Holcroft, H., *An Outline of Great Western Locomotive Practice 1837-1947*, Locomotive Publishing Co Ltd, 1957

Holcroft, H., *The Armstrongs of the Great Western*, Railway World Ltd, 1953

Judge, C. W., *The History of Great Western AEC Diesel Railcars*, Oxford Publishing Co, 1986

Lewis, John, *Great Western Steam Rail Motors*, Wild Swan Publications Ltd, 2004

Lewis, John, *Great Western Auto Trailers Parts 1 & 2*, Wild Swan Publications Ltd, 1991/1995

MacDermot, E. T., *History of the Great Western Railway Volumes I & II*, Ian Allan Ltd, 1927 (rev 1964)

Nock, O. S., *William Stanier*, Ian Allan Ltd, 1964

Railway Correspondence & Travel Society, *The Locomotives of the Great Western Railway*, Railway Correspondence & Travel Society, 1951-1993

Railway Research Service, 15 year Statistical Report on Railway Industry, 1938

Robertson, Kevin, *The Great Western Railway Gas Turbines – A Myth Exposed*, Sutton Publishing, 1989

Rutherford, Michael, *Great Western 4-6-0s*, Ian Allan Ltd, 1995

Sixsmith, Ian, *The Book of the Castle 4-6-0s*, Irwell Press Ltd, 2009

Sixsmith, Ian, *The Book of the County 4-6-0s*, Irwell Press Ltd, 2012

**ABOVE** In the 21st Century, out-sourcing of specialised services and short or long term hire/lease of capital equipment is normal commercial practice, proven to be financially advantageous in many situations. An early example on the GWR was the hire of individual Pullman cars in 1929 for use with Plymouth-Paddington boat trains, soon followed by two eight-coach rakes to form the short-lived "Torbay Pullman Limited". Apart from footplate crew and guard, the train staff were Pullman employees; the supplement charged to passengers was shared with the GWR.

Felix Pole in his book tactfully states that he never understood the basis for the Chairman's antipathy to this arrangement. Other sources suggest that Lord Churchill resented a high profile decision that had been instigated by Pole while he was absent overseas. Official grounds were that the arrangement was too expensive, and that the GWR could do as well with its own stock.

The resultant Super Saloons were fine vehicles but considering their high capital cost, concomitant depreciation, and limited utilisation, it is doubtful whether they ever earned their keep. Their creation was a classic example of "recreation of the wheel" for purposes of prestige but with little consideration for actual market demand. The progressively-minded Southern Railway hired Pullman vehicles and personnel for a wide variety of services over many years, to mutual satisfaction. It was evidently lucrative to serve Brighton and Bournemouth with luxury carriage stock but Torquay only had a regular service of this quality for the 1929 season. It would be interesting to know whether any feasibility assessment was conducted to substantiate the policy change

This episode is thought to be an example of the progressively-minded Pole finding himself at odds with conservative elements in the company's senior ranks, and contributory towards his departure from the company. *BR*

**ABOVE** On 26 May 1964 No 9463 climbs the Lickey hauling a failed four-car Class 123 'Inter-City' diesel multiple unit (built at Swindon in 1963). *F. R. Sherlock*

# INDEX